Developing Learning Skills through Children's Literature:

An Idea Book for
K-5 Classrooms and Libraries

Developing Learning Skills through Children's Literature:
An Idea Book for K-5 Classrooms and Libraries

By Mildred Knight Laughlin
and Letty S. Watt

ORYX PRESS
1986

The rare Arabian Oryx is believed to have inspired the myth of the unicorn. This desert antelope became virtually extinct in the early 1960s. At that time several groups of international conservationists arranged to have 9 animals sent to the Phoenix Zoo to be the nucleus of a captive breeding herd. Today the Oryx population is over 400, and herds have been returned to reserves in Israel, Jordan, and Oman.

Copyright © 1986 by
The Oryx Press
2214 North Central at Encanto
Phoenix, AZ 85004-1483

Published simultaneously in Canada

Printed and Bound in the United States of America

∞ The paper used in this publication meets the minimum requirements of American National Standard for Information Science—Permanence of Paper for Printed Library Materials, ANSI Z39.48, 1984.

Library of Congress Cataloging-in-Publication Data

Laughlin, Mildred.
    Developing learning skills through children's literature.

    Bibliography: p.
    Includes index.
    1. Children—Books and reading.   2. Children's literature—Study and teaching.   3. Elementary school libraries—Activity programs.   4. Libraries, Children's —Activity programs.   5. Libraries and education.
6. Children's literature—Bibliography.   I. Watt, Letty S., 1947– .   II. Title.
Z1037.A1L315 1986   011'.6250544   86-2554
ISBN 0-89774-258-3

Contents

Introduction: The Need for a Literature Program

CHILDREN'S LITERATURE AND ITS ROLE IN CHILD DEVELOPMENT

The term "children's literature" is not a new one. Countless teachers and librarians have enrolled in a college course with that label, yet few attempt to define it or set about in an organized fashion to impart its values to children. Perhaps this lack of definition or clear delineation of value may be at the root of the haphazard approach to children's literature evidenced in most elementary schools.

Webster's Seventh New Collegiate Dictionary defines literature as "writings in prose or verse; esp. writings having excellence of form or expression and expressing ideas of permanent or universal interest." Does this definition apply to children as well as adults? Rebecca Lukens in *A Critical Handbook of Children's Literature*[1] reminds her readers that "literature for children differs from literature for adults in degree, but not in kind. Literature for children can and should do the same things for young readers as literature does for adults." Thus, educators must be concerned with selecting works that have excellence of form or expression, that express ideas of interest to all children at a particular level of experience and maturation, and that accomplish the same things for children that they do for adults.

What values are inherent in literature? If a group of elementary teachers met to consider the reasons for sharing literature with children, a number of ideas would probably emerge.

Most important, literature must provide enjoyment. The experience may provide additional rewards, but unless the child finds pleasure in the work, s/he will, depending upon reading ability, fail to listen intently, leave the work unfinished, or complete the work but fail to consider its theme, savor the beauty of the writing style, or take away ideas to be long remembered.

Literature helps to develop the imagination by drawing children into fictional and fantasy worlds, demanding suspension of disbelief. The follow-up activities in which children can engage following the introduction of books and authors of many genres allow a variety of imaginative experiences.

Through vicarious journeys into other times and places literature reveals the forces that shape people's actions. The conflicts caused by extremes of nature or demands of present and past societies bring out qualities of character that can be assessed, resulting in new understanding of forces that shape people's lives. Speculation about "Would I have reacted in the same way in similar circumstances?" encourages personal experience in making choices.

Literature should help children understand the common ties that unite people everywhere. Through sharing quality literature about children in other lands that shows the needs of all people rather than the stereotypes promoted by the uninformed, a real contribution to human understanding and ultimate peace may be made.

Sharing literature provides opportunities for the development of thinking skills. In 1964 the Educational Policies Commission asserted that the central purpose of education is to teach children to think. As children acquire abilities in understanding theme, assessing character development, evaluating the influence of setting, and noting unique aspects of an author's style, they are developing lifelong skills that will enable them to experience the magic of words and become personally involved in ideas.

Children's literature can actively contribute to successive stages of growth and development. Those who subscribe to Piaget's views about the growth patterns of children realize that an understanding of the characteristics of children at a specific stage is needed if one is to have reasonable expectations about a child's capabilities at a given level. That understanding allows adults to select literature appropriate for a child's interests and to provide experiences that allow children to mature until they finally achieve abstract thinking abilities.

In her *The Child as Critic*[2] Glenna Sloan observes that the literate person is "not one who knows *how* to read, but *one who reads* fluently, responsively, critically, and because he [or she] wants to." It is impossible to teach or learn literature; it must be experienced. The full impact of literature is felt through encountering it in a cumulative approach, not merely as a list of apparently unconnected poems and stories.

If the task of helping each child become a literate person is to be accomplished, it must begin with oral sharing in a sequential pattern as soon as the child enters school. All educators must work together and be aware of the objectives and the approaches of other teachers. How many teachers in an elementary school know each week what the school library media specialist shares in the library with the students? Does the school library media specialist have any idea what books the teacher read aloud last week or last year? With so many good books and a plethora of exciting ideas for sharing, it is unfortunate that titles and approaches are constantly duplicated. Most elementary school teachers would not attempt to teach mathematics or social studies without a scope and sequence, and we should not depend on a haphazard approach for literature.

The identification of goals for a literature program is the first step in the development of a literature scope and sequence. The reasons for sharing literature explored in the previous pages will provide a springboard, and each school faculty will want to add or change to address unique needs.

Broad approaches to the accomplishment of these goals must be identified. Specific authors and illustrators on any grade level should be agreed upon. At this point the school library media specialist and/or a committee of teachers can outline a variety of activities relating to specific available books and materials that are appropriate to the needs and interests of children of a particular grade level.

HOW THIS BOOK IS ORGANIZED AND HOW IT CAN BE USED

The units that follow are suggested ideas for sharing literature that may be utilized in developing a scope and sequence of literature experiences for children in grades K–5. For primary grades K–2 the activities are primarily arranged through sharing the works of a particular author or illustrator. Through this deliberate exploration the child begins to know that person as a friend. S/he is excited about new books by that same author or illustrator and discusses books on a level not often achieved if authors are approached only haphazardly. Those included represent a variety of classic and current authors and illustrators "too good to miss" who have made a particular contribution to literature for young people. A variety of literary and artistic styles are represented, lending themselves to purposeful follow-up activities designed to increase each child's awareness of the enjoyment and value in reading and sharing good books. The roots of literary criticism lie in these grades, for as young people share "the best," they gradually build an experiential background which helps them to consciously or unconsciously turn aside from mediocre "grocery store" books that do not measure up to the art and literary style evidenced in the titles shared from a carefully selected library collection.

It is also the responsibility of media specialists and teachers on these levels to introduce parents to the inexpensive quality paperbacks available from Puffin, Dell, and other publishers which can provide the beginning of a home library for each child. Reliable paperback book clubs managed by the teacher or school library media specialist may be one mode of monthly introduction to home ownership of good books. If free copies mailed to the adults responsible for ordering are pooled, multiple copies can be assembled in a teacher workroom to be used for small third- through sixth-grade book discussion groups led by the school library media specialist. Such groups provide opportunity for simple discussion of character, identification of theme, evaluation of aspects of style, assessment of the appropriateness of the ending, and other approaches useful later in in-depth literary analysis.

For each of the authors or illustrators suggested in the following chapters, it is important that the school library media specialist and/or teacher read a biographical account (if available) in preparation for the group introduction. By choosing events in the author's or illustrator's early life that would interest children, the author "lives" for the young person and the interest in his or her books is heightened. In addition, if events that may have influenced later writing are shared and discussed, the roots of psychological criticism are introduced in a pleasurable, meaningful way. Biographical sources are listed in units about particular authors, with complete bibliographic information in Appendix I. In addition, publishers often have free or inexpensive leaflets about authors and illustrators available upon request that can be organized in an author file. The *School Library Journal, The Horn Book Magazine,* and *Top of the News* often report these items.

The activities that follow for each grade level are organized in a similar pattern. Each individual unit identifies behavioral objectives to be accomplished by utilizing increasingly difficult materials. Knowledge and comprehension skills are basic for the objectives, with higher levels of application, analysis, synthesis, and evaluation becoming more evident as progress through the grades is made. It suggests books to use with the unit, provides a teacher/school library media specialist group introductory activity, and shares follow-up ideas for teacher and students to engage in on subsequent days. Not all works by an author/illustrator are included, so the teacher and library media specialist may want to examine their own collection for additional titles that may be used. For kindergarten and first grade the material will be shared aloud and the activities directed by the teacher. In the second grade some suggested activities may be carried out by individuals or small groups with less adult participation or supervision. As students become more proficient in reading, the follow-up activities can become more self-directed. All students in the class need not engage in *all* suggested follow-up activities, as participation will depend upon the interests and abilities of the children involved. The activities are designed for a variety of levels of ability, and teachers should choose those appropriate for their class. These can be photocopied and laminated if desired and made available for students to choose.

The brief annotations for the suggested books to be used are descriptive in nature, as the activity related to the book provides a more detailed utilization guide. Additional resources may be suggested for use in specific activities if available, but they are not necessary in achieving unit objectives. Some out-of-print books have been included if it was felt that past popularity would make them generally available in school media centers.

Obviously, all distinguished children's authors and illustrators could not be included in the 60 units suggested on the following pages. Favorite authors and illustrators of teachers, the school library media specialist, and students should by all means be included in each school's own literature scope and sequence. The enthusiasm of teacher and school library media specialist for a specific author or illustrator is beginning assurance that the children will enjoy and remember the literature experiences that evolve. Only authors and illustrators whose works have been included in current and retrospective selection tools have been included. It is hoped that by introducing activities to be used with books of both older and more recent copyright dates, all school library media centers will have some of the books available now, and if the sharing is pleasurable and profitable for the students, the remaining titles may serve as a potential buying guide. The ideas and activities suggested for the materials included on the following pages are not necessarily unique for a specific book and may be adapted and used in follow-up activities for books by other authors and illustrators.

The units suggested for the third to fifth grades are developed around authors and illustrators, genres of literature, themes, and types of books found in the Dewey Decimal arrangement of the school media center. It is hoped that, when appropriate, the location of these works within the library arrangement will be discussed.

At the end of the fifth-grade school year a class group should be able to share a group of books with the spine labels covered and decide from the content into which general Dewey classification the work belongs. This ability to classify and document their rationale for the choice is a good demonstration of utilization of higher levels of thinking and application of skills learned in a pleasurable sharing session. By calling attention through the years to the arrangement of books in the media center, children will acquire a broad understanding of major areas through use, *not* memorization of the Dewey Decimal arrangement. This final classifying exercise will provide excitement as well as reinforcement; in addition, children will leave the fifth grade with a basic understanding of library arrangement and a sense of "belonging" that invites literature exploration in a strange school or public library.

In all grades it is important to correlate the literature experience with the curriculum content of the individual school. For example, if the social studies curriculum is using England as a content base on a specific grade level, then the literature experiences should involve the folk tales, poetry, music, art, and fiction of the country as well as its geography and history. The activities included for the intermediate grades are only suggestions and must be recombined and altered to meet the needs of the individual school. In many cases titles should be substituted to reflect appropriate reading levels, and in all situations titles should be added which reflect current holdings of the school media center.

The suggested follow-up activities do not exhaust the potential, but should, rather, inspire the addition of other ideas, so that *all* students can participate in an enjoyable experience relating to the concept introduced by the school library media specialists or teacher. Follow-up activities should involve a choice so that all children can engage in an activity or activities that satisfy personal needs and interests. Only then will children develop a true involvement in a love for literature.

At all levels there should be concern that each student develop the many thinking, listening, and communicating library skills identified by Ruth Davies in *The School Library Media Program.*[3] This should not be done in isolation but should be correlated with curriculum activities demanding that skill, so it is relevant to the moment and so that the knowledge gained can be reinforced immediately through application. The literature activities suggested involve thinking, listening, and communicating, but the emphasis must remain that of a pleasurable literature experience and never result in worksheets or drills.

The adopted reading texts for any school include excerpts from children's fiction or poetry by well-known writers. The school library media specialist and teacher can extend these brief reading introductions into appropriate literature units in which the total book from which the excerpt was taken can be introduced; additional works by the same author, poet, or illustrator may be shared; and other materials on the same theme can be enjoyed. In each instance appropriate varied follow-up activities should be planned.

The media center literature activities for all grades should provide many opportunities for reading, listening, and viewing; for creative endeavors in drama, art, music, dance, writing, puppetry, and storytelling; for visual literacy development; and for formal and informal participation in small and large group book discussions. In the activities suggested on the following pages, rational power development is evidenced in such terms as listing, predicting, illustrating, analyzing, imagining, and evaluating, thus reflecting Bloom's Taxonomy translated into enjoyable literature sharing.

The above-mentioned modes of expression are included as introductory techniques or in follow-up suggestions. For teachers and school library media specialists desiring more information on any of these sharing techniques, an annotated bibliography of appropriate reference works is included in Appendix II.

The units that follow have been given appropriate specific grade designations for organizational purposes. Careful examination by teachers and school library media specialists in a specific school is essential, for many may be deemed more useful at a different level for a particular group of children. In all instances the objectives *must* be planned jointly by teachers and school library media specialists and the follow-up ideas carried out in the classroom or media center as time, space, and type of activity dictate. With such an approach literature is team taught *without* a structured time in which each segment of the literature program must be completed on any grade level. Flexibility to meet the needs and interests of young people is essential, and enjoyment of literature must be a major objective.

REFERENCES

1. Rebecca Lukens, *A Critical Handbook of Children's Literature,* 2d ed. (Glenview, IL: Scott, Foresman, 1982), p. 8.

2. Glenna Sloan, *The Child as Critic* (New York: Columbia Teachers College Press, 1975), p. 1.

3. Ruth Davies, *The School Library Media Program* (New York: Bowker, 1979), pp. 304–07.

Developing Learning Skills through Children's Literature:
An Idea Book for K-5 Classrooms and Libraries

Chapter 1
Kindergarten/First Grade

Concepts with Tana Hoban

STUDENT OBJECTIVES:

- Have experience pantomiming concepts
- Arrange and project simple objects
- Discuss the dedication page in a book
- Clarify the concept of opposites
- Recognize shapes

RECOMMENDED READING:

Hoban, Tana. *A, B, See!* Greenwillow, 1982.
  Arrangements of photograms of objects to illustrate each letter of the alphabet.

———. *Big Ones, Little Ones.* Greenwillow, 1976.
  Black-and-white illustrations of large and small zoo and farm animals.

———. *Circles, Triangles, and Squares.* Macmillan, 1974.
  Black-and-white illustrations of familiar, yet often surprising examples of the three shapes.

———. *Dig, Drill, Dump, Fill.* Greenwillow, 1975.
  Textless book of large equipment shown engaged in title activities.

———. *I Walk and Read.* Greenwillow, 1984.
Photographs of signs children may see while walking down the street.

———. *Is It Larger? Is It Smaller?* Greenwillow, 1985.
Animals and objects photographed in two or more sizes so comparisons can be made.

———. *Is It Rough? Is It Smooth? Is It Shiny?* Greenwillow, 1984.
Photographs of objects with different textures, such as hay, eggs, bubbles, and cotton candy.

———. *Look Again.* Macmillan, 1971.
A square cutout in a white page reveals a portion of the black-and-white photo on the next page so users can guess what the object is before turning the page. The third page gives a second approach to the object.

———. *Over, Under and Through and Other Spatial Concepts.* Macmillan, 1973.
Black-and-white photographs illustrate the identified concepts.

———. *Push, Pull, Empty, Full. A Book of Opposites.* Macmillan, 1972.
Black-and-white photos demonstrate a variety of opposite terms.

———. *Take Another Look.* Greenwillow, 1981.
A portion of the photographs of nine objects and animals are first seen through a circle in a white page so the observer can try to identify the whole from the part. The following page shows the object or animal in an appropriate setting.

———. *Where Is It?* Macmillan, 1974.
Simple rhyme and photographs record the bunny's search for something special.

BIOGRAPHICAL SOURCES:

For more information on Tana Hoban, see *Fourth Book of Junior Authors & Illustrators,* 178–79; *Something about the Author,* 22:158–59.

GROUP INTRODUCTORY ACTIVITY:

Share *Over, Under and Through and Other Spatial Concepts* with the children. Urge them to look at each illustration carefully, for Tana Hoban says that her books are about ordinary things that people often overlook. She tries to rediscover them and share them in her books. One must do more than just glance at her pictures, she says, because she always tries to include something new.[1] Talk about the meaning of each concept. Have children pantomime concepts illustrated, using classroom objects, for members of the class to interpret. Suggest that the children find pictures in magazines or draw one of the concepts for a Hoban bulletin board.

FOLLOW-UP ACTIVITIES FOR TEACHER AND STUDENTS TO SHARE:

1. Read Hoban's *Where Is It?* to the class. Suppose the story was about a dog. Where would it search? What might it find? Pretend something is hidden in the school for a child to find. Where might s/he look? What might they find?
2. Share Hoban's *A, B, See!* with the class. Identify the objects arranged. Suggest that each child bring magazine pictures from home or cut out small construction paper objects that begin with the same letter. Arrange them attractively on the overhead and project for the class to identify.

   Share the dedication "This one is for Miela." Talk about who Miela might be. See if Hoban's other books also have a dedication.
3. Share Hoban's *Circles, Triangles and Squares* with the class. Note the book dedication: What might it mean? Take a walk around the school or outside. Look for objects or parts of objects with a circle, triangle, or square shape.
4. Share Hoban's *Is It Larger? Is It Smaller?* with the class. Let different children identify each object compared and describe the relative size. Let them think of other larger/smaller comparisons such as father and son.
5. Share Hoban's *Look Again* and *Take Another Look.* Let different children guess what each object will be, turn the page, then anticipate the setting in which each object will be placed.

   Make a *Look One More Time* book. Have children find a picture from a magazine that they want to include. Have them cut out a triangular hole from the sheet of white paper that, when placed over the picture, will reveal a bit of the object; children can thus try to identify the whole from the part. All triangular openings need not be in the center of the page. Staple the book and make a cover. Perhaps the class may want to share it with another kindergarten or first-grade class in the school.
6. Share Hoban's *Dig, Drill, Dump, Fill.* Discuss the exact tasks of each of the items of equipment illustrated. Using the plan of this book as a guide, suggest that the class think of a car book they could make to demonstrate other concepts such as fast, slow, high, low. Specific cars or settings might be used to demonstrate the concepts.
7. Share Hoban's *Big Ones, Little Ones* with a class or small group. Have them look on the way home or at home for all the

big/little items they can find. Make a list on the board of all the ideas they bring back. See if you can get 100 items in the list.

8. Share Hoban's *Is It Rough? Is It Smooth? Is It Shiny?* with the class. Have the children identify each familiar object and describe the texture. If possible, have a few of the pictured objects available for touching. Then let them discuss the texture of objects around them. Have them bring small objects from home or take a walk and discover objects that can be placed in a texture display of rough, smooth, sticky, etc.

9. Share Hoban's *Push, Pull, Empty, Full* with the class. Have children recall the illustrations so a list of opposites can be made on the blackboard. Children can think of other opposites to list during this sharing session as well as in days to come.

10. Share Hoban's *I Walk And Read* with the class. Let the children identify each sign and talk about where it might be seen. Follow up with a discussion of other signs they can recall. Draw those suggestions on the blackboard or overhead projector acetate for all to see. Take a walk and look for signs on cars, trucks, and streets, and in yards.

Nursery Rhyme Adventures

STUDENT OBJECTIVES:

- Compare the illustrations of a favorite rhyme in different books
- Learn a nursery rhyme and record it on tape
- Illustrate a favorite rhyme for a class bulletin board or book
- Participate in choral speaking and singing of rhymes

RECOMMENDED READING:

The Bells of London. Illustrated by Ashley Wolff. Dodd, Mead, 1985. Linoleum-block illustrations tell the story of how two children save the pet dove that the little girl must sell.

Brian Wildsmith's Mother Goose. Oxford University Press, 1982. Familiar and little-known verses with stunning watercolor illustrations.

The Comic Adventures of Old Mother Hubbard and Her Dog. Illustrated by Tomie de Paola. Harcourt, Brace, Jovanovich, 1981.
The adventures are given a stage setting with other nursery rhyme characters watching the show—ready to be identified by the reader.

James Marshall's Mother Goose. Farrar, Straus & Giroux, 1979.
Thirty-five rhymes with humorous cartoon-style illustrations are included.

Marguerite de Angeli's Book of Nursery and Mother Goose Rhymes. Doubleday, 1954.
Over 250 illustrations accompany the almost 400 rhymes in this oversized collection.

Mother Goose. Illustrated by Frederick Richardson. Rand-McNally, 1976.
A new version of the classic 1915 Volland edition.

Mother Goose. Illustrated by Tasha Tudor. Walck, 1944.
Seventy-seven verses are enhanced by old-fashioned illustrations.

Real Mother Goose. Illustrated by Blanche Fisher Wright. Rand-McNally, 1916, 1944.
Illustrations on every page add to the enjoyment of over 300 rhymes.

Singing Bee! Illustrated by Anita Lobel. Lothrop, 1982.
A colorfully illustrated collection of 125 favorite children's songs, including many familiar nursery rhymes.

The Tall Book of Mother Goose. Illustrated by Feodor Rojankovsky. Harper & Row, 1942.
A gaily illustrated volume in a unique shape.

GROUP INTRODUCTORY ACTIVITY:

Share Brian Wildsmith's illustrations in his Mother Goose book. See if children can guess each rhyme from the illustrations. Let the one who guessed correctly try to say the rhyme. Then all repeat as a choral reading. Pantomime "Little Bo Peep," "Little Miss Muffet," "Jack Be Nimble," etc., with those students not actively involved in the pantomime repeating the rhyme.

FOLLOW-UP ACTIVITIES FOR TEACHER AND STUDENTS TO SHARE:

1. Introduce Lobel's illustrated *Singing Bee.* Sing some of the familiar nursery rhymes.

2. Pick subjects such as animals, boys, girls, flowers, etc. If volunteer adults or older students are available for assistance, divide the class into small groups to search in available collections for rhymes to fit each classification. The teacher can copy each of these rhymes on a page for children to illustrate and organize into a class rhyme book.

3. Read Wolff's *The Bells of London* to the children, giving them time to carefully look at each picture. Then share the illustrations again, this time having the class tell the story Wolff has given in the pictures. Let them discuss how the little girl must have felt to have to sell the dove. What clues to her feelings do the illustrations give? How did the dove get away? From what dangers did the children save the dove? Was it a happy ending?

4. Share the poem "Humpty Dumpty." Ask students to think of reasons he may have fallen off the wall. A small group of students may want to search for illustrations to see if any suggest a reason. The children may want to illustrate some of the reasons they suggested.

5. With the help of older children or adult volunteers let a small group pick a favorite rhyme and find as many illustrations as possible for that rhyme. Urge the children to determine which illustrations they like best. Keep a record of the favorite illustration of each small group to see if one book's illustrations are favorites.

6. Urge each child to learn a favorite rhyme and share it orally with the class. Afterwards, have each of the students audiotape or videotape that favorite rhyme with the assistance of the library media specialist. Share with the class and also with parents at an open house.

7. Share de Paola's *The Comic Adventures of Old Mother Hubbard and Her Dog* with the class. See how many other rhymes the class can identify from the small illustrations on each page. Repeat those rhymes in unison.

Fun with Pat Hutchins's Books

STUDENT OBJECTIVES:

- Compare one book with another
- Compare the same story through the media of film and book
- Create animal sounds
- Extend a story by imagining new outcomes
- Translate a message whispered from child to child

RECOMMENDED READING:

Hutchins, Pat. *Changes, Changes.* Macmillan, 1971.
The wooden man and woman arrange and rearrange wooden blocks.

——. *Good-night, Owl!* Macmillan, 1972.
Animals who kept the owl awake all day with their noises are awakened at night by the owl's screech of revenge.

——. *Rosie's Walk.* Macmillan, 1968.
Few words are needed to create the suspense of a stalking fox who has failed in each attempt to catch Rosie the hen.

——. *The Surprise Party.* Macmillan, 1969.
Rabbit's whispered message about a party is altered as it is passed on and, until properly decoded, causes refused invitations.

——. *The Tale of Thomas Mead.* Greenwillow, 1980.
Thomas makes a lot of trouble for himself because he refuses to learn to read.

——. *Titch.* Macmillan, 1971.
Titch's brother and sister always make him feel inadequate until a little seed brings him reassuring success.

——. *The Very Worst Monster.* Greenwillow, 1985.
Hazel Monster tries to prove to her family that she is worse than her brother.

——. *The Wind Blew.* Macmillan, 1974.
The mischievous wind snatches away many items before tiring of playing with them and blowing off to sea.

BIOGRAPHICAL SOURCES:

For more information on Pat Hutchins, see *Fourth Book of Junior Authors & Illustrators,* 189–91; *Something about the Author,* 15:141–45; *Twentieth-Century Children's Writers,* 2d ed., 402–03.

GROUP INTRODUCTORY ACTIVITY:

Read Hutchins's story *Good-night, Owl!* aloud. Tell the children that Pat Hutchins was born in England, and during her childhood, her mother often cared for injured animals. Her family had all kinds of pets, even a hedgehog. To escape their sometimes noisy house Pat and her pet Sooty the crow would sometimes go to the fields where she would sketch. When she was 16 she received a scholarship at an art school. Pat enjoys doing her own illustrations for her books, since she likes to be involved from the first idea to the finished product.[2] Dramatize *Good-night, Owl!* with each child making one of the animal sounds.

Ask the children to think of other noises that keep them awake at night and make the sound for others to guess.

FOLLOW-UP ACTIVITIES FOR TEACHER AND STUDENTS TO SHARE:

1. Read Hutchins's *Titch* aloud to the group. Have the children think of advantages to being the youngest and make an "I'm Glad I'm Titch" list or illustrated book.
2. Let children share in reading Hutchins's picture story *Changes, Changes.* Then, if available, view the film *Changes, Changes* (Weston Woods, 1974, 6 min., color, 16 mm.), which is based on the book. Talk about the advantages of one medium over the other in presenting the story.
3. Share Hutchins's *The Tale of Thomas Mead* with the class. Have them think of other troubles that people might have if they could not read specific signs. Make the signs on the blackboard.
4. Read Hutchins's *The Surprise Party* to the class. Try passing on a whispered message. See what the final message is. Let each child tell what s/he thought was whispered. See how many times the message changed.
5. Read Hutchins's *The Wind Blew* to the class. Follow this by reading Doris Lund's *Attic of the Wind* (Parents Magazine Press, 1966, o.p.). Were any of the same things mentioned in both stories? How did the endings differ? If the Lund book is not available, have the children pretend the wind has a "storehouse"

of blown-away things up in the sky above the clouds. What could be in the storehouse? Make a sky, clouds, and a big open storehouse on the bulletin board. Have the children draw and/or cut out and place inside pictures of objects the wind might blow away.

   Note the "For Mark" dedication in *The Wind Blew*. Discuss who Mark might be.

6. Let the children read the pictures for Hutchins's *Rosie's Walk* and tell the story. What if Rosie had been walking around the school and/or schoolyard stalked by the fox? What events could have happened? How would the fox have been stopped from catching Rosie each time?

7. Read Hutchins's *The Very Worst Monster* to the class. Discuss other attempts Hazel might have made to prove she was the very worst monster. Let children suggest what the baby monster might have done to cause him to be returned to his parents.

Play with Marie Hall Ets's Characters

STUDENT OBJECTIVES:

- Dramatize a story
- Invent and demonstrate an imaginary game
- Pantomime ways one can talk without words

RECOMMENDED READING:

Ets, Marie Hall. *Another Day*. Viking, 1953. o.p.
   A little boy helps the forest animals decide which activity is best.

———. *Gilberto and the Wind*. Viking, 1963.
   Gilberto plays games with the wind and finally falls asleep.

———. *In the Forest*. Viking, 1972.
   A small boy with a horn and paper hat leads imaginary animals in a forest parade.

———. *Just Me*. Viking, 1965.
   A small boy wants to play with the animals by imitating the way each moves.

————. *Play with Me.* Viking, 1955.
A little girl finds that trying to catch the animals is not the way to play with them.

————. *Talking without Words.* Viking, 1968. (o.p.)
Identifies many ways people and animals talk to each other without words.

Ets, Marie Hall, and Labastida, Aurora. *Nine Days to Christmas.* Viking, 1959.
Caldecott Award–winning book in which the reader shares with a little Mexican girl the anticipation of her own *posada* and the children's excitement in breaking the piñata.

BIOGRAPHICAL SOURCES:

For more information on Marie Hall Ets (deceased), see *Books Are by People,* 61–63; *The Junior Book of Authors,* 2d ed., 115–16; *Something about the Author,* 2:102–03; *Twentieth-Century Children's Writers,* 413–15; *Twentieth-Century Children's Writers,* 2d ed., 266–67.

GROUP INTRODUCTORY ACTIVITY:

Read the story *Play with Me* to the class. Then dramatize the story, allowing children to select an animal each wants to interpret. Let more than one child pretend to be the same animal so the whole class can participate.

Share with the class the childhood of Marie Hall Ets. She has said that the happiest memories of her childhood were of summers in the Wisconsin North Woods. "I loved to run off by myself into the woods and watch for the deer with their fawns and for porcupines and badgers and turtles and frogs and huge pine snakes and sometimes a bear or a copperhead or a skunk. When I was old enough to be trusted alone in a flat bottomed boat I used to explore the lake shore or the channels between the lakes."[3] Suggest that as they share more of her books they note how many times the plot involves playing alone with animals.

FOLLOW-UP ACTIVITIES FOR TEACHER AND STUDENTS TO SHARE:

1. Read Ets's *In the Forest* to the class. Recall with their help her early childhood. Talk about how she might have got the idea for the story. Note the end of the story. Explore what Ets may have

meant by the promise "I'll hunt for you another day." (*Another Day* was a sequel.)

Discuss other games the animals might have played at the picnic. Suggest that the children pretend to be forest animals and play one of the games they talked about.

Have an animal parade, pantomiming appropriate actions.

2. Read Ets's *Another Day* to the group. Invent other activities the little boy may have chosen and demonstrate each. Discuss why laughing was or was not a better choice than those demonstrated.

   Imagine activities different farm animals would do and dramatize the story using the farm animals suggested instead of those in Ets's story.

3. Before reading Ets's *Gilberto and the Wind* to the group, tell them how the story was written. Ets was on vacation in California and was looking for a story model. She saw a little boy that attracted her but she had no camera or drawing materials with her. Then the little boy ran across the street and threw his arms around her legs. In broken Spanish, she asked him to take her to his mother. The little boy was Gilberto, who became the model for the story.[4] Pantomime the games Gilberto played with the wind. Think of other games he could have played and demonstrate each.

   Suggest they draw pictures of a "wind/child" game.

4. Read Ets's *Just Me* to the class. Imagine other endings the story might have had to cause the boy to end his play.

   Dramatize the story, using several children as each animal when desired.

   Think of zoo animals and pantomime their movements. Ask children why Ets did not have the little boy play with zoo animals in her story.

5. Share Ets's *Talking without Words* with the class. Instead of verbalizing other activities one might do without words, pantomime them for others to guess. The children may want to draw pictures of ideas suggested and make a class *Talking without Words* book.

6. If Ets is shared during the December holiday season, tell her *Nine Days to Christmas,* sharing the illustrations as the story is told. For a follow-up fill a cardboard or papier mâché piñata with wrapped candies and break it.

Bearables

STUDENT OBJECTIVES:

- Make a stick puppet and use it in a storytelling activity
- Observe the moon and help record its shape
- Participate in the choral reading of a book
- Record his/her ideas on tape and play back for the class
- Discuss what a pseudonym is and why an author would use one

RECOMMENDED READING:

Asch, Frank. *Moon Bear.* Scribner's, 1978, o.p.
Bear sees the moon getting smaller and tries to feed it honey so it will become round again.

———. *Mooncake.* Prentice-Hall, 1983.
Bear builds a rocket because he wants to taste the moon.

———. *Moongame.* Prentice-Hall, 1984.
Moon hides behind a cloud while playing hide-and-seek with Bear, causing all the animals to join in a search.

Freeman, Don. *Beady Bear.* Viking, 1954.
Beady the toy bear tries to live alone in a cave but misses something.

———. *Bearymore.* Viking, 1976.
Bearymore discovers that sleeping and working on a new act may cause problems.

———. *Corduroy.* Viking, 1968.
Despite an unsuccessful search for a lost button, Corduroy, a department-store toy bear, is purchased by the little girl Lisa.

———. *A Pocket for Corduroy.* Viking, 1978.
Corduroy spends the night in the laundromat while searching for a pocket.

Gage, Wilson. *Cully Cully and the Bear.* Greenwillow, 1983.
Cully Cully and the bear are very confused about who is chasing whom around the tree.

Lemieux, Michele. *What's that Noise?* Morrow, 1985.
Brown Bear hears an unidentifiable noise and, in the pursuit of its origin, discovers many other intriguing sounds.

Mack, Stan *10 Bears in My Bed.* Pantheon, 1974.
> A counting-down story in which the bed is finally cleared of bears.

Maris, Ron. *Are You There, Bear?* Greenwillow, 1985.
> After a search for a toy bear in a darkened bedroom, he is found reading a book.

McPhail, David. *The Bear's Toothache.* Little, Brown, 1972.
> A little boy succeeds in helping a bear get rid of an aching tooth.

GROUP INTRODUCTORY ACTIVITY:

Read Lemieux's *What's that Noise?* to the class. As you read, ask the children to make each of the italicized sounds when you point to them. (Point to the class right after you read each sound.)

After reading the story, have the children recall the sounds that were made and identify each. Encourage the children to think of other animals or things the bear might have identified as making a sound. Have them make each sound.

FOLLOW-UP ACTIVITIES FOR TEACHER AND STUDENTS TO SHARE:

1. Read Freeman's *Beady Bear* to the class. Discuss with the class the sequence of events and let two volunteers act out the story.

   Have children think of things *they* might have taken from their house to make a cave seem like home.

   Help children make stick puppets of Beady Bear and Thayer. Suggest they act out the story with a partner, using the puppets.
2. Share Maris's *Are You There, Bear?* with the class. Let children guess what will be found in each place before the toy is revealed. After reading the story, let the children again look at the illustration on the cover of the book Bear is reading. Have the children make up a title for the book.

   Urge the children to think of a story their parents may have shared that a bear might tell. If someone names *The Three Bears,* let them reconstruct the scenes in that story and act it out if desired.
3. Read Freeman's *Bearymore* aloud. Have students pretend they are Bearymore and suggest a circus act that could be done. Let them demonstrate if possible.
4. Read Mack's *10 Bears In My Bed* aloud. Then read it again, having the class be the chorus for each "Roll over, Roll over." Suggest that they notice on this reading the various ways the

bears left the bedroom. Let children recall the ones pictured and then think of other ways the bears could have chosen to leave.

5. Read Freeman's *Corduroy* to the class. Ask the children to suggest things they would do for fun if locked in a department store overnight.

   Assist small groups in thinking of ways that Lisa and Corduroy might play together. Have them act out the ideas for the class.

6. Read Freeman's *A Pocket for Corduroy* aloud. Suggest that the children may want to think of some other difficulty Corduroy might have encountered during a night at the laundromat. Share the ideas as a class. Ahead of time make a pair of overalls for a stuffed bear. Give each child a paper pocket to decorate. Pin a new pocket on the bear's overalls each day.

7. Read Asch's *Moon Bear* aloud to the class. After reading the story let children discuss why Bear loved the moon. Why did most of the birds not want to tell Bear what was causing the honey to disappear? How did the little bird keep Bear from being sad at the end of the story?

   Read to the children pages 10–19 in Franklyn Branley's *The Moon Seems to Change* (Crowell, 1960) or another simply written book about why the moon changes. Ask the children to look at the moon that night and see what stage the moon is in. Make a bulletin board of Bear and stages of the moon. Label with the date as children report that the moon is in each stage from new to full.

8. Read Asch's *Mooncake* to the class. Have children think of other ways besides building a rocket that Bear might have tried to reach the moon. Ask the children what Bear thought the moon would taste like. If Bear had been a mouse instead, what might he have thought the moon would taste like? Why do the children suppose Asch named the book *Mooncake*? Have the children think of other animals and suggest what each animal thought the moon would taste like.

   Share with the children poems from *The Man in the Moon as He Sails the Sky* (Dodd, Mead, 1979), being sure to read "The Moon's the North Wind's Cooky."

9. Read Asch's *Moongame* to the class. As the book is read let children guess what each yellow object was that the Bear saw while hunting the moon. Then show the pictures of the daisy, the cheese, and the balloon.

   Look again at the double-spread picture of all the animals searching for the moon. Let children note what some of the animals were using to assist them in the search. What else might they have used?

10. Read McPhail's *The Bear's Toothache* to the class. Recall the ways the little boy tried to help the bear get rid of the tooth. What other ideas do the children have of things he might have

tried? Why did the boy put the bear's tooth under his pillow? Let the children describe how their own teeth that did not fall out have been removed.

11. Read Gage's *Cully Cully and the Bear.* Discuss what made the bear and Cully Cully think there was more than one of each. Ask the children if they have ever run in a circle until they were dizzy. Did they react as the bear did? If they banged their noses, would they use cool mud to bring relief? What might they use?

Tell the children that Wilson Gage's name is really Mary Steele and that her husband was also an author. Explain what a "pseudonym" is, and let them think of reasons why she might have chosen to write under a pseudonym.

Imagine . . . As You Can

STUDENT OBJECTIVES:

- Develop a bulletin board relating to a book title
- Pantomime a story
- Create and describe shadow pictures cast on the wall
- Demonstrate visual literacy by translating pictures into words before text is read

RECOMMENDED READING:

Burningham, John. *Come Away from the Water, Shirley.* Crowell, 1977.
While Shirley's parents sit on the beach and yell out instructions, Shirley goes off on a fantasy adventure fighting pirates and digging for buried treasure.

———. *Mr. Gumpy's Motor Car.* Crowell, 1973.
Mr. Gumpy gets stuck in a muddy road, much to the dismay of all of his passengers, who must help push the car to the top of the hill.

———. *Mr. Gumpy's Outing.* Holt, Rinehart & Winston, 1971.
Mr. Gumpy's boat ride involves 10 characters who, despite causing the boat to overturn, manage to create a pleasant ending.

———. *The Shopping Basket.* Crowell, 1980.
On the return home from the store with his purchases, Steven meets a number of animals that demand food from him.

———. *Time to Get out of the Bath, Shirley.* Crowell, 1978.
Unmindful of her mother's discourse about bathing, Shirley's fanciful imagination takes her to the land of kings and queens.

———. *Would You Rather....* Crowell, 1978.
Several hypothetical questions are introduced, such as "Would you rather be lost in a fog, or at sea, in a desert, in a forest or in a crowd?", with preposterous results.

Christopher, Eileen. *Henry and the Dragon.* Clarion, 1984.
After Henry Rabbit hears a story about dragons, he sees shadows in his room and begins to imagine a dragon living near his house.

Gackenbach, Dick. *Harry and the Terrible Whatzit.* Houghton Mifflin, 1978.
When Harry goes searching for his mother in the cellar, he comes face to face with the whatzit.

Oram, Hiawyn. *In the Attic.* Holt, Rinehart & Winston, 1985.
Bored, a little boy uses his fire truck ladder to escape to the attic and discovers marvelous places to explore.

Strauss, Joyce. *Imagine That!!! Exploring Make Believe.* Human Sciences Press, 1984.
Questions that lead the reader into a make-believe situation are asked to stimulate the reader's imagination.

GROUP INTRODUCTORY ACTIVITY:

Read aloud or share the sound filmstrip of Burningham's *Mr. Gumpy's Outing.* (Weston Woods, 1973, color, 5 min.) After sharing the tale, urge the children to retell the story by asking, "Whom did we meet first in the story?" "Whom next?" etc. Select a child to be Mr. Gumpy. Then, as each of the characters are named, pick a volunteer to be that character. After the animals practice their noises, reread the story with the children pantomiming the characters.

FOLLOW-UP ACTIVITIES FOR TEACHER AND STUDENTS TO SHARE:

1. Before reading Burningham's *Mr. Gumpy's Motor Car,* talk to the children about how Burningham makes his books—that he likes to draw his pictures first and then tell a story through the drawings. When he is satisfied with the story that his picture tells, he adds words.[5]

Introduce Mr. Gumpy, recalling that the children have met him earlier in *Mr. Gumpy's Outing.* Instead of reading the story, use a piece of tagboard to cover the words on each page or paper clip construction paper strips over the words throughout the books. Let the children absorb the pictures on each page, then uncover the words and read how Burningham tells his story. As the children get excited about the story, let them say what they think is happening before reading the words.

2. As Burningham's *Would You Rather . . .* is read aloud and the illustrations are shared, have the children participate in each of the situations by responding with a yes or no. Place the words "Would You Rather" on a bulletin board. Ask the children to think of an idea and illustrate it. Then place the illustrations on the bulletin board. As each child finishes the picture and describes it to the teacher, it can be labeled with an appropriate line, i.e., "eat a hot dog on a stick." The picture should come first, then the words.

3. Before reading Burningham's *The Shopping Basket* to the class, have the store items mentioned in the book ready to use on the flannel board. To help illustrate the numerical sequences from the story, display the items on the flannel board exactly as they are in the book. When Steven meets each character and loses an apple, orange, banana, etc., take the item off the flannel board. Let the children draw other items Steven could have purchased at the store.

4. Set the scene for sharing Burningham's *Time to Get out of the Bath, Shirley* by talking to the children about the ways to have fun while bathing and what they can pretend to do by floating specific toys. Then introduce Shirley as a little girl who travels in a pretend world. Make sure when reading about Shirley that the children have begun to visualize her trip down the drain pipe. After reading the story discuss Shirley's pretend trip. What was her mother doing? On the last page is a full-color spread of Shirley's imaginary pipe system. Let the children recall aspects of the story by identifying objects in the illustration.

5. Shirley is off again on high-seas adventures in Burningham's *Come away from the Water, Shirley.* After sharing the story, encourage the children to talk about experiences they may have had or could have on the beach. Help them get the feel for the beach by making caves and castles in a large framed table covered with a few inches of sand, if one is available in the classroom. If that is not possible, try sandpainting. Put a mixture of half glue and half water in a tin can. Using paint brushes and the glue-water mixture, the children can paint a design on heavy paper. Sprinkle sand on their designs and let dry.

6. After sharing Shirley's pretend trips in Burningham's *Come away from the Water, Shirley* and *Time to Get out of the Bath, Shirley,* take the children on other types of imaginary trips.

Enjoy an exploration with Sandra Sivulich's *I'm Going on a Bear Hunt* (Dutton, 1973). Follow up by "Going on a Lion Hunt" after reading *Andy and the Lion* by James Daugherty (Viking, 1938) or a hippo hunt following the reading of *The Boy Who Was Followed Home* by Margaret Mahy (Watts, 1975). For a very unusual picture trip share Ann Jonas's *Round Trip* (Greenwillow, 1983).

7. Using different-sized boxes as windows, let the children look through them to imagine what they see just as the little boy in Oram's *In the Attic* did when he opened the windows to other worlds. After sharing the story aloud, have the children share what they imagined they saw. A large refrigerator box may be decorated and placed where children can be alone to read and imagine other worlds.

8. After reading Gackenbach's *Harry and the Terrible Whatzit* let the children share imaginary experiences in meeting terrible whatzits. Then place clear acetate on the overhead projector and let children use colored vis-à-vis pens to draw their idea of a whatzit. Let children take turns adding parts, and when a creature is completed, let those who have participated in drawing describe what it eats, where it lives, etc. Continue the activity over the next few days until all have had a chance to participate. Be sure to leave the projector on while they are drawing so others can watch the creature come into being.

9. Each question in Strauss's *Imagine That!!!* leads to an appropriate group experience. For instance, let the children create someone of their own age and describe what that person is like. Have each child lie down on butcher paper and have someone draw around him/her. Then each child can decorate his/her own character to suit the personality of the one described. As a class, children can discuss activities they enjoy sharing with friends.

10. After sharing Christelow's *Henry and the Dragon,* have the children do what Henry did when he discovered his shadow dragon. Use either a flashlight or an overhead projector to cast a light on the wall. Have the children use their arms or other objects to cast shadows on the wall and describe what they imagine them to be.

Friends Created by Jose Aruego and Ariane Dewey

STUDENT OBJECTIVES:

● Develop the idea of making friends with book characters
● Associate author with the text and illustrator with the pictures
● Pantomime a story
● Prepare a collage picture based on a story experience
● Recall the components of a title page

RECOMMENDED READING:

Aruego, Jose. *Look What I Can Do.* Scribner's, 1971.
   The attempts of two carabaos to outdo each other almost end in disaster.

Aruego, Jose, and Dewey, Ariane. *We Hide, You Seek.* Greenwillow, 1979.
   After the rhino accidentally uncovers others in a jungle hide-and-seek game, he hides himself.

Ginsburg, Mirra. *The Chick and the Duckling.* Illustrated by Jose and Ariane Aruego. Macmillan, 1972.
   Wherever the duckling goes or whatever it does, the chick follows and chirps, "Me, too."

———. *Where Does the Sun Go at Night?* Illustrated by Jose Aruego and Ariane Dewey. Greenwillow, 1981.
   Animals follow the sun from sunset to dawn to find out where the sun goes at night.

Kraus, Robert. *Another Mouse to Feed.* Illustrated by Jose Aruego and Ariane Dewey. Windmill, 1980.
   Mr. and Mrs. Mouse have a difficult time supporting 31 children, but when the thirty-second arrives the children volunteer to help by getting after-school jobs and doing the housework.

———. *Whose Mouse Are You?* Illustrated by Jose Aruego. Macmillan, 1970.
   A young mouse rescues his mother from the cat and his father from the trap, finds his sister, and wishes for a brother, since he has none.

Shannon, George. *Dance Away.* Illustrated by Jose Aruego and Ariane Dewey. Greenwillow, 1982.
Rabbit, who loves to dance, rescues his friends from the fox with his dancing song.

BIOGRAPHICAL SOURCES:

For more information on Jose Aruego, see *Fourth Book of Junior Authors & Illustrators,* 14–16; *Something about the Author,* 6:3–5.
For more information on Ariane Dewey, see *Fourth Book of Junior Authors & Illustrators,* 115–17; *Something about the Author,* 7:63–65.

GROUP INTRODUCTORY ACTIVITY:

Before sharing Shannon's *Dance Away,* talk about friends (book characters) who live between the covers of a book. Identify some of your book friends such as Thomas Mead in *The Tale of Thomas Mead* and Hazel Monster in *The Very Worst Monster,* both from the "Fun with Pat Hutchins's Books" unit. Ask the children if they remember any special book friends.

Then introduce *Dance Away,* telling the class it is about a rabbit who saves his friends by dancing. Turn to the title page, pointing out the title, that the author George Shannon wrote the story, and that the pictures were drawn by Jose Aruego and Ariane Dewey. Reinforce the meaning of the words "author" and "illustrator" by having them repeat each. Throughout the unit talk about who is the author and illustrator of each book.

Tell the children that as they look at the illustrations in this unit, they should feel encouraged. Ariane Dewey said that when she tried to paint a picture in the fourth grade, she repainted it so many times that the paper tore. She did not give up and after making her first book for a class, she knew she would always paint.[6]

Jose Aruego first became a lawyer, probably because others in his family were lawyers. That seems a strange background for someone who now enjoys drawing funny animals doing laughable things.[7]

As *Dance Away* is shared, urge the children to participate in the "left two three kick" chant. Talk about the plot, then pantomime or dramatize the story with the children as rabbits and fox participating in the dance.

Talk about why the rabbits became tired of their dancing friend. Would they be friends again after the fox problem?

FOLLOW-UP ACTIVITIES FOR TEACHER AND STUDENTS TO SHARE:

1. Share Ginsburg's *The Chick and the Duckling* with the class. Open the book to the title page. Point out the title, author, and illustrators. When reading the story, emphasize the "Me, too" with a high-pitched voice. The children will soon join in.

   After completing the story, ask the children what other activities these two friends could do together. Then compose their ideas into a sequence such as:

   > "I found a ———," said the duckling.
   > "Me, too," said the chick.
   > "I want a ———," said the duckling.
   > "Me, too," said the chick.
   > "I am ———," said the duckling.
   > "Me, too," said the chick...etc.

   Ask the children for ideas about what a friend is. Encourage them to tell what they do with their friends.

2. Before reading Kraus's *Whose Mouse Are You?* prepare a bulletin board with the title of the book across the top. The first picture of the mouse sticking his head out of the mouse hole can be enlarged by using the opaque projector, and that can be featured on the board. Share *Whose Mouse Are You?* aloud, pointing out the author and illustrator on the title page.

   After the story let the children talk briefly about their families. Urge them to bring a picture of their family, if possible, to place on the bulletin board after they share it with the class.

3. The children will delight in Mr. and Mrs. Mouse's dilemma in Kraus's *Another Mouse to Feed.* Jose Aruego's illustrations depict the dozens of jobs the children obtain. Point out each illustration while reading the story to see if the class understands what the jobs are.

   After sharing the story discuss the jobs outside the home that their parents have. What can the children do to help their families? What jobs can they do in the classroom to help the teacher?

4. Jose Aruego wrote the book as well as drawing the pictures in *Look What I Can Do.* Point that out to the children before reading the brief text. Ask the children to suppose the story had been about two dogs. What might they have done to try to outdo each other? How could the dog story end?

5. Jose Aruego and Ariane Dewey were the author/illustrators of *We Hide, You Seek.* Share this book with pairs or small groups of children. Ask them to find and name the animals that are

hidden. Urge them to examine the illustrations closely and keep a record of which group finds the most.

6. By now the children should be able to recognize and identify with the illustrations of Jose Aruego and Ariane Dewey in Ginsburg's *Where Does the Sun Go at Night?* Share the book aloud with the class. Complete the unit with an art activity. Using brightly colored art paper as background, give the children cotton balls to create their own "cloudimals." Lightly glue the cotton shapes to the paper.

Everyday Experiences through the Books of Rosemary Wells

STUDENT OBJECTIVES:

* Identify rhyming sounds
* Express feelings about friends
* Talk about responsibilities of family members
* Explore and/or reinforce word and number concepts

RECOMMENDED READING:

Wells, Rosemary. *Benjamin and Tulip.* Dial, 1973.
Tulip beats up Benjamin every time he passes her until they discover they both like watermelon.

———. *A Lion for Lewis.* Dial, 1982.
Lewis, the littlest sibling, gets tired of playing all the minor roles in games with his brother and sister.

———. *Max's First Word.* Dial, 1979.
In this first of four small board books Max's older sister Ruby tries in vain to teach him his first word.
Others in the series are:
Max's New Suit. Dial, 1979.
Max's Ride. Dial, 1979.
Max's Toys. Dial, 1979.

————. *Morris's Disappearing Bag: A Christmas Story.* Dial, 1975.
Morris is so disappointed in his Christmas present that he invents a disappearing bag which gets the attention of his brother and sisters.

————. *Noisy Nora.* Dial, 1973.
Rhymed verse describes Nora's attempts to get her family's attention.

————. *Stanley and Rhoda.* Dial, 1978.
In three short stories the reader meets a clever older brother, Stanley, and his little sister Rhoda.

————. *Timothy Goes to School.* Dial, 1981.
Tired of tolerating Claude, the overachiever, Timothy plans to quit school, until he finds a friend with similar problems.

BIOGRAPHICAL SOURCES:

For more information on Rosemary Wells, see *Fourth Book of Junior Authors & Illustrators,* 343–45; *Something about the Author,* 18:296–98; *Twentieth-Century Children's Writers,* 2d ed., 810–11.

GROUP INTRODUCTORY ACTIVITY:

Share *Timothy Goes to School* with the class. Tell the class Rosemary Wells always loved to draw, even in school when she should have been studying. Her parents encouraged her, and in a house full of books and no television, it is no wonder she got her first job in book publishing at 19. There she was "discovered" as an author/artist.[8] Ask the children to express how Timothy feels about Claude, Claude about Timothy, Violet about Grace, and Grace about Violet. Their facial expressions are useful clues.

Follow the discussion with a "feelings box." In a shoebox collect pictures from magazines showing feelings as evidenced in facial expressions. As each picture is drawn from the box, ask the children to decide how the person feels. Think of reasons the person pictured might feel that way.

FOLLOW-UP ACTIVITIES FOR TEACHER AND STUDENTS TO SHARE:

1. Share Wells's book or the sound filmstrip *Noisy Nora* (Weston Woods, 1973, 28 fr., col., 10 min.). Let children discuss Nora's feelings. Why was she being noisy? Print the words to *Noisy Nora* in poetry form on a large poster board. Tape a piece of

paper over the last rhyming word in each stanza. When the verses are read aloud, have the children guess what each last word is. When the correct word is given, show the word to the class.

2. Read *A Lion for Lewis* aloud to the students. Follow with a discussion about Lewis's feelings on being the youngest and their own feelings about the problems faced by the youngest child. Then read aloud Steven Kellogg's *Much Bigger than Martin* (Dial, 1976). Have the class compare the problem of Lewis and Henry and how it was solved in each case.

3. Share Wells's book or the sound filmstrip *Morris' Disappearing Bag* (Weston Woods, 1978, 38 fr., col., 6 min.) before the holiday season. Have an empty bag to share with children after the story. Ask the children to imagine a gift they want that could be in the bag. One by one have the children reach into the bag, find an imaginary object, and without telling the other children what it is, describe it to the class. See if the class can guess each object.

4. Read aloud Wells's *Benjamin and Tulip* or share the filmstrip (Weston Woods, 1975, 38 fr., col., 4 min.) Remind the children to notice the faces of Benjamin and Tulip. Let children talk about ways to meet and keep friends. Find food likenesses the children have in common. Have a tea party for the class in which fruit juice is served.

5. Read aloud and laugh along with Wells's *Stanley and Rhoda.* Point out the title page and explain that the book has three different stories about a brother and sister. (This book would be ideal for a unit on families.) Discuss responsibilities of each member of a family. Share ideas of ways families work and play together as a team. Have the children cut out pictures from magazines and newspapers showing families and friends working and playing together. Have the children explain what they think the people in the pictures are doing. A treat of "Bunny Berries" (jelly beans) would be an enjoyable close to the sharing of the story.

6. In a reading center use Wells's four board books about Max. Enlarged pictures of Max for decoration can easily be made using an opaque projector. Each book deals with a single concept. Have picture cards to show what Max's sister was trying to teach Max to say in *Max's First Word* and in *Max's Ride.* If children are having a difficult time dressing as Max did in *Max's New Suit,* have large dolls available to dress and old shoes with shoelaces on which to practice. Have beads and sticks at the center so children can count along with Max in *Max's Toys.*

Steven Kellogg's Characters Come to Life

STUDENT OBJECTIVES:

- Recognize a problem and a solution in a story
- Compare two books on the same subject
- Predict the outcome of a story
- Extend understanding of the months of the year
- Conceptualize large numbers

RECOMMENDED READING:

Kellogg, Steven. *Can I Keep Him?* Dial, 1971.
> Arnold just wants a playmate; but each time he makes a sugges-
tion, his mother responds with "No, Dear."

——. *The Mysterious Tadpole.* Dial, 1977.
> The tadpole that Louis receives for his birthday from his uncle in
Scotland grows into a most unusual creature.

——. *The Mystery of the Missing Red Mitten.* Dial, 1974.
> Annie imagines many possible uses for her lost red mittens as she
and her dog search for them.

——. *The Mystery of the Stolen Blue Paint.* Dial, 1982.
> Belinda's attempt to paint a blue picture for her room is foiled
when the paint disappears.

——. *Pinkerton, Behave!* Dial, 1979.
> As a puppy that is the size of a pony, Pinkerton is sent to
obedience school, where he causes many problems.

——. *A Rose for Pinkerton.* Dial, 1981.
> Pinkerton's life is lonely until Rose the cat arrives and creates a
great deal of turmoil in Pinkerton's family.

——. *Tallyho, Pinkerton.* Dial, 1982.
> Aleasha Kibble's private hunting class and Pinkerton collide head
on to create a riotous fox hunt.

Noble, Trinka Hakes. *The Day Jimmy's Boa Ate the Wash.* Illustrated
by Steven Kellogg. Dial, 1980.
> A could-be-boring class trip to a farm becomes an adventure
when Jimmy's pet boa constrictor finds the hen house.

Schwartz, David M. *How Much Is a Million?* Illustrated by Steven Kellogg. Lothrop, 1985.
Illustrations and text help children conceptualize the terms "million," "billion," and "trillion."

BIOGRAPHICAL SOURCES:

For more information on Steven Kellogg, see *Fourth Book of Junior Authors & Illustrators,* 208–09; *Something about the Author,* 8:95–97.

GROUP INTRODUCTORY ACTIVITY:

A flyer available from Dial Press quotes Steven Kellogg as saying that he was born with a picture in his head and a crayon in his hand. He scribbled all over as a kid, both in legal and illegal places. He literally scribbled his way through elementary school. He also says that as a child he loved telling stories to his little sisters. They would have sessions called "telling stories with pictures." With a stack of paper in his lap he would make up a story and scribble little illustrations as he told it. He did not have a pet as a child and instead made a series of drawings of dogs and other mammals. As a result of his unfulfilled desire to have a dog, he wrote *Can I Keep Him?, The Mysterious Tadpole,* and the Pinkerton series.

Kellogg now lives in a pre–Revolutionary War farmhouse in Sandy Hook, Connecticut. He and his wife Helen have six children; three cats named Second Hand Rose, Dr. Pepper, and Madame Butterfly; and the Great Dane Pinkerton.

After sharing facts about Kellogg, read aloud his *Can I Keep Him?* Ask the children to identify Arnold's problem and the solution to it. What will Arnold's mother say about the bird he brings home as the story ends? Extend the story by urging the children to think of other animals Arnold could have suggested. Where would he find them? What would his mother say?

Make a *Can I Keep Him?* bulletin board. Let children make illustrations of animals they would like to bring home. They may want to look at magazines such as *Ranger Rick* or *National Geographic World* to get ideas.

FOLLOW-UP ACTIVITIES FOR TEACHER AND STUDENTS TO SHARE:

1. Read Kellogg's *The Mysterious Tadpole* or share the sound film-strip of that title (Weston Woods, 1980, 41 fr., col., 9 min.) After viewing the filmstrip or reading the book, review the story by examining Kellogg's illustrations. Be sure to give the children time to note the calendar that appears in several illustrations to show time passing as Alphonse, the tadpole, grows. Turn the pages of a calendar in the room to help the children realize the time span during which the mysterious tadpole grows. Ask them to predict what will happen with Louis's new birthday gift.

2. Read Kellogg's *Pinkerton, Behave!* to the students, taking time for the students to see the action in the illustrations. Point out that the story's pictures begin on the title page. Be sure to note the dedication and have the children try to recall who Helen is. After sharing the story urge the children to think of other commands to which Pinkerton could have been introduced in obedience school. What might have been Pinkerton's reaction to each? If someone in the community trains dogs, invite that person to the class to demonstrate how a dog should be trained to obey.

3. Kellogg's *A Rose for Pinkerton* introduces Rose, another family pet of the Kellogg family. Share this story, allowing time to point out humorous details in the illustrations such as a book called *Kittens,* whose author is Sarah Chattercat. After reading the story have the children describe the problems that resulted from the cat's arrival. How were the problems solved? As small groups of children sit down with the book after the discussion, they may want to note the two pages showing goldfish, birds, and kittens in almost hidden picture format. They also may want to count the animals that are illustrated.

4. Share Kellogg's third Pinkerton book, *Tallyho, Pinkerton,* with the children. After sharing it aloud, ask the children to tell what they think is the funniest part of the story. What other adventures of Pinkerton do you remember that are funny? By now it should be obvious to the children that Steven Kellogg loves animals and enjoys sharing them in his books. The last page of *Tallyho Pinkerton* shows a multitude of animals. Enlarge the picture by placing the book in the opaque projector so the children can identify them. List them and, if possible, plan a field trip to the zoo or a walk in the park to find as many as possible from the list. Were any other animals sighted that Kellogg did not picture?

5. Read aloud Noble's *The Day Jimmy's Boa Ate the Wash,* illustrated by Steven Kellogg. This story, like others illustrated by Kellogg, begins before the title page. The little girl in the story

tells her mother that they never found out why the farmer's wife was screaming. The readers find out why. Ask the class to imagine what life was like on the farm with a pet boa constrictor. Talk about what might have happened. Pretending they are the farmer and his wife, write a letter to Mrs. Stanley's class explaining what happened after they left.

6. Read Schwartz's *How Much Is a Million?* urging children to listen and examine the illustrations carefully. Then have them think about how tall it would be if a million children stood on one another's shoulders to build a single tower. Have the children look at the seven pages of stars as you show the pages 10 times. If the children imagine the stars not visible because of the balloon illustration on each page, they will now have seen a million tiny stars.

7. Share Kellogg's *The Mystery of the Missing Red Mitten.* Note the dedication, exploring who Laurie may be. After reading the book, the children may want to discuss where they have found mittens they have lost. Make the shape of a tree on the blackboard. Label it "OUR LOST MITTEN TREE." Suggest that children bring from home a mitten which has no mate.

   If available, read Laura Bannon's *Red Mittens* (Houghton Mifflin, 1946, o.p.) and/or Alvin Tresselt's *The Mitten* (Lothrop, 1964). Talk about what the stories have in common.

   Set up a "red" center in the classroom or media center. Use books about the color red in addition to the red mittens books. Children may want to have a "red" day in which they wear something red, make a red picture, share the poem "What Is Red" from Mary O'Neil's *Hailstones and Halibut Bones* (Doubleday, 1961) and other types of "red" activities.

8. Read Kellogg's *The Mystery of The Stolen Blue Paint* to the class. Discuss what a mystery story is and how the mystery was solved. Think of other things that could have happened to the paint.

   The children may each want to paint a blue picture after sharing the story.

Think about Mercer Mayer's Stories

STUDENT OBJECTIVES:

- Use their imaginations to create a silly story
- Use finger paints to create their own monsters or "no-things"
- Tape record their own version of a wordless picture book
- Act out stories after reading the pictures
- Think about special things to do for people
- Detect humor in illustrations

RECOMMENDED READING:

Mayer, Mercer. *Ah-Choo.* Dial, 1976.
In this textless tale a poor elephant's allergy to flowers causes a trouble-creating sneeze, but all ends well when someone who is equally allergic is encountered.

———. *Appelard and Liverwurst. Illustrated by Steven Kellogg.* Four Winds, 1978.
Appelard's farm in Cyclone County becomes the center of prosperity when Liverwurst the rhinosterwurst comes to live with him.

———. *Frog, Where Are You?* Dial, 1969.
This wordless picture book tells the adventures the boy and his dog have as they search for their lost pet frog.

———. *If I Had . . .* Dial, 1968.
A small boy who is faced with bullies imagines having a gorilla or an alligator for a friend to help him out of tough situations.

———. *Just for You.* Golden Press, 1975.
The little monster tries unsuccessfully to do something nice for his mother; finally a kiss brings pleasure to both of them.

———. *Liverwurst Is Missing. Illustrated by Steven Kellogg.* Four Winds, 1981.
The action builds as Appelard, the Wackatoo Indians, the Koala scouts, and the retired Forth-ninth Cavalry go in search of Liverwurst, who has been stolen from the Zanzibus Circus by the dastardly Archibald McDoot III.

————. *A Silly Story.* Parents Magazine, 1972. o.p.; Scholastic, 1980.
A young boy begins to wonder throughout the day "What if I'm
not me?" One silly thought leads to another.

————. *Terrible Troll.* Dial, 1968.
To fight evil dragons and rescue fair ladies from bad knights is
the wish of a young boy—until he faces the troll.

————. *There's a Nightmare in My Closet.* Dial, 1968.
A young boy confronts his nightmare only to find out that his
nightmare is afraid.

BIOGRAPHICAL SOURCES:

For more information on Mercer Mayer, see *Fourth Book of
Junior Authors & Illustrators,* 259–61; *Something about the Author,*
32:130–36.

GROUP INTRODUCTORY ACTIVITY:

Share with the children Mercer Mayer's thoughts on imagination.
He says that often when he speaks to young people he tells them that
a book can be written from any point of view. To illustrate, he asks
the audience to imagine a tiny green frog sitting on top of an apple,
the apple on top of an alligator, and the alligator on top of an
elephant. He then asks them to imagine the elephant standing on a
ball. Now he has everyone imagining the same thing, but they are all
seeing it from a different point of view, all imagining the scene a
little differently.[9]
Read aloud to the class Mayer's *A Silly Story.* Then encourage
the children to consider the little boy's first thought: "Once I had a
silly thought while sitting in the shade." Using an overhead projector,
acetate, and marking pens, write down the children's silly thoughts so
they can see their thoughts in writing. Expand these thoughts into a
fan book. Take butcher paper (14" width) and fold it back and forth
so it resembles a fan. Give the book a title page with proper credits.
Print each child's silly thought on the left page, leaving the right page
empty. Have each child illustrate his or her own silly thought. A
finished book with all the children's illustrated silly thoughts will be
the result.

FOLLOW-UP ACTIVITIES FOR TEACHER AND STUDENTS TO SHARE:

1. After sharing Mayer's *There's a Nightmare in My Closet* with the class, ask the children what other nightmares may lurk in the little boy's closet. Do any of the children have nightmares they need to confront? Mercer Mayer says that as a child he was afraid of the "thing" that lived in his closet. His parents told him there was nothing in his closet. He knew what "a thing" was, but what was a "no-thing"? So the story idea was really about him versus his own little monster.[10] Using finger paints, let the children create their own monsters, dragons, or "no- things."

2. Share Mayer's wordless picture book *Frog, Where Are You?* with a small group. Using the other wordless picture books in this series (*A Boy, A Dog, and A Frog; A Boy, A Dog, A Frog, and A Friend; Frog On His Own; Frog Goes to Dinner* and *One Frog Too Many*) set up a reading center in the classroom. Have the children read the stories individually or in pairs. In a quiet part of the room have a cassette recorder and blank tapes set up. When a child decides on a favorite story let him/her tell that version of the story on tape. Be sure all children get to hear their own story played back. This is an excellent activity to have set up for parents' night.

3. Read Mayer's *Terrible Troll* aloud, being sure to allow the children time to absorb the humor in the illustrations. The fight with the knights and dragons actually takes place after the little boy confronts his cat in the trash can on the first page and extends to the last page when he holds the cat in his arms and is glad to be where he is. Pose the question "When the little boy is fighting the cat, what is he pretending?" Let the children act out scenes from this story or create their own make-believe dreams.

4. Sharing Mayer's *Just For You* aloud with the children will be a special experience; the teacher thinks of all the things children try to do to please adults. Have the children name some of the things they might try to do for their parents and what might happen if they did. The teacher may want to make a chart showing the ideas they shared.

WANTED TO DO	DID
1. Make coffee in the morning	1. Spilled the can of coffee because it was too heavy

5. Mayer's story *Appelard and Liverwurst* actually begins on the first illustrated page before the title page. Before reading the

book point out on the title page that Mercer Mayer wrote the book but Steven Kellogg illustrated it (refer to unit "Steven Kellogg's Characters Come to Life"). Because of the detailed illustrations, read the book to the entire class showing the pictures as you go. Be sure to leave this book in the room for the children to view again and again. Especially study the illustrations on pages 31–33 when the circus people gather for the Appelard and Zanzibus Circus. Steven Kellogg's humor is evident. On a large poster board create a circus tent. Give the circus a name and let the children draw one by one their imagined circus characters.

6. Share Mayer's *Liverwurst Is Missing,* a type of cumulative tale. As Appelard searches for Liverwurst, several colorful groups of characters join the hunt. After children recall the sequence of events, have the students act out the search and rescue. The main characters may wear illustrated name tags for identification with the remainder of the class being secondary characters.

7. If the Liverwurst stories have already been shared, follow with Mayer's book *Ah-Choo.* Note the dedication, "To dear friends: Steve, Helen, and the whole brood of Kelloggs." Talk about who these people are. If this book is shared with the whole class use the opaque projector to enlarge the pictures. To help the children with sequencing, ask them to retell the story in their own words. Then act it out.

8. Read aloud to the class Mayer's *If I Had . . .* Take a close look at the illustrations by Mercer Mayer. Explain that in most of his books Mayer does his own illustrations and that often he illustrates books for other people.

   After sharing this story, the boys and girls may want to think of other ideas for *If I Had . . .*

Culminating Activities after Kindergarten/First Grade

Discuss with the entire class the literature experiences they have shared. What authors and illustrators do they recall? What books did each person named write or illustrate? What book characters do the students remember?

What literature activities did the students particularly enjoy? Do the students remember any facts about specific authors or illustrators?

What is a dedication? How many nursery rhymes can they recite? What is the difference between an author and an illustrator?

REFERENCES

1. Doris de Montreville and Elizabeth D. Crawford, eds., *Fourth Book of Junior Authors & Illustrators* (New York: H.W. Wilson, 1978), p. 178.

2. de Montreville and Crawford, pp. 189–90.

3. Lee Bennett Hopkins, *Books Are by People* (New York: Citation Press, 1969), p. 61.

4. Hopkins, p. 62.

5. D.L. Kirkpatrick, ed., *Twentieth-Century Children's Writers* (New York: St. Martin's Press, 1978), p. 210.

6. de Montreville and Crawford, p. 115.

7. de Montreville and Crawford, pp. 14–15.

8. de Montreville and Crawford, pp. 343–44.

9. *Newsletter,* Follett Library Book Company, (Chicago, Winter 1983), p. 1.

10. *Newsletter,* p. 3.

Chapter 2
First Grade/Second Grade

Charlotte Zolotow Shares Family Feelings

STUDENT OBJECTIVES:

- Examine positive sibling relationships
- Enjoy stories about everyday experiences
- Participate in imaginative play
- Compare his/her own feelings to those of a book character
- Relate an author's own experiences to his or her writing

RECOMMENDED READING:

Zolotow, Charlotte. *Do You Know What I'll Do?* Harper & Row, 1958.
A sister offers to share with her little brother all of her experiences with nature.

———. *The Hating Book.* Harper & Row, 1969.
A little girl who thinks she hates her friend because the friend ignores her finds out that their problem was caused by a misunderstanding.

———. *If It Weren't for You.* Harper & Row, 1966.
If it weren't for the younger brother the older child could have such things as a room of his own and a whole bottle of pop, but then he'd have to be alone with the adults.

———. *Mr. Rabbit and the Lovely Present.* Harper & Row, 1962.
With the help of Mr. Rabbit a little girl gives her mother a basket of colors for her birthday.

———. *My Friend John.* Harper & Row, 1968.
Two boys are the best of friends even though one can't spell and the other can't multiply.

———. *One Step, Two,* rev. ed. Lothrop, 1981.
A mother and young daughter take a walk and notice the sounds and sights as they count their steps.

———. *Over and Over.* Harper & Row, 1957.
When the first snow of winter falls the little girl is curious about what holiday and season will be next.

———. *The Quarreling Book.* Harper & Row, 1957.
A gray, rainy day causes a chain reaction of unhappy people until at last the sun comes out and frowns turn to smiles.

———. *The Song.* Greenwillow, 1982.
A bird's song that Susan hears stays with her through summer sunshine, the gray skies of winter, and the pink clouds of spring apple blossoms.

———. *When the Wind Stops.* Harper & Row, 1975.
As a mother explains such concepts as where the sun goes, her son begins to realize that everything begins somewhere else.

———. *William's Doll.* Harper & Row, 1972.
William's father buys him toys, but a sensitive grandmother buys him what he wants—a doll.

BIOGRAPHICAL SOURCES:

For more information on Charlotte Zolotow, see *Books Are by People,* 334–36; *More Junior Authors,* 235; *Something about the Author,* 35:237–45; *Twentieth-Century Children's Writers,* 1385–88; *Twentieth-Century Children's Writers,* 2d ed., 855–56.

GROUP INTRODUCTORY ACTIVITY:

Introduce Charlotte Zolotow as an author of over 50 picture books that portray young children enjoying everyday experiences and discovering the world around them. Zolotow says, "Writing came quite naturally to me. I can recall winning a silver pencil in grade three for a composition I wrote. Actually, all I could do was write. I couldn't add or subtract, nor could I remember names and dates."[1] She continued to write while raising a family and suggests that the activities of her children and their friends often reminded her of her own childhood, producing themes for her books. She also loves to garden and finds it difficult to decide whether to grow vegetables or flowers.

Read Zolotow's *Mr. Rabbit and the Lovely Present* aloud to the class. Have a basket and fruits available and, as the story is read, fill the basket with the colored fruit mentioned in the story. When the story is completed discuss what other colors, fruits, and vegetables the little girl and the rabbit could have used. Call attention to the Maurice Sendak illustrations and tell children he has won two Caldecott awards for *Where the Wild Things Are* and *Outside over There*. Make them available for children to examine at their leisure.

Based on the information shared about Charlotte Zolotow, urge children to generalize about where she got her ideas for *Mr Rabbit*. If time allows, Marjorie Flack's *Ask Mr. Bear* (Macmillan, 1932) can be read, followed by a discussion of any similarities in the two children's approaches to acquiring a birthday present for mother.

FOLLOW-UP ACTIVITIES FOR TEACHER AND STUDENTS TO SHARE:

1. Before reading Zolotow's *My Friend John* to the class, ask the children to talk about what the word "friend" means to them. After sharing the story discuss differences there may be between friends that do not in any way deter close friendships. Then discuss other everyday activities not mentioned by Zolotow that children may do together. Children may want to illustrate these ideas and label the activity to make a Friendship Book.

2. Read Zolotow's *The Hating Book* to a small group of children. Let children briefly discuss the cause of the bad feelings. Then read Janice Udry's *Let's Be Enemies* (Harper & Row, 1961). Compare the similarities in the two stories.

3. Let the class listen to the song "William's Doll" on Marlo Thomas's sound recording *Free To Be...You and Me* (Arista Records, 1972, AL 4003). After hearing the song read Zolotow's book *William's Doll*. Let children tell about special gifts they have received from family or friends. Have children evaluate William's feelings and those of his father. Let the children pretend they are William and write a thank you note to his grandmother.

4. Read aloud Zolotow's *The Quarreling Book* to the class. Let children suggest how they think Zolotow got the idea for the book. This book is excellent for inspiring role playing. Children can act out how they think the day went for each of the characters: Mr. James, Mrs. James, Jonathan, Sally, Marjorie, and little Eddie. They may also want to discuss morning activities that can start the day off well for everyone. Be sure that

children note that Arnold Lobel did the illustrations in the *Quarreling Book.*

5. Read aloud Zolotow's *If It Weren't for You* and *Do You Know What I'll Do?* Both books deal with sibling relationships but from different perspectives. Children may want to create their own version of *If It Weren't for You.* Children who have no brothers or sisters may want to write and illustrate *If You Were My Sister.*

   Children may want to bring pictures of their brothers and sisters for a show-and-tell in which they share some funny or serious incident involving those pictured.

6. Read Zolotow's *One Step, Two* to the children. Go walking with small groups. If older children are available, enlist their help. At some point in the walk start counting steps, and after one step say "What can you see?" Record each child's observations. After two steps more record what they hear. Ater three steps, record what they can touch or smell. Repeat until 10 steps have been taken and recorded. A "What I Observed" list may be made for which children can prepare a border and then place on the bulletin board. Of course, the children will want to share some of their observations with the class.

7. Have a calendar available when Zolotow's *Over and Over* is shared aloud. As the girl asks, "What comes next?" point to or turn the calendar pages and ask the students what comes next. Assist children in making their own "Over and Over" list or book, starting with 11 months before their birthday and recording months with special holidays in order. They can copy the name of the month on a page and create their own holiday illustration. Since the beginning place is dependent upon each child's birthday, those with birthdays in the same month may want to work together as a committee.

8. Zolotow's *The Song* also involves seasons and may be related to the previous book when sharing it. Since many children may not be familiar with songbirds, compare the song that played in Susan's head with a tune they may have learned and continued to hum. Do they have songs they sing inside themselves when they are happy or sad? Listen to bits of music and let children discuss how it makes them feel.

   Help children become aware of birds and their music. If possible, bring a bird to class for a few days to allow children to listen and observe.

9. Before reading Zolotow's *When the Wind Stops* ask the children, "Did you ever wonder where the wind comes from or why turtles have shells? A little boy in this story had lots of questions to ask, and this is how his mother answered."

   After reading the story they may want to make a simple booklet to illustrate. Fold a sheet of typing paper in fourths. Number the pages at the top left hand corner. With a large-print typewriter, type four of the questions the little boy asks. Have the children illustrate their answers to each question.

A Child's World through Leo Lionni's Eyes

STUDENT OBJECTIVES:

- Enjoy descriptions of nature through illustrations and figurative language
- Create an imaginary animal
- Visualize on paper a personal reaction to a story
- Examine the themes in stories
- Derive a lesson exemplified in a fable

RECOMMENDED READING:

Lionni, Leo. *The Biggest House in the World.* Pantheon, 1968.
A father snail tells his son a story about why some things are better small.

———. *Fish Is Fish.* Pantheon, 1970.
Fish wishes to be like his friend the frog and see the world, but a crisis makes him content with his life in the sea.

———. *Frederick.* Pantheon, 1967.
Frederick is a poet mouse who shares nature's beauties with his friends during the dull winter days.

———. *Inch by Inch.* Obolensky, 1960.
A clever inchworm inches his way out of trouble when asked to measure the nightingale's song.

———. *Let's Make Rabbits.* Pantheon, 1982
Two rabbits created with scissors and pencil become friends and decide that because they cast a shadow, they are real.

———. *Little Blue and Little Yellow.* Obolensky, 1959.
Little blue and little yellow become such good friends that they blend to form green; and although their parents are disturbed for a while, all ends well.

————. *Pezzettino.* Pantheon, 1975.
Pezzettino travels across the sea to a barren island only to discover that as small as he is, he still has importance.

————. *Swimmy.* Pantheon, 1963.
Swimmy, who looks different from his brothers and sisters, teaches other small fish how to explore the ocean floor.

BIOGRAPHICAL SOURCES:

For more information on Leo Lionni, see *Books Are by People,* 149–51; *Third Book of Junior Authors,* 179–80; *Something about the Author* 8:114–15; *Twentieth-Century Children's Writers,* 784–86; *Twentieth-Century Children's Writers,* 2d ed., 484–85.

GROUP INTRODUCTORY ACTIVITY:

To introduce Leo Lionni, tell children that he was born in Holland in 1910 and taught himself to draw by visiting museums in Amsterdam and studying the works of great artists. He came to America with his wife and children in 1939. He says he doesn't make books for children; rather, he feels that good children's books are for all people who have not lost their joy in life, for the part of everyone who is still a child.[2]

Read Lionni's story *Frederick* to the class. As a follow-up give children gray paper and let them tear a Frederick. In honor of Frederick, create a Poet Tree on the bulletin board. Read at least one poem daily to the children, then put the poem on a leaf or blossom and place it on the tree.

FOLLOW-UP ACTIVITIES FOR TEACHER AND STUDENTS TO SHARE:

1. Read Lionni's *Let's Make Rabbits* to the class. After the story, let children make rabbits either with a pencil or scissors. Notice the end papers of the book. They look like a wallpaper pattern. Perhaps old wallpaper books could be used in making the scissors rabbit.
2. Share Lionni's *Little Blue and Little Yellow* with the class. Tell them the source of the story as recorded in the note in *Let's Make Rabbits:* While riding on a slow commuter train in 1958, Lionni entertained his restless grandchildren by tearing small circles from some colored paper and making up a story about two characters, Little Blue and Little Yellow.

After reading the story, have torn pieces of all colors of tissue paper, including blue and yellow, to place in front of each child at a table or desk. Be sure they have plenty of pieces so each can make up a game they can play or a new story about the pieces.

3. Read Lionni's *Swimmy* to the class. Urge them to especially listen for the descriptions of the medusa, lobster, strange fish, eel's tail, anemones, and seaweeds. Have children try to recall these descriptions when the story is over.

   Using bits of paper doilies, wallpaper, cotton, and tissue paper, let children create a collage "forest of seaweeds growing from sugar candy rocks." Some children may want to paint a "medusa made of rainbow jelly" or "strange fish, pulled by an invisible thread."

4. Share Lionni's *Fish Is Fish* with the children. Just as the fish imagined fish birds and fish people, let the children imagine and draw people fish or people space creatures.

5. Read Lionni's *Pezzettino* to the class. Since Pezzettino means "little pieces," let children use colored squares to create animals and/or objects.

6. Read Lionni's *Inch by Inch* to the class. Talk about other things (such as happiness) that an inchworm cannot measure. Discuss the cleverness of the inchworm in surviving danger. Talk about the fact that if *Inch by Inch* were made into a sound filmstrip or movie, background music would be selected to heighten the mood. Let children listen to various recordings and choose one that seems most appropriate. Then ask an upper-grade student to tape record the story using the selected music as background. Children may then want to listen to the tape recording at their leisure while they look at Lionni's illustrations.

7. Read Lionni's *The Biggest House in the World* to the class. Talk about fables and suggest that the story the snail's father told is really a fable with a lesson or moral. What was that lesson? Did any of Lionni's other stories have a theme they could identify?

   In the art center have milk and egg cartons, tissue rolls, small boxes, and other objects. Divide the class into small groups and have each group create their own elaborate biggest house.

Be a Nature Detective with Millicent Selsam

STUDENT OBJECTIVES:

- Recognize certain animal tracks
- Classify animals using individual's own criteria
- Identify different breeds of animals
- Use a microscope
- Read and report facts on animals

RECOMMENDED READING:

Selsam, Millicent. *All about Eggs.* Illustrated by Stephanie Fleescher. Addison-Wesley, 1980.
Illustrations and brief text identify many animals that hatch from eggs.

———. *Benny's Animals, And How He Put Them in Order.* Illustrated by Arnold Lobel. Harper & Row, 1966.
Benny's curiosity about animals leads him to discover how animals are classified.

———. *Greg's Microscope.* Illustrated by Arnold Lobel. Harper & Row, 1963.
Greg prepares slides and observes household items under the microscope.

———. *How Kittens Grow.* Illustrated by Esther Bubley. Four Winds, 1973.
The first eight weeks of a kitten's life are shown through photographs and a brief explanation.

———. *How Puppies Grow.* Illustrated by Esther Bubley. Four Winds, 1972, 1971.
Photographs and narration take the reader through the first six weeks with a litter of puppies.

———. *How to Be a Nature Detective.* Illustrated by Ezra Jack Keats. Harper & Row, 1966.
By being nature detectives, children learn how to identify the tracks of a dog, cat, fox, frog, turtle, seagull, and other animals.

————. *Is This a Baby Dinosaur? And Other Science Picture-Puzzles.* Harper & Row, 1971.
Through picture puzzles and explanations children are helped to realize that science and nature can be found everywhere.

————. *Terry and the Caterpillars.* Illustrated by Arnold Lobel. Harper & Row, 1962.
By observation Terry learns how caterpillars go from caterpillar to cocoon to moth to egg and back to caterpillar.

————. *When an Animal Grows.* Illustrated by John Kaufman. Harper & Row, 1966.
A comparison of the growth and development of a baby gorilla and lamb are given, followed by a similar comparison of a sparrow and mallard duck.

Selsam, Millicent, and Hunt, Joyce. *A First Look at Cats.* Walker, 1981.
Through illustrations and brief explanation the reader discovers why cats belong to a group of mammals called carnivora.

BIOGRAPHICAL SOURCES:

For more information on Millicent Selsam, see *Books Are by People,* 247–49; *More Junior Authors,* 180–81; *Something about the Author,* 29:173–75.

GROUP INTRODUCTORY ACTIVITY:

Introduce Millicent Selsam's science books, explaining that she wants to write books that encourage children to research things for themselves. She likes to have children participate in learning and make personal discoveries. Selsam became interested in nature while taking biology class trips in high school and college. Some of the plant experiments she included in her early books were ones she carried out on the windowsills of her New York apartment.[3]

Introduce *How to Be a Nature Detective* by having the children discuss the meaning of the term "detective." Now read the book aloud. Give the children time to view the tracks so they can try to identify which animal makes them. Be sure children note that Ezra Jack Keats made the illustrations in the book.

Using as a guide the tracks on the last four pages of the book, make a poster depicting animal tracks. Using pictures of those animals found in magazines, let children match the pictures to the tracks. Encourage the children to document what clues they used in making the selection.

Take a nature walk around the schoolyard or to a neighborho park. Record what animals and clues were discovered.

As an art follow-up use a stamp pad and have the children put their thumb prints on a piece of paper. With the thumb prints as a basis have them draw their own imaginative animals. Ed Emberley's *Great Thumbprint Drawing Book* (Little, Brown, 1977) has excellent ideas that may help some children to get started.

FOLLOW-UP ACTIVITIES FOR TEACHER AND STUDENTS TO SHARE:

1. Using Millicent Selsam's books, set up a science corner. Have as many of her books as possible for children to share. Also have available animal pictures from the vertical file and/or pictures cut from old magazines. Share *Benny's Animals and How He Put Them in Order* with small groups. Then let the children classify the pictures as Benny did.

2. Enjoy Terry's excitement over her caterpillars as a small group shares in reading Selsam's *Terry and the Caterpillars.* Note that Arnold Lobel made the illustrations. If possible, have caterpillars for the class to observe. If that is not possible, some children may want to draw the metamorphosis that Terry observed: caterpillar, cocoon, moth, egg, caterpillar.

3. Use Selsam's *All about Eggs* with small groups of children. Let them observe the illustrations and suggest what will hatch from each egg as the book is read. Urge them to identify the clues that were the basis of each decision. If possible set up an incubator with chicken eggs that the children can observe. A field trip to a hatchery is also a possibility.

4. Millicent Selsam's books excite children about science through observation and participation. Let small groups share in the reading of *Greg's Microscope.* Point out that Arnold Lobel made the illustrations. After the book is read, set up a microscope and have the children do some of the same experiments that Greg did. What other items can the children think of to observe under the microscope? Ask them to draw what they saw when the salt and sugar crystals were examined.

5. Use Selsam's *When an Animal Grows* with a group of readers. Children can begin to do research with this book. Ask them to each read either the comparison between the gorilla and lamb or between the sparrow and mallard duck. Have them select one of the four topics. On the front of the page write the word, such as "gorilla," and draw a picture of that animal. On the back of the page write two facts: what the baby animal eats and when it is old enough to live without its mother.

6. Share *A First Look at Cats*. This is another book explaining scientific classification. Refer to the two stacks of pictures from *Benny's Animals*. Pull out the cat pictures. Ask the children to bring pictures of cats from magazines at home if that is possible. When enough pictures of cats have been gathered, identify as many as possible and make a "Cat Detective" bulletin board.

7. Share aloud with the class both *How Kittens Grow* and *How Puppies Grow*. Encourage the children to discuss their pets, talking about how to care for them properly. They may want to bring pictures of their pets to share in the days that follow. It is also an appropriate time to share rhymes about cats and dogs such as those selected by Lenore Blegvad for *Mittens for Kittens and Other Rhymes about Cats* (Atheneum, 1974) and *Hark! Hark! The Dogs Do Bark, and Other Rhymes about Dogs* (Atheneum, 1976).

8. Use Selsam's *Is This a Baby Dinosaur? And Other Science Picture-Puzzles* to lead the children into spontaneous discussion about the puzzles. Challenge them to give a reason for their responses. Read aloud and discuss each of the puzzles. Have some lentils and potatoes on hand. Set up a "Nature Detective" center where the children can observe how the potatoes change as they grow. If a hot plate or stove is available, cook the lentils for soup one day.

   If the children enjoyed the picture-puzzles, follow up with those found on the back page of issues of *National Geographic World*.

9. Send a small group of students to the library to work with the library media specialist in locating pictures of specific animals. Expose the children to as many resources as possible such as the vertical file, study prints, encyclopedias, filmstrips, magazines, and nonfiction books located by subject in the card catalog.

10. As a culminating activity, refer back to being a nature detective and have children record what they have learned about animals. Ask each child to find a picture of an animal they learned something about. Help them write or tape one sentence about that animal. The pictures may be mounted on blank language master cards and the fact they found can be recorded, such as "A mountain lion is also called a cougar."

Clever Cats

STUDENT OBJECTIVES:

- Extend the action of a story
- Pantomime an action for others to guess
- Participate in choral responses
- Carefully examine the illustrations to see how they extend the text
- Anticipate a story ending

RECOMMENDED READING:

Brett, Jan. *Annie and the Wild Animals.* Houghton Mifflin, 1985.
  After losing her cat, Annie tries to feed the wild animals and find a new pet.

Brown, Ruth. *A Dark, Dark Tale.* Dial, 1981.
  A black cat finds a hidden animal among the abandoned toys in an old house.

Flack, Marjorie. *Angus and the Cat.* Doubleday, 1931.
  Angus tried to get rid of the strange cat, but he missed it when it was gone.

Gag, Wanda. *Millions of Cats.* Coward, McCann & Geoghegan, 1928.
  The very old man and very old woman acquired millions and billions and trillions of cats before getting one of their very own.

Potter, Beatrix. *The Tale of Tom Kitten.* Warne, 1907.
  Tom and his two sisters do not stay clean while waiting for company.

Seuss, Dr. *The Cat in the Hat.* Random House, 1957.
  Limited vocabulary tale of a fun-loving cat who shared his tricks with two children on a rainy day.

Stein, Sara Bonnett. *Cats.* Harcourt Brace Jovanovich, 1985.
  The habits and daily activities of a family pet are presented with illustrations and brief text.

Turkle, Brinton. *Do Not Open.* Dutton, 1981.
  Miss Moody opened a bottle washed up on the beach and was able to trick its evil occupant.

GROUP INTRODUCTORY ACTIVITY:

Read *Millions of Cats* to the class. Have the children help with the reading by saying the "hundreds of cats" refrain whenever it appears in the text. Talk about why the little cat was saved when the others were killed. How do people get pet cats today? Let children think of a name for the little cat who became the old people's pet. Urge children who have pet cats in their home to bring pictures of their cats for the bulletin board. Label each picture with the cat's name. Have each child share with the class how the name was chosen.

FOLLOW-UP ACTIVITIES FOR TEACHER AND STUDENTS TO SHARE:

1. Read Brown's *A Dark Dark Tale* to the class. Urge the children to watch the illustrations to find the black cat as it wanders through the room. Let the children guess what was in the box before the last page is shared. Let the children talk about why the book was named *A Dark Dark Tale.* How do the illustrations contribute to the title? Have the children think about what will happen when the cat sees the mouse. Will they become friends? If so, what is one game they might play in this old, abandoned house? If not, how will the mouse escape?
2. Read Brett's *Annie and the Wild Animals* to the class. Then share the illustrations again, urging the children to look at the borders very carefully. What season was it when the story began? What border clues do the children see to make them know it is spring when the story ends? Why did Annie name her cat Taffy? Let the children suggest what Annie will name the kittens. Make a list of the suggested names and let the children vote on their favorite name for each kitten.
3. Read Dr. Seuss's *The Cat in the Hat* aloud to the class. Talk about other bad tricks Thing One and Thing Two might have tried. Let a child pantomime something the Cat in the Hat or Thing One and Thing Two did. See if the class members can guess the action. If children in the class can read, urge them to read Dr. Seuss's *The Cat in the Hat Comes Back* (Random House, 1958). Perhaps a group of students can share reading it aloud to the rest of the class.
4. Read Stein's *Cat.* Let children talk about cat facts given in the book. Then let them share other things they know about cats: what they eat, places they sleep, and games they play.
5. Read Turkle's *Do Not Open* to the class. Let the children discuss whether they would have opened the bottle. Why did Miss

Moody pretend to be afraid of mice? Let children discuss treasures that could be found on a beach. Suggest they draw what they would wish for if they had one wish. Put the labeled pictures on an "If I Had One Wish" bulletin board.

6. Read Flack's *Angus and the Cat* to the class. Let them suggest places where a cat might have been hiding when Angus couldn't find it. Why was Angus glad to see the cat? Let children look at the pictures again to see how Angus showed the cat he was glad it was back. What games will Angus and the cat play now that they are friends?

7. Read Potter's *The Tale of Tom Kitten* to the class. Then let the children try to march to duck rhythm. Potter suggests that she should have made another book recounting a new Tom Kitten adventure. Let the children make up another story, this time with Peter Rabbit or another familiar Potter animal as a character instead of Jemima Puddle-Duck.

Introducing Anita and Arnold Lobel

STUDENT OBJECTIVES:

- Use the content page to locate a story
- Compare illustrations in different books illustrated by the same person
- Make a record of books they have read
- Participate in an a, b, c activity
- Read aloud in small groups
- Recall a fable

RECOMMENDED READING:

Lobel, Arnold. *Fables.* Harper & Row, 1980.
   Twenty original animal fables.

———. *Frog and Toad Are Friends.* Harper & Row, 1970.
   First of four "I Can Read" books in which two very good friends share enjoyable experiences.
      Some other books about Frog and Toad:
      Days with Frog and Toad. Harper & Row, 1979.

    Frog and Toad All Year. Harper & Row, 1976.
    Frog and Toad Together. Harper & Row, 1971.

————. *How the Rooster Saved the Day.* Illustrated by Anita Lobel. Greenwillow, 1977.
A clever rooster saves his life from robbers by telling a story.

————. *Mouse Tales.* Harper & Row, 1972.
An "I Can Read" account of a papa mouse who puts his seven children to bed by telling them stories, one for each child.

————. *On Market Street.* Illustrated by Anita Lobel. Greenwillow, 1981.
A young boy who is lured by the wonders on Market Street buys gifts from A to Z for a friend.

————. *The Rose in My Garden.* Illustrated by Anita Lobel. Greenwillow, 1984.
Poetic text in a "House that Jack Built" sequence that introduces the flowers growing near a rose upon which a bee sleeps.

————. *A Treeful of Pigs.* Illustrated by Anita Lobel. Greenwillow, 1979.
The wife of a lazy farmer cleverly tricks her husband into helping her raise the pigs.

BIOGRAPHICAL SOURCES:

For more information on Anita and Arnold Lobel, see *Books Are by People,* 156–59; *Something about the Author,* 6:146–48; *Third Book of Junior Authors,* 180–82; *Twentieth-Century Children's Writers,* 796–99; *Twentieth-Century Children's Writers,* 2d ed., 491–93.

GROUP INTRODUCTORY ACTIVITY:

Introduce the author and the illustrator, Anita and Arnold Lobel, by telling the children that they are married and work side by side in the same studio. They met in art school and worked separately for a while before collaborating.[4] Ask the children to think of reasons it would be advantageous to have the illustrator of the book you wrote working in the same room. What might be the disadvantages?

Share Lobel's story *A Treeful of Pigs.* Discuss how else the farmer's wife could have made the pigs fall like rain.

Find a tree branch to pot or construct a bulletin board with a tree on it. Make pigs out of construction paper and let a child add one to the tree each time they read a Lobel book. Place the name of the book on one side of the pig and the child's name on the other.

FOLLOW-UP ACTIVITIES FOR TEACHER AND STUDENTS TO SHARE:

1. Share with the class Lobel's *How the Rooster Saved the Day.* Lobel's story is based on a stained glass rooster that his wife Anita made. Using an opaque projector, enlarge Anita's rooster on a poster or find a similar one in a coloring book. As a class project make a mosaic using all types of beans and seeds. Glue colored yarn to outline the major portions of the rooster.

2. Share Lobel's *On Market Street* with small groups of children so all can have the opportunity to study the intricate designs. Notice that the drawings are done with a picture frame effect. Compare the illustrations in *On Market Street, How the Rooster Saved the Day* and *A Treeful of Pigs.*

   Identify the vegetables the V merchant is made of. What musical instruments were part of the M man? What others could have been included? Think of 10 favorite books that could have been used for the B book person.

   Think of new items the merchants could be selling. See how many letters can be identified in new ways.

3. You need not read all 20 stories in *Fables*; some may not be suitable for this level. Instead, pick a few relevant fables to read or tell to the class. For instance, in "The Baboon's Umbrella," the baboon learns that advice from friends is sometimes good and sometimes bad. Ask the children to relate a time when they received advice from a friend that may have caused them to get into trouble. Follow up with "The Bear and the Crow." The bear wanted so badly to impress everyone with his clothes that he forgot to think about what he was doing. These two fables are excellent for leading into a discussion of decision making.

   Be sure to urge the children to examine the illustrations, because *Fables* won the Caldecott Medal in 1981. Talk about the meaning of the word "fable." Urge the children to ask their parents to recall a fable that they remember and tell it to the class the following day. It will be interesting to see if several tell the same fable.

4. Read Lobel's *The Rose in My Garden.* Then read again, having one child point out each flower mentioned while the others repeat as a chorus "That sleeps on the rose in my garden" at the appropriate time. After completing the reading, show the children the pictures of the flowers to see if they can recall the names and any phrases Lobel used, such as bluebells "with petals like lace" or daisies "as white as the snow." Also have them locate and trace the progress of the little snail.

   If a seed catalog is available let the children find and cut out the flowers mentioned in *The Rose in My Garden* for a labeled blackboard border.

5. Share one of the stories in *Frog and Toad Are Friends*. Show them how to use the table of contents to select a tale. Then urge the class to divide into four small groups and share reading one of the "Frog and Toad" books aloud to each other—*Frog and Toad Are Friends, Frog and Toad Together, Frog and Toad All Year* and *Days with Frog and Toad*. After each group has read one book, they can select a project to present to the class as a whole. For example, they might dramatize one of the stories; write a letter to a friend as Frog did to Toad; or tell the story of the lost button as children place buttons of all sizes on the overhead projector to create a shadow show of buttons.

6. Read aloud Lobel's *Mouse Tales* to the class. If a picture of Lobel is available, share it with them, for the children might recognize him as the father in *Mouse Tales*. To encourage children to read more stories, give each child a mouse made out of construction paper to hang over his or her desk with the tail hanging down. As the children read books by Arnold and Anita Lobel or other "Easy to Read" books, they can write the title on a bow-shaped piece of paper and tape it to the tail.

Sharing the Books of Beatrice Schenk De Regniers

STUDENT OBJECTIVES:

- Pantomime a story
- Compare two stories to find common elements
- Illustrate new ideas relating to stories read
- Share poetry chorally
- Create shadow pictures

RECOMMENDED READING:

De Regniers, Beatrice Schenk. *Everyone Is Good for Something.* Illustrated by Margot Tomes. Houghton Mifflin, 1980.
Jack and his cat prove their worth.

———. *Laura's Story.* Illustrated by Jack Kent. Atheneum, 1979.
Laura imagines a story in which she rescues her mother and cares for her. Then bedtime comes and reverses the roles.

———. *A Little House of Your Own.* Illustrated by Irene Haas. Harcourt Brace Jovanovich, 1954.
The author describes little places where one can have an opportunity to be alone.

———. *May I Bring a Friend?* Illustrated by Boni Montresor. Atheneum, 1964.
A little boy brings different zoo animals to visit the king and queen each day.

———. *Red Riding Hood.* Illustrated by Edward Gorey. Atheneum, 1972.
Tale of "Red Riding Hood" in verse, ending with the hunter's cutting open the wolf to rescue the two victims, then filling the wolf with stones and sewing him up again.

———. *The Shadow Book.* Illustrated by Isabel Gordon. Harcourt Brace Jovanovich, 1960.
Black-and-white illustrations of shadows enhance the simple text of things shadows can do.

———. *The Snow Party.* Illustrated by Reiner Zimnik. Pantheon, 1959.
A blizzard brings the little old farm woman the party for which she wished.

———. *Something Special.* Illustrated by Irene Haas. Harcourt Brace Jovanovich, 1958.
Nine poems that provoke participation and imaginative play.

———. *Waiting for Mama.* Illustrated by Victoria de Larrea. Clarion, 1984.
Amy waits for her mother outside the grocery store and passes the time by imagining a future of waiting.

BIOGRAPHICAL SOURCES:

For more information on Beatrice Schenk De Regniers, see *Books Are by People,* 52–55; *More Junior Authors,* 65; *Something about the Author,* 2:90–92; *Twentieth-Century Children's Writers,* 366–68; *Twentieth-Century Children's Writers,* 2d ed., 239–41.

GROUP INTRODUCTORY ACTIVITY:

Share *May I Bring a Friend?,* calling attention to the fact that the illustrations won a Caldecott Medal. Let children think of five different animals the boy could have taken to visit the king and queen. What problems would each animal cause? Substitute the new animals and their problems into a new story and pantomime it, using the newly created characters while the library media specialist tells the newly created tale.

FOLLOW-UP ACTIVITIES FOR TEACHER AND STUDENTS TO SHARE:

1. Read De Regniers's *Everyone Is Good for Something* aloud to the class. Then read Marcia Brown's *Dick Whittington and His Cat* (Scribner's, 1950). Identify the elements the two stories have in common.
2. Read aloud De Regniers's *A Little House of Your Own.* Share with the children De Regniers's comment that anyone who reads *A Little House of Your Own* knows something about her. Some of Irene Haas's drawings look so much like De Regnier that a stranger was able to recognize her as the author of the book just by walking into the office where she worked. The tree house illustrated in the book was really in her childhood back yard in Crawfordsville, Indiana. She says she finds it natural to write children's books because she remembers how she felt at the age of her book characters.[5]

   Discuss reasons why people need secret houses. Children may want to think of secret houses not mentioned by De Regniers and illustrate them for the bulletin board.
3. Read aloud De Regniers's *The Snow Party.* Discuss the scenes in the story and play out as a follow-up. Children may create additional dialogue as they feel the need.
4. Share each poem in De Regniers's *Something Special* in a separate session, using an appropriate follow-up for each. Children will participate in "What Did You Put in Your Pocket?" and "What Can You Do" as a choral, but each poem can be followed by a discussion and description of things equally appropriate, ending in new poems.

   "If You Find a Little Feather" and "If I were Teeny Tiny" can result in imaginative descriptions and/or drawings of other ideas of things you could do in those situations. "What's the Funniest Thing You Can Think Of" can also be used to evoke new possibilities and additional verses to the poem.
5. Read De Regniers's *Red Riding Hood* aloud. Compare the story with Paul Galdone's *Little Red Riding Hood* (McGraw-Hill, 1974) or other nonillustrated versions. Which is most satisfying?
6. Share De Regniers's *The Shadow Book.* Discuss other ways shadows can be helpful. Using the overhead projector children can create shadows on the wall with their hands or with cut paper, perhaps indicating appropriate movements. If the sun is out children can go out shadow hunting and come in to record their observations through art or on the tape recorder.

7. Read De Regniers's *Laura's Story* aloud. Have children share new ideas of what Laura could do if she were large and her parents were small. Assist children in creating a new story using their ideas. Why is De Regniers's ending a satisfying one? Can they think of one that is equally appropriate?
8. Read De Regniers's *Waiting for Mama* aloud. Then let students tell their experiences in waiting for someone. How did they feel? What other ways might Amy have used to pass the time in the story?

Brian Wildsmith Creates Animals and Shapes

STUDENT OBJECTIVES:

- Participate in research seeking appropriate words for groups of specific animals
- Compare a, b, c illustrations in a number of books and assist in synthesizing the findings
- Have experiences with round, triangular, and rectangular shapes
- Infer reasons for the use of specific words in identifying groups of animals
- Observe a small portion of an animal and describe what the whole looks like
- Increase his or her vocabulary

RECOMMENDED READING:

Wildsmith, Brian. *ABC.* Watts, 1963.
   A,B,C's are presented through simple pictures of animals and objects on one side of the page with the identifying word in both upper- and lower-case letters on the opposite page.

———. *Animal Games.* Oxford University Press, 1980.
   Brief text identifies the game each of 12 animals play.

———. *Brian Wildsmith's Circus.* Watts, 1970.
   Textless panorama of the acts of animals and people that provide the unique excitement of the circus.

————. *Brian Wildsmith's 1, 2, 3's.* Watts, 1965.
The circle, rectangle, and triangle are employed to prepare increasingly more complicated pictures to present the numbers one through 10.

————. *Brian Wildsmith's Puzzles.* Watts, 1970, (o.p.)
Illustrated double-spread pages depict visual puzzles to solve or problems to answer.

————. *Daisy.* Pantheon, 1984.
Daisy the cow wanted to see the world, but after doing so she realized that her farm home was better.

————. *Pelican.* Pantheon, 1982.
Split pages hide part of the activity, adding to the suspense as a pelican hatched on a farm must be taught to fish.

————. *Wild Animals.* Oxford University Press, 1979, 1967.
Vivid colors attract viewers to these groups of animals identified with the group name for each type.

BIOGRAPHICAL SOURCES:

For more information on Brian Wildsmith, see *Books Are by People,* 312–15; *Something about the Author,* 16:277–83; *Third Book of Junior Authors,* 300–01.

GROUP INTRODUCTORY ACTIVITY:

Before sharing *Animal Games* tell children that Brian Wildsmith lives in England. Locate the country on the globe. Tell them that Wildsmith originally thought he wanted to be a chemist. Then one day he happened to paint a picture that made him decide his career should be art. The next day he left the school he was attending and enrolled in art school.[6] After sharing the books let children discuss which of the games they also play. In what ways would the rules be different?

Urge them to think of games other animals not illustrated by Wildsmith might play. Children may want to illustrate the animals and games they suggest and make a class "Animal Games" book.

FOLLOW-UP ACTIVITIES FOR TEACHER AND STUDENTS TO SHARE:

1. Share Wildsmith's *Pelican* with the class. Explore the reasons Wildsmith may have had for using the split-page format. How

would the story have been different if some other bird had hatched from the egg? Have the class select a type of bird that could have hatched and make a group story using the selected bird instead of a pelican.

2. Share Wildsmith's *Daisy* with the class. Let them discuss why they think Wildsmith used split-page illustrations for the book. Let them think of other TV commercials Daisy might have made. What might be some roles Daisy could have played in movies?

3. Share *Brian Wildsmith's Puzzles* with a small group so each can more easily participate in the activities suggested. Follow up by sharing pictures of animals with only part of the animal showing. See if the children can guess the type of animal and describe the appearance of the whole animal.

4. Share Wildsmith's *Wild Animals.* Talk about the usual use of words such as "nursery," "ambush," "pride," "corps," "troop" and "family." Does "pride" seem appropriate for a group of lions? Make a list of farm animals and try to recall the group name for each. Have children enlist the aid of parents overnight in determining the accurate words. Draw or find pictures of farm animals and label each as Wildsmith did to make a class Farm Animals book.

5. Share *Brian Wildsmith's 1, 2, 3's* with a small group. Have them participate in the exercises involving shapes that are included in the last four double-spread pages. Let children select a number and make its shape using circles, squares, and/or triangles. Color the outcomes.

6. Share Wildsmith's *ABC.* Record on the blackboard the animal or object used for each letter. Have children examine other ABC books and, as they find different animals or objects, record those also. Was there any letter in which the same word was always illustrated? Let children draw and illustrate their own ABC book using the most commonly used word for each letter.

7. Examine *Brian Wildsmith's Circus* in small groups. Study the illustrations carefully to see how many circus acts can be identified. As a group discuss which acts they feel are especially enjoyable for the spectators. Which are especially dangerous for the performers? Can anyone think of circus acts that Wildsmith did not illustrate?

The Words and Pictures of Eric Carle

STUDENT OBJECTIVES:

- Listen for pleasure
- Interpret a wordless picture story
- Reinforce 1–10 number concept by recalling story sequence
- Create a new book based on an author's idea
- Reinforce the concept of days of the week and hours of the day

RECOMMENDED READING:

Carle, Eric. *Do You Want to Be My Friend?* Crowell, 1971.
A wordless picture book of a lonely little mouse who follows various animals while seeking a friend.

———. *The Grouchy Ladybug.* Crowell, 1977.
Each hour as the day progresses the hungry ladybug challenges successively larger animals to a fight.

———. *The Mixed-Up Chameleon,* rev. ed. Crowell, 1984.
A chameleon adds parts of other animals to its body as it wishes for their qualities until it is no longer able even to catch a fly for food.

———. *1, 2, 3 to the Zoo.* Philomel, 1968.
Wordless picture book in which succeeding pages show 1 elephant, 2 hippopotomi, 3 giraffes, etc. on a train headed for the zoo.

———. *The Secret Birthday Message.* Crowell, 1971.
A little boy, given precise directions for finding a birthday gift, peers through holes in the page as he pursues his quest.

———. *The Very Busy Spider.* Philomel, 1984.
Despite the animals' requests that she engage in other activities, the spider spins a beautiful, useful web and then falls asleep.

———. *The Very Hungry Caterpillar.* Collins, 1970.
Holes in the pages of the book evidence the hunger of the caterpillar, who eats a variety of foods from Sunday to Saturday, then forms a cocoon and emerges a butterfly.

Green, Norma. *The Hole in the Dike.* Illustrated by Eric Carle. Crowell, 1975.
Vivid double-spread illustrations enhance the drama of the familiar tale of the small boy who saved Holland from flooding.

BIOGRAPHICAL SOURCES:

For more information on Eric Carle, see *Fourth Book of Junior Authors & Illustrators,* 68–69; *Something about the Author,* 4:41–43.

GROUP INTRODUCTORY ACTIVITY:

Before sharing Carle's *The Secret Birthday Message* tell the children about Eric Carle's childhood. He went to kindergarten in Syracuse, New York, where there were large sheets of paper, bright colored paints, and big brushes for the children to use. When he was six his parents moved to Germany, where his school has small sheets of paper, rulers, and hard pencils; and he was warned not to make mistakes. He went to a German school for 10 years and all he remembers liking was a wonderful art teacher and a kind librarian. He had almost no books as a boy, so now he finds himself making books for himself—the ones he longed for as a child.[7] Have the children anticipate what gift will be received in the story. After reading the story let children think of a place in the house where it might be appropriate to hide a birthday gift. Suggest places in the other rooms where clues might be hidden. What might the clues say?
Have hidden in the library or classroom the stack of Carle books that the class may share later in the week. Hide numbered clues that the children will take to the teacher for reading. They must be shared so that students will be directed to specific areas in which to search for each clue.

FOLLOW-UP ACTIVITIES FOR TEACHER AND STUDENTS TO SHARE:

1. Share Carle's *Do You Want to Be My Friend?* with the class. Read the introduction to teachers before sharing in order to create an appropriate narration. The first time through, the children can try to guess each animal by its tail.
   Compare this story with Margaret Wise Brown's *Home for a Bunny* (Simon & Schuster, 1956). In what ways are they similar?
   Help children plan the illustrations for another wordless animal story where a little animal seeks a friend. Suggest they

illustrate it using collage as the art style, since that was Carle's choice for illustrating his book.

2. Introduce Carle's *The Mixed-Up Chameleon* by letting children discuss what they think Carle's dedication means: "Dedicated to all children who have worked with me on this book." Then share facts from the note on the back page which explains the dedication.

   After reading the book let children think of the unique characteristics of other animals for which the chameleon might have wished. As a group, draw the animal, with each child adding a part of the mixed-up chameleon based on their suggestions of new animals. Have them think of other reasons the chameleon decided it would rather be itself.

3. Read Carle's *The Grouchy Ladybug*. Using the hours-of-the-day format, make a list of how "The Happy Child" helps his/her family on Saturday. The teacher can print the brief text needed to identify each activity.

4. Share Carle's *1, 2, 3 to the Zoo* with the class. What do the children suppose the little mouse was saying to each of the animals? What questions was he asking them? Recall the picture in which the little mouse was sitting on the animal. Why? Using the little train on the last page, let children try to remember which animals went in each car.

   Make a 1, 2, 3 book in which farm animals go on trucks to the fair. Have the children make collages as illustrations.

4. Share *The Very Hungry Caterpillar* with the class. Then have the children recall the foods the caterpillar ate each day. What foods do the children like so much they could eat them until they got sick? How would their story end?

   If the caterpillar had been a mouse, what might it have eaten? How might the mouse story end?

   Share Millicent Selsam's book *Terry and the Caterpillars* (Harper & Row, 1962). Why was the ending different from that of *The Very Hungry Caterpillar*?

   Why do you suppose Eric Carle dedicated the story to his sister Christa?

6. Read Carle's *The Very Busy Spider* to the class. Let the children make the sounds of the animals as you read. Let the children react to why they think Carle made the web illustrations raised. Ahead of time lightly sketch a web on transparency. Then let the children play out the story as one child with a paper spider taped to a felt-tip pen makes the web on transparency on a lighted overhead projector.

7. Read Green's story of *The Hole in the Dike* to the class. Discuss how Eric Carle's illustrations helped to make the story more meaningful. Let children explore ways a modern child might do a brave act to help others.

Getting Acquainted with Robert McCloskey

STUDENT OBJECTIVES:

- Create a picture in monochrome
- Act out a portion of a story
- Share the excitement of losing a first tooth
- Examine watercolor and lithographs
- Interpret in art form an unfamiliar setting introduced by a story

RECOMMENDED READING:

McCloskey, Robert. *Blueberries for Sal.* Viking, 1948.
Little Sal and Little Bear each follow the wrong mother as they eat blueberries on Blueberry Hill.

———. *Burt Dow, Deepwater Man.* Viking, 1963.
Burt Dow and his giggling pet gull face a crisis when they encounter a huge whale while sailing in a leaky dory.

———. *Lentil.* Viking, 1940.
A small boy's harmonica helps save the day when the band cannot play for Colonel Carter.

———. *Make Way for Ducklings.* Viking, 1941. 4BA Mrs. Mallard and her eight ducklings take an amazing walk through the Boston streets to their new home in the Public Garden.

———. *One Morning in Maine.* Viking, 1952.
Sal's first tooth is lost but she uses a successful alternative approach to make her wish come true.

———. *Time of Wonder.* Viking, 1957.
Hurricanes and quiet times during the summer season on a Maine island are seen through the eyes of two children who explore and share in the beauty.

BIOGRAPHICAL SOURCES:

For more information on Robert McCloskey, see *Books Are by People,* 164–68; *The Junior Book of Authors,* 2d ed., 203–04; *Something about the Author,* 39:138–48; *Twentieth-Century Children's*

Writers, 849–51; *Twentieth-Century Children's Writers,* 2d ed., 525–26.

GROUP INTRODUCTORY ACTIVITY:

Before reading aloud the 1942 Caldecott Award–winning *Make Way for Ducklings,* explain to the children that in order for McCloskey to be able to draw the mallards in motion, he felt he had to closely observe some ducks for a period of time. Since he lived in a New York apartment and lacked access to ducks, he purchased two mallards and kept them in his apartment. For weeks he followed them around the apartment on his hands and knees with his sketchbook, watching them move and even swim in his bathtub. He later acquired six baby ducklings and made hundreds of sketches in the same way.[8]

Ahead of time, prepare eight 8½" x 11" signs with the names Jack, Kack, Lack, Mack, Nack, Ouack, Pack, and Quack printed on them. Select eight children to sit in front holding the signs in order. Then, each time their names are called have them stand with their sign and face the audience. Have the entire group join in saying each name aloud.

To prepare the illustrations McCloskey used lithographic pencils on grained zinc. Let the children retell the story using the pictures. Urge them to observe closely the facial expressions on the mallards. Point out that the illustrations are "monochromatic" and explain what this means. Have them explore why he used the brown tones.

Urge each child to prepare monochrome illustrations of his or her favorite parts of the story.

FOLLOW-UP ACTIVITIES FOR TEACHER AND STUDENTS TO SHARE:

1. If there is a park with a lake or pond in your town where ducks might live, let small groups of children look at the city map. Help them chart a way for the ducks to walk from the school to the park. What dangers would they encounter? How could they overcome each problem?

2. View the sound filmstrip of *Blueberries for Sal* (Weston Woods, n.d., 47 fr., col., 9 min.) or read McCloskey's book to the class. Tell the children that the experiences related in *Blueberries for Sal, One Morning in Maine,* and *Time of Wonder* grew out of things that happened to the author's own family.[9] Like those in *Make Way for Ducklings,* the illustrations are also done monochromatically. Have the children discuss why the color blue was used.

Let four children play the parts of Sal, her mother, Little Bear, and his mother. Pantomime the scenes where each child is following the wrong mother. Let the audience in chorus repeat the words each horrified mother says when she discovers the mix-up.

3. In McCloskey's *One Morning in Maine,* Sal is introduced again as she loses her first tooth. Share the book with the class. Stop the story on page 39 long enough to predict what might happen now that Sal has really lost her tooth. After briefly discussing the possibilities, complete the story.

   After the story let children share their first experiences losing a tooth. How did they lose it? What did they do with it? The ideas may be compiled in a Losing My First Tooth experience chart and shared with another class.

   If the sound filmstrip *One Morning in Maine* (Viking, distributed by Live Oak Media, 1979, 65 fr., b/w, 19:28 min.) is available, it may be set up and used by small groups who want to share the story again in another medium.

4. In 1958 Robert McCloskey again won the Caldecott Medal, this time for *Time of Wonder.* Share the book with the class. Ask the children if they can guess who the family might be.

   Send a small group of students to the library to find information on Maine that describes the Penobscot Bay area, then summarize the information. Do McCloskey's books about Maine, *Time of Wonder* and *One Morning in Maine,* enhance an understanding of the area? Then, reread the beginning paragraphs in *Time of Wonder.* Give the children the opportunity to imagine themselves on a Maine island in a specific season of the year. Then using watercolors, have them illustrate what they imagine.

5. Share McCloskey's story *Burt Dow, Deep Water Man.* Discuss Burt Dow's attempts to upset the whale's stomach. What colors were used? Let children use paints to illustrate the inside of the whale's stomach just before the whale's burps.

6. Read *Lentil* to the class. Give each child a lemon section to suck. See if they can whistle. What instruments do they think they could play even though their lips are puckered? Discuss why Mr. Sneep played the lemon trick. What else could he have done to spoil the welcome?

The Picture Stories of Ezra Jack Keats

STUDENT OBJECTIVES:

- Use imagination to create a paper animal and tell a story about it
- Plan a party and invite another class
- Pantomime animal tricks appropriate for a stage show
- Create and/or decorate a hat for a parade
- Share a choral poem
- Read a story without words

RECOMMENDED READING:

Keats, Ezra Jack. *Clementina's Cactus.* Viking, 1982.
> A wordless tale of a child whose discovery of a cactus is interrupted by a storm, but who finds it in full bloom in the morning.

———. *Dreams.* Macmillan, 1974.
> Collage and acrylic painting enhance this tale of the paper mouse that frightened the big dog by casting a shadow.

———. *Hi Cat.* Macmillan, 1970.
> Archie and Peter try to feature a dog and cat in a show for their friends.

———. *Jennie's Hat.* Harper & Row, 1966.
> The birds help Jennie make her plain hat into a beautiful Easter bonnet.

———. *A Letter to Amy.* Harper & Row, 1968.
> Peter has a difficult time trying to invite Amy to his birthday party.

———. *Pet Show.* Macmillan, 1972.
> Archie's cat runs away and he has to find a new pet to take to the show.

———. *Peter's Chair.* Harper & Row, 1967.
> Although Peter takes his chair and runs away before father can paint it for his baby sister, he returns to find that he is loved and needed.

———. *Regards to the Man in the Moon.* Four Winds, 1981.
> The junkman's son uses his imagination and junk to create a spaceship, and the adventures that ensue turn his companions' jeers into respect.

————. *The Snowy Day.* Viking, 1962.
Peter spends a happy day playing in the snow.
————. *Whistle for Willie.* Viking. 1964.
Peter finally learns to whistle in order to call his dog.

BIOGRAPHICAL SOURCES:

For more information on Ezra Jack Keats (deceased), see *Books Are by People,* 116–20; *More Junior Authors,* 120; *Something about the Author,* 14:99–103; *Twentieth-Century Children's Writers,* 678–80; *Twentieth-Century Children's Writers,* 2d ed., 420–21.

GROUP INTRODUCTORY ACTIVITY:

Share the book *Hi Cat.* Tell the children Keats has said that his reason for writing books for children was so he could share his own experiences with them, either from the real world or from fantasy. He hoped that children would discover that they are important, resourceful, and that they can have hope and self-esteem.[10]

Discuss appropriate animals one could use in a show. Suggest to children that they pretend they are a specific animal, then describe and/or demonstrate a trick that would be appropriate for a show.

FOLLOW-UP ACTIVITIES FOR TEACHER AND STUDENTS TO SHARE:

1. Share Keats's *The Snowy Day.* Then, if available, view the sound filmstrip (Weston Woods, 1965, 27 fr., col., 6 min.). Discuss whether a book or filmstrip would be better for a given situation, i.e., bedtime story, large group story hour at the public library, etc.

   Talk about collage as an art medium. Suggest the children make collage pictures or a group mural of children having fun in the snow. Cotton and bits of cloth as well as paper can be used.

2. Read Keats's *A Letter to Amy* to the class. Note that the book was dedicated to Augusta Baker. Tell the class that she is a storyteller and, if available, show them one of her story collections. Discuss reasons why Ezra Jack Keats might have dedicated it to her.

   Talk about games often played at birthday parties. What presents might the children have brought Peter?

   Plan a party for another class in your school. Discuss invitations, refreshments, and games. Perhaps the class may want to have the party at the end of the unit on Keats and share his books in some ways as entertainment.

3. Read Keats's *Regards to the Man in the Moon*. Look at a recent picture of a spaceship and discuss ways in which the children's spacecraft was different in the book. Discuss the meaning of the word "junk" and think of ways junk is sometimes used—as car parts or art forms made from discarded objects. Collect a box of junk such as bits of wire, cotton from tops of bottles, scraps of colored paper or cloth, bottle caps, wood scraps, etc. and encourage children to make collage pictures or sculpture from it.

4. Show children Keats's wordless picture book, *Clementina's Cactus*. Let them examine it individually and tape the story plot as they see it. Play back their versions. Note points in which all are alike.

5. If available, share the 16mm film *Ezra Jack Keats* (Weston Woods, 1970, 1 reel, col., 17 min.). Discuss the way he used paint for the background of his illustrations. Examine his books to find which illustrations resulted from this technique. Talk about Ezra Jack Keats's use of his own neighborhood to get his art and story ideas. If he could have walked around your neighborhood, what might he have seen that would have interested him?

6. Read Keats's *Pet Show* to the class. Let the children describe what they would bring if the class had a pet show. Have the children bring, draw, or find in magazines pictures of the pets described and make a wall pet show.

7. Share Keats's *Dreams* with the children. Urge children to make paper animals and think up dream stories about them. The children may want to record these stories on tape. These stories could be played as part of teacher conferences with parents or at school open house.

8. Before reading *Whistle for Willie* share the poem "Whistles" by Dorothy Aldis in Nancy Larrick's *Paper Pipe that Song Again* (Random House, 1965, o.p.). After reading it several times urge the children to repeat it together as a choral.

   After reading the story let the children suggest reasons that whistling might "come in handy." Place their list of reasons on the blackboard.

9. Read Keats's *Jennie's Hat* to the class. Fold paper hats and decorate them with crayons or scraps of ribbon, cloth, etc. from the junk box. Have a "hat" parade.

10. Read Keats's *Peter's Chair*. Discuss why Peter ran away. What did he take with him? If he had intended to go very far, what else would he have needed? Why did he go back into the house? What made him change his mind about the chair? Play out the story, adding appropriate dialogue as needed.

Culminating Activities after First Grade/Second Grade

Discuss with the entire class the literature experiences they have shared. What authors and illustrators do they recall? What books did each person named write or illustrate? What book characters do the students remember?

What literature activities did the students particularly enjoy? Do the students remember any facts about specific authors or illustrators?

What does it mean to win the Caldecott Medal? Name a medal-winning book. What is collage? Which illustrator used collage in creating the pictures for a book?

What is a fable? What are some specific names for a group of the same kind of animal? What facts do they recall about specific animals?

REFERENCES

1. Lee Bennett Hopkins, *Books Are by People* (New York: Citation Press, 1969), p. 334.

2. Anne Commire, ed., *Something about the Author* (Detroit: Gale Research, 1976), vol. 8, p. 114.

3. Muriel Fuller, ed., *More Junior Authors* (New York: H.W. Wilson, 1963), p. 180.

4. Doris de Montreville and Donna Hill, eds., *Third Book of Junior Authors* (New York: H.W. Wilson, 1972), p. 182.

5. Fuller, p. 65.

6. de Montreville and Hill, p. 300.

7. Doris de Montreville and Elizabeth D. Crawford, eds., *Fourth Book of Junior Authors & Illustrators* (New York: H.W. Wilson, 1978), pp. 68–69.

8. Elizabeth Montgomery, *The Story behind Books* (New York: Dodd, Mead, 1949), pp. 35–41.

9. D.L. Kirkpatrick, ed., *Twentieth-Century Children's Writers* (New York: St. Martin's Press, 1978), p. 850.

10. Kirkpatrick, p. 679.

Chapter 3
Second Grade/Third Grade

Imaginative Situations Created by Maurice Sendak

STUDENT OBJECTIVES:

- Discuss dreams, fears, and fantasies
- Draw what s/he imagines
- Locate a story by using the table of contents
- Participate in the action of a story as it is reread
- Note title page and table of contents

RECOMMENDED READING:

Minarik, Else. *Little Bear.* Illustrated by Maurice Sendak. Harper & Row, 1957.
    Four stories show Little Bear wanting to wear clothes in the winter, making himself some soup, explaining an imaginary trip to the moon, and listening to his mother tell him a goodnight story.
        Others in the Little Bear series:
        Father Bear Comes Home. Illustrated by Maurice Sendak. Harper & Row, 1959.
        Kiss for Little Bear. Illustrated by Maurice Sendak. Harper & Row, 1968.
        Little Bear's Friend. Illustrated by Maurice Sendak. Harper & Row, 1960.
        Little Bear's Visit. Illustrated by Maurice Sendak. Harper & Row, 1961.

Sendak, Maurice. *Alligators All Around.* Harper & Row, 1962.
Alligator acts out the alphabet from "alligators all around" to "zippity zound."

———. *Chicken Soup with Rice.* Harper & Row, 1962.
A rhymed book of months.

———. *In the Night Kitchen.* Harper & Row, 1970.
In his dreams Mickey falls through the dark into the night kitchen where the jovial bakers prepare their goods while everyone else sleeps.

———. *One Was Johnny.* Harper & Row, 1962.
Johnny counts from one to 10 and back again.

———. *Outside Over There.* Harper & Row, 1981.
While Ida watches her baby sister, a goblin steals the baby and leaves a changling; but Ida discovers the change and goes to the rescue.

———. *Pierre.* Harper & Row, 1962.
Pierre learns a lesson about caring in a cautionary tale.

———. *Where the Wild Things Are.* Harper & Row, 1963.
After Max is sent to his room because he has made mischief, his dreams take him to the place where the wild things are.

BIOGRAPHICAL SOURCES:

For more information on Maurice Sendak, see *Books Are by People,* 250–54; *More Junior Authors,* 181–82; *Something about the Author,* 27:181–201; *Twentieth-Century Children's Writers,* 1098–1101; *Twentieth-Century Children's Writers,* 2d ed., 685–87.

GROUP INTRODUCTORY ACTIVITY:

Introduce facts about Sendak's life. If possible share some of the illustrations in Selma Lanes's *The Art of Maurice Sendak,* particularly those of the toys he, his brother, and his sister made as children.[1]

Maurice Sendak was born June 10, 1928, the same year as Mickey Mouse, in Brooklyn, New York. He was the third youngest child of Jewish immigrants. Sendak's main interests as a student were art and English. He says he wanted to be an illustrator very early in life and loved the smell of new books. (Get a new book from the library and pass it around for children to smell.)

In a December 1972 article in *Harper's Bazaar* Sendak said that his books are journeys, literally, trips into fantasy. It's his one theme. Through their imaginations children get away from a situation: out of a house where they feel no one is interested in them or out of a place where they are bored. He says that children and the characters in his books accept life if they know they can go away for a few minutes, have a real fantasy, do all the things that are pent up, and get it out of their systems.[2]

Read Sendak's *Where the Wild Things Are* to the class. Then let each child pretend he or she is a wild thing. Let them demonstrate roaring terrible roars, gnashing terrible teeth, rolling terrible eyes, and showing terrible claws without making a sound. Select a child to be Max and another to be his mother, and with the rest of the children as wild things, pantomime the story as it is reread.

FOLLOW-UP ACTIVITIES FOR TEACHER AND STUDENTS TO SHARE:

1. Read Sendak's *In the Night Kitchen* to the class. Discuss the ways that Mickey is like Max in *Where the Wild Things Are.* Recall what Maurice Sendak said about the value of imagination. If the children could take a dream trip some night, where would they go? What adventures might they have? Perhaps they may want to select one dream and illustrate it as a class project mural.

2. *Outside Over There* needs to be read aloud, allowing time for the children to see the story developing in the illustrations. Tell the children that Sendak considers this the third in the trilogy of *Where the Wild Things Are* and *In the Night Kitchen.* Urge them to talk about how the stories are alike. After the children determine that all three are fantasy journeys to escape the present, note what the child in each was trying to escape. Ask the children to go to their desks, and after turning off the lights, ask them to close their eyes and imagine where they wish they could be at this moment. While they are imagining with eyes closed, place a large sheet of drawing paper on each desk. Then ask them to draw their "outside over there" place using paints or crayons, whatever they imagine it to be.

3. Set up a Little Bear Reading Corner. Place in it the five books by Else Minarik—*Little Bear, Little Bear's Friend, Little Bear's Visit, Father Bear Comes Home* and *Kiss For Little Bear.* Ask the children to bring stuffed bears from home to make the corner more attractive. Introduce *Little Bear* by reading an episode aloud to the class. Before doing so, show the class the title page and identify each item of information given there. Then turn to the contents on page two and select the episode to read. After sharing the episode, show the children the other Little Bear books and a dittoed "sharing form" that includes space for recording title of book, author, illustrator, name of story in book, page on which story begins, and colors used in the illustration. Ask each child to read a number of episodes

from the Little Bear books and fill out a sharing form for each episode read. After this sharing activity is completed, let the children discuss and/or recall the episodes they enjoyed most.

4. If available, share the Sendak-narrated sound filmstrip *Chicken Soup with Rice* (Weston Woods, 1976, 26 fr., col., 5 min.). If the book is used instead, share it with a small group so all can see. As a project, let the children prepare a calendar for each month and decorate it.

5. Alligator acts out the letters of the alphabet in Sendak's *Alligators All Around.* Listen to the song "Alligators All Around" on the record *Maurice Sendak's Really Rosie* by Carole King and Maurice Sendak (Caedmon, 1981, disc, TR5368). This jazzy song is easily picked up by the children. As you turn the pages of the story, sing "Alligators All Around." Each child can be assigned a letter of the alphabet. As the letter is sung, that child can stand up and act it out.

6. Read aloud Sendak's *One Was Johnny,* a counting book. Point out the facial expressions of Sendak's characters as the action evolves in the story. Give each child a piece of 8½" X 11" drawing paper. Ask them to fold the paper into fourths, then open the paper to lie flat. Have each child draw his or her own counting book with one to four on the front side and four back to one on the reverse side. As a language activity they can add words to the story if desired.

7. If a small copy from Sendak's Nutshell Library (Harper & Row, 1962, 4 v.) that includes Sendak's *Pierre* is available, show it to the children. Explain that even in such a small book there is a title page, table of contents, and prologue. Discuss what is included in each. As you read *Pierre* aloud, have the children join in with the line "I don't care." Discuss the lesson Pierre learned.

8. After having read all the available books that Maurice Sendak has illustrated examine the books again. A committee of children will want to check the card catalog under "Sendak" to be sure they have available all the books that Sendak illustrated. Classify the books by style of illustration to note in which books the characters resemble each other. In which books are babies illustrated? In which books is a dog found?

Meet Judith Viorst through Her Books

STUDENT OBJECTIVES:

- Become aware of other people's feelings
- Discuss ways of earning and spending money
- Distinguish points of view
- Locate other stories and poetry dealing with friendship
- Identify with characters and events in books

RECOMMENDED READING:

Viorst, Judith. *Alexander and the Terrible, Horrible, No Good, Very Bad Day.* Illustrated by Ray Cruz. Atheneum, 1972.
Alexander's day goes from bad to worse as he gets gum stuck in his hair, sings too loud, has a cavity in his tooth, and must wear his hated railroad train pajamas to bed.

————. *Alexander Who Used to Be Rich Last Sunday.* Illustrated by Ray Cruz. Atheneum, 1978.
In a matter of days Alexander goes from being rich (with $1.00) to having only bus tokens.

————. *If I Were in Charge of the World, And Other Worries.* Illustrated by Lynne Cherry. Atheneum, 1981.
In this collection of poetry children's feelings from wishes and worries to wicked thoughts are explored.

————. *I'll Fix Anthony.* Illustrated by Arnold Lobel. Harper & Row, 1969.
Anthony's little brother decides that when he is six years old he'll be able to do everything better than Anthony.

————. *My Mama Says There Aren't Any Zombies, Ghosts, Vampires, Creatures, Demons, Monsters, Fiends, Goblins, or Things.* Illustrated by Kay Chorao. Atheneum, 1973.
A young boy's mother reassures him that there aren't any mean-eyed monsters or tall white ghosts; but even mothers are sometimes mistaken.

————. *Rosie and Michael.* Illustrated by Lorna Tomei. Atheneum, 1974.
Rosie and Michael are the best of friends even if sometimes he is dopey and she is grouchy.

————. *The Tenth Good Thing about Barney.* Illustrated by Erik Blegvad. Atheneum, 1971.
   After the death of his pet cat, Barney, a little boy, realizes how many good things there are about Barney.

BIOGRAPHICAL SOURCES:

For more information on Judith Viorst, see *Fourth Book of Junior Authors & Illustrators,* 333–35; *Something about the Author,* 7:200–01; *Twentieth-Century Children's Writers,* 1290–91; *Twentieth-Century Children's Writers,* 2d ed. 796–97.

GROUP INTRODUCTORY ACTIVITY:

Read *Alexander and the Terrible, Horrible, No Good, Very Bad Day.* Let the children discuss their feelings about what makes a very bad day. Share your feelings about what makes an adult day bad.
   After discussing an Alexander-type day, introduce Judith Viorst to the children. Judith Viorst said that she started writing when she was seven. She said that hers were terrible poems about dead dogs, mostly. She became a successful author when she began to write about her family to fulfill specific needs. To help her son Alexander get through the day a little better she wrote *Alexander and the Terrible, Horrible, No Good, Very Bad Day.* A discussion of death resulted in *The Tenth Good Thing about Barney.* For her son Nick, who used to be scared of monsters, she wrote *My Mama Says There Aren't Any Zombies . . . .*[3]

FOLLOW-UP ACTIVITIES FOR TEACHER AND STUDENTS TO SHARE:

1. After having heard about Alexander's bad day and discussing such days, have the children draw a cartoon sequence of the worst things that could have happened to them at school during the past week. Briefly label each and place in an Alexander Bad Day book.
2. Read aloud the poem "Fifteen, Maybe Sixteen Things To Worry About" in *If I Were in Charge of the World, And Other Worries.* Urge children to predict the situation that made Viorst write this poem. Have children suggest 16 things about which children worry for a teacher-recorded class list. They may want to examine each to see if the need for that worry can be refuted.

3. Read aloud Viorst's *Alexander Who Used to Be Rich Last Sunday.* With children sequencing the action, make a chart showing how Alexander spent his money. Have children compare how Alexander spent his money with how they might spend a dollar. Can they suggest ways Alexander might earn a dollar? Read aloud Shel Silverstein's poem "Smart" in *Where the Sidewalk Ends* (Harper & Row, 1974). Compare how the character Alexander spent his money with the boy in the poem "Smart."

4. Share with the class Viorst's friendship story, *Rosie and Michael.* Perhaps a girl can read Rosie's lines and a boy Michael's. Compare their point of view about situations and people. What act of friendship did the children like best? Why?

5. Have a small group of students extend Viorst's *Rosie and Michael* by finding in the library some riddles that Rosie and Michael might have shared. Let each share their favorite with the class. Another group may want to check the card catalog under the subject heading "Friendship" to locate other books about friendship that class members could read silently. Another group of children may want to extend the story by discussing name changes. Michael thought about changing his name to Ace, Tiger, or Lefty. Rosie wanted to change the spelling of her name to Rosi or Wrosie. Each child could identify a nickname or a different spelling they might prefer, indicating the reason for the preference.

6. Read Viorst's *My Mama Says There Aren't Any Zombies . . .* to the class. Follow up with an art activity in which children can create their own monster masks or construction paper creatures.

7. After reading aloud Viorst's *The Tenth Good Thing about Barney,* which deals with the death of a pet cat, allow the children to share their feelings about the story or about their own pet. The little boy in the book had difficulty thinking of a tenth good thing. Ask the class to list as many good things as they can about a pet or make-believe pet. Read aloud *Petey* by Tobi Tobias (Putnam's, 1978) and have the children indicate the likenesses and differences between the two stories.

8. In her book *If I Were In Charge of the World, And Other Worries,* Viorst shares easily recognizable humorous situations. Share the poems in this book over a period of time. After the poems have been shared, have the children select favorites. Make transparencies of these poems and let children make a border decoration or an illustration. Using the transparencies share these poems again as a choral, using a small group or entire class as readers.

9. Read aloud Viorst's *I'll Fix Anthony,* paying special attention to expressing the little brother's feelings with your voice. Talk with the children about the importance of reading with expression as opposed to a monotone. If the class wants to, let pairs of children practice voice and facial expression and read the story

aloud to other class groups at a later time.

   After reading the story have the children relate their own feelings about older brothers and sisters.

10. As a culminating experience let children discuss what stories or events in her books might have happened in the Viorst home. After discussing these events let children select one or two, recall the scenes, and act out.

On the Farm with Roger Duvoisin's Friends

STUDENT OBJECTIVES:

- Participate in a choral reading activity
- Imagine other characters or incidents in a story
- Develop vocabulary by listening for figurative language and thinking of different ways a particular objective could be described
- List family names that denote objects from nature
- Explore the contributions of animals to farm life

RECOMMENDED READING:

Duvoisin, Roger. *The Crocodile in the Tree.* Knopf, 1973.
   Crocodile makes friends with the farmer's wife by bringing her flowers.

———. *Crocus.* Knopf, 1972.
   When Crocus regains her teeth and spirit, the animals realize that they all need something to make them feel worthwhile.

———. *The Importance of Crocus.* Knopf, 1980.
   Crocus learns to be proud of his individual accomplishment.

———. *Petunia.* Knopf, 1950.
   Petunia discovers that merely possessing a book does not ensure wisdom.

———. *Petunia Beware.* Knopf, 1958.
   Petunia faces danger as she seeks the grass that seems greener on the other side of the fence.

———. *Petunia, I Love You.* Knopf, 1965.
Petunia escapes being eaten by the wily raccoon and saves the raccoon's life instead.

———. *Petunia's Christmas.* Knopf, 1952.
Petunia earns money to buy the gander's freedom.

———. *Petunia's Treasure.* Knopf, 1958.
Petunia's contemplated riches cause the animals to fight over the gifts they want.

———. *Two Lonely Ducks.* Knopf, 1955.
A counting book about two ducks who are no longer lonely after their 10 eggs hatch.

———. *Veronica.* Knopf, 1961.
Veronica's wish to be different comes true when she visits the city—but not in the way she had imagined.

BIOGRAPHICAL SOURCES:

For more information on Roger Duvoisin (deceased), see *Books Are by People,* 64–68; *The Junior Book of Authors,* 2d ed., 106–07; *Something about the Author,* 30:101–07; *Twentieth-Century Children's Writers,* 391–94; *Twentieth-Century Children's Writers,* 2d ed., 256–57.

GROUP INTRODUCTORY ACTIVITY:

Before sharing *Petunia Beware* tell the children that, before his death in 1980, Roger Duvoisin said he enjoyed talking with children, for he could learn from them as well as teach them. He loved children's questions, drawings, and letters. He was delighted that nowadays children are encouraged to create and to express themselves. He felt that the childhood that was still alive in both himself and his wife Louise Fatio, also a children's author, (*The Happy Lion,* McGraw-Hill, 1954) helped them both create for children.[4]

Share *Petunia Beware* with the class. Urge them to participate by joining in when the repetitive refrain about the grass is read:

The grass *wasn't* a bit greener,
It *wasn't* a bit tastier,
It *was* the *same* grass.

Recall with the children the sequence of events and play out the story, using a portion of the group to be the "grass chorus."

FOLLOW-UP ACTIVITIES FOR TEACHER AND STUDENTS TO SHARE:

1. Read Duvoisin's *Petunia* aloud. Ask the children to think of other disasters that could have happened to Petunia and her friends because she pretended to read signs on box labels. Record on tape and pantomime if desired.
2. Read Duvoisin's *Petunia's Christmas* aloud to the group. Introduce an example of figurative language such as "The new snow was soft like a kitten's fur" before reading. Ask the children to hold up their hand if they notice any other expressions that compare two things as the story progresses. After reading the story, urge children to think of other ways Duvoisin could have described the softness of the snow and other examples of figurative language that they noted.

   Discuss other ways Petunia could have acquired money to buy the gander's freedom.
3. Read Duvoisin's *Petunia's Treasure* aloud. Suggest that the children draw another gift that one of the farm animals could have wanted.
4. Share Duvoisin's *Two Lonely Ducks* with the group. Reread, this time asking them to repeat as a choral expression such as "gleaming in the corner of the barn" and "She sat one day," etc.

   As a group think of nine different ways to describe the eggs that were "gleaming in the corner of the barn." The teacher may want to write down the responses, insert them in the story, and on the following day use the students for the choral portions while rereading their new story of two lonely ducks.
5. Introduce Duvoisin's *Veronica* to the group. After sharing the story, let children think of specific misadventures Veronica might have if visiting Petunia's farm instead of the city.

   Perhaps a committee of students could make a mural of *Veronica* in the midst of one of these misadventures.
6. Read Duvoisin's *Crocus* to the class. Let children discuss what made each of the other animals feel important. Let children think about what zoo animals they feel could make a contribution to farm life. Why would some specific animals not be chosen?
7. Share Duvoisin's *The Importance of Crocus* with the class. After reading the story, go back to the first two pages and reread, having the children listen for the figurative language. Talk about how each description makes them feel.

   Recreate the plot line of the story, noting what each animal could do. Then dramatize the story.

   Think of some other farm animal that was not mentioned. Draw a picture illustrating what that animal could contribute to the farm.

8. Read Duvoisin's *Petunia I Love You* to the class. Have the class recall each of the ways the raccoon tried to kill Petunia. In each instance, did Petunia save herself or was it an accident that she escaped? What was the raccoon's one wish? Why did he change his mind at the end of the story? Let children think of a new trick the raccoon might have used to try to capture Petunia. How could she have escaped that time?

9. Read Duvoisin's *The Crocodile in the Tree.* Let the children verbalize about where they might hide a crocodile if it came to their house. What could the crocodile do to please each of their mothers? If it lived in their area, what wildflowers might the crocodile bring? Do any of those mentioned by Duvoisin grow near their houses? Why do the children suppose Duvoisin gave the family the name Sweetpeas? What other flower last names might he have used? Are any of those mentioned by the children found in the local telephone book?

Fun with James Stevenson

STUDENT OBJECTIVES:

- Identify those elements of a story that make it a tall tale
- Participate in an imaginative animal concert
- Create a situation and recount how it could have been worse
- Discuss cartoon illustrations and try to create a new cartoon idea
- Research constellations and try to locate them in the night sky

RECOMMENDED READING:

Stevenson, James. *Clams Can't Sing.* Greenwillow, 1980.
    Easy-to-read story of two clams that participate in the annual concert even though they can't sing.

———. *"Could Be Worse!"* Greenwillow, 1977.
    Even though grandpa's "guess what" adventures are fantastic, the children respond with grandpa's favorite expression, "Could be worse!"

———. *Emma.* Greenwillow, 1985.
    Emma's friends help her trick the witches that made fun of her.

————. *Howard.* Greenwillow, 1980.
A duck that survives the New York City winter through the assistance of a frog and some mice evidences the meaning of true friendship.

————. *The Sea View Hotel.* Greenwillow, 1978.
Hubert is bored with the vacation site until he meets Alf, the handyman. Then there is plenty to do.

————. *That Terrible Halloween Night.* Greenwillow, 1980.
Grandpa weaves a tall tale of why he doesn't scare easily because of the frightening Halloween adventure he had as a boy.

————. *We Can't Sleep.* Greenwillow, 1982.
When Grandpa completes his tall tale about the night he couldn't sleep, Mary Ann and Lorrie are asleep.

————. *The Wish Card Ran Out!* Greenwillow, 1981.
A credit card from International Wish does not prove to be as delightful as Charlie imagined.

BIOGRAPHICAL SOURCES:

For more information on James Stevenson, see *Fifth Book of Junior Authors & Illustrators,* 303–04; *Something about the Author,* 34:191.

GROUP INTRODUCTORY ACTIVITY:

Read the story *Clams Can't Sing* to the class. With children creating the actions and making the appropriate sounds, have a big concert. Now pretend it is a farm animal concert. Think of the role each animal could play. What animal might at first be told it could not participate? What *could* that animal do? Hold the farm concert.

Suggest that children pantomime the story in the classroom with one of the children reading the book.

FOLLOW-UP ACTIVITIES FOR TEACHER AND STUDENTS TO SHARE:

1. Before reading *Could Be Worse* tell the children that although Stevenson wrote and drew when he was young, he doesn't feel his work was influenced by books he read as a child. "I think that my experiences and creative mind have been formed much more by movies and comic books," he says. "I like the idea of a story board and I like the idea of a movie and all the different angles from which things can be viewed."[5]

Have children watch the pictures carefully as you read, noting that his pictures resemble comic-strip format and do illustrate viewing things from different perspectives. See if they can find an example of seeing from a different perspective.

After reading the story *Could Be Worse!* to the class, have the children recall incidents in the story and think of ways each could have been worse.

2. Read *That Terrible Halloween Night* to the class. List all the adventures that happened to grandpa. Introduce the idea of a tall tale as one which recounts adventures that could not happen in real life. Could any of the adventures listed actually be possible? Make your own Halloween story of someone who went into a deserted house.

3. Read the story *Howard.* What event indicated that Howard had discovered the meaning of true friendship? If a duck were separated from the flock flying south in your town or city, who might be its friend? What adventures could it have?

4. Read *The Wish Card Ran Out* to the class. Suggest that each think of three things they would do with a wish card and use a tape recorder to record the thoughts of each child. Share with the class and record how many ideas were created. Make wish cards by printing WISH CARD across the top of an index card and the student's name underneath. After the children decorate the card, laminate or cover with contact paper.

5. Read *We Can't Sleep* to the class. Discuss possible alternatives to a tall tale if they can't sleep at night. Would the tale grandpa told have put the class to sleep? Why? Why not? Ask the library media specialist for sleepy time poems, songs, and stories that might be used for sleepless nights. Share those with the class and let them decide which they like best. Make a WE CAN'T SLEEP bulletin board and let children find or draw pictures to give ideas for solutions to the problem.

6. Read *The Sea View Hotel* to the class. List all the things Hubert learned from Alf. How did they play "Duck on the Rock"? What other games could they have played?

Tell children that James Stevenson is a well-known cartoonist. Discuss the location of the text in a cartoon. Are there any obvious characteristics of cartoon illustrations? Examine the illustrations in all his books. Suggest that the children may want to draw a cartoon of something else Hubert might have learned from Alf.

Hubert learned about the star Arcturus and the constellation Cassiopeia. Let a committee of children go to the library and find a book illustrating other constellations they might see. Urge the children to look at the stars with their family and try to find Cassiopeia or others they researched.

7. Read *Emma* to the class. Let children recall how Emma tricked the witches. What else might she have done? Have the children look at the illustrations and see if they remind them of *The Sea View Hotel.* If so, how?

Sharing Books by James and Edward Marshall

STUDENT OBJECTIVES:

● Record an original story told by students
● Dramatize portions of a story
● Draw pictures relating to new incidents for the stories
● Interpret a dance as done by an animal
● Find simple French words and use in classroom conversation

RECOMMENDED READING:

Marshall, Edward. *Space Case.* Illustrated by James Marshall. Dial, 1980.
The "thing" shared Halloween with Buddy, then became the best science project at school.

———. *Three by the Sea.* Illustrated by James Marshall. Dial, 1981.
An easy-to-read attempt of three friends at storytelling.

———. *Troll Country.* Illustrated by James Marshall. Dial, 1980.
An easy-to-read story about Elsie Fay and her mother, who tell of their encounter with the same troll, even though father insists trolls do not exist.

Marshall, James. *George and Martha.* Houghton Mifflin, 1972.
Five short stories about the friendship of two hippopotami.
Other George and Martha books are:
George and Martha Encore. Houghton Mifflin, 1973.
George and Martha, One Fine Day. Houghton Mifflin, 1978.
George and Martha, Rise And Shine. Houghton Mifflin, 1976.
George and Martha, Tons of Fun. Houghton Mifflin, 1980.

BIOGRAPHICAL SOURCES:

For more information on James Marshall, see *Fourth Book of Junior Authors & Illustrators,* 253–54; *Something about the Author,* 6:161; *Twentieth-Century Children's Writers,* 2d ed., 513–14.

GROUP INTRODUCTORY ACTIVITY:

Introduce the George and Martha series. Marshall says the stories really began as he was sitting on his Texas patio drawing idly while watching television. His rough sketches finally became recognizable as hippopotami, and because they needed names, he gave them the names of the characters in the play he was watching.[6] Before reading *George And Martha* to the group, suggest that they may want to do the follow-up activities in committees instead of as a whole class. They could take turns reading the books and, under teacher direction, discuss the stories and carry out art activities.

After reading *George And Martha* to the group have the children make up a new story about what happened to George when he tripped on his roller skates. Record the story.

What if George had been able to float away in the balloon? Let children suggest ideas of what might have happened to him.

Suggest that they each draw a picture of how else George might have gotten rid of the split pea soup.

FOLLOW-UP ACTIVITIES FOR TEACHER AND STUDENTS TO SHARE:

1. Read Marshall's *George and Martha, Rise and Shine* as a committee activity or to the group as a whole. Discuss how else Martha might have taken George to the picnic without wearing herself out.

   Dramatize the story of the picnic or pantomime it while the story is read.

   Make up a new story about what happens when Martha starts studying bees. The teacher may want to write it down to share with another class or group.

2. Read Marshall's *George and Martha Encore* as a committee activity or to the group as a whole. Children may want to do the Mexican Hat Dance as George would have done it. Others may want to try Martha's Dance of the Happy Butterfly.

   What might George have done to help Martha have an instant garden instead of buying cut tulips? Draw a picture of what it would look like.

Find a book in the library that would tell how George said "goodbye" in French. Make up a story in which George asked Martha out to dinner. Use the French words for "yes" and "thank you."

3. Share Marshall's *George and Martha, One Fine Day* as a small group or class. As a group think of an entry for Martha's diary.

Lay a string on the floor. Let children pretend they are Martha doing fancy footwork on the tightrope.

What might Martha have done to scare George without waiting until they went to the amusement park? Draw a picture of how he would have reacted. Some children may want to draw a picture of George and Martha on another ride in the amusement park.

4. Share Marshall's *George and Martha, Tons of Fun*. Notice the bookstore illustration. Find some familiar authors. Check to see what books are in the library by those authors. Examine them and decide which book Martha might have given George.

Think of other ways Martha might have made George cut down on sweets.

5. Share Marshall's *Space Case* as a small group or class. Suppose the "thing" comes back at Christmas. What might it bring Buddy?

How long is a zyglot? Check with the library media specialist and find other space terms related to time or distance.

6. Use Marshall's *Three by the Sea* for a small group read-aloud. Let children discuss which of the three stories they like best. As a group think of a story about a cat or a rat that Lolly or Sam might have told.

Urge children to try telling the spider's story. Use the tape recorder and play back to get ideas for improvement. Then tell the story to friends or another class.

7. Use Marshall's *Troll Country* for a small group read-aloud. Note that Edward Marshall wrote *Space Case, Three by the Sea* and *Troll Country*. James Marshall made the illustrations. After reading *Troll Country* let children discuss what they would do if they met a troll. What trick might be played to allow escape?

Act out the portion of the story where Elsie meets the troll.

Karla Kuskin, Artist and Poet

STUDENT OBJECTIVES:

- Identify orchestra instruments
- Generalize why poets write specific poems
- Dramatize a story
- Create poetry individually or as a group
- Identify animals and the sounds they make
- Translate riddles from prose to poetry form

RECOMMENDED READING:

Kuskin, Karla. *Any Me I Want To Be.* Harper & Row, 1972.
Appealing riddle-type animal poems.

———. *Dogs and Dragons, Trees and Dreams.* Harper & Row, 1980.
A collection of poetry with notes on introduction through reading, writing, and listening.

———. *James and the Rain.* Harper & Row, 1957.
James sets out to find out what rainy day games the animals play.

———. *Near the Window Tree.* Harper & Row, 1975.
Thirty-two poems introduced by Kuskin's description of how she felt when the poem was written.

———. *The Philharmonic Gets Dressed.* Illustrated by Marc Simont. Harper & Row, 1982.
The activities of 105 orchestra members are described as each gets ready for a performance.

———. *Roar and More.* Harper & Row, 1956.
Brief rhymes introduce the sounds of the animals.

Winn, Marie. *What Shall We Do and Allee Galloo!* Illustrated by Karla Kuskin. Harper & Row, 1970.
A collection of songs and singing games, each with an activity described to enhance the sharing experience.

BIOGRAPHICAL SOURCES:

For more information on Karla Kuskin, see *Something about the Author,* 2:169–70; *Third Book of Junior Authors,* 167–69; *Twentieth-Century Children's Writers,* 722–24; *Twentieth-Century Children's Writers,* 2d ed., 448–49.

GROUP INTRODUCTORY ACTIVITY:

Introduce Karla Kuskin by telling the children that one of her favorite activities as a child was reading. She says that there were times when books took the place of people for her. Her mother liked to read aloud, expecially poetry. Karla made up verses and stories before she could write, so she dictated them to her mother. Her father was a writer and used to write letters to her in verse. She says she became a read-aloud addict and loved the rhythm of words.[7] As children read her stories and poems, see if they can find evidence of her liking for rhythm.

If available, share the first part of the sound filmstrip *Poetry Explained by Karla Kuskin* (Weston Woods, 1980, 43 fr., col., 16 min.) so the children can meet Karla Kuskin. Then introduce some of the poems in *Near the Window Tree.* Introduce page 37, in which children are urged to listen to the sound of words. After reading the cow poem (p. 39), talk about other words that are light, heavy, musical, and funny. Using one of the words suggested, make a short class poem about that word.

Then talk about words that "look and sound like their meaning" (p. 40). Read Kuskin's poem about the worm (p. 41). Using one of the words suggested by the children, make a class poem about the word.

Read the bug introduction and the bug poems (pp. 42–47). Talk about which poem they like best. Think of some funny words. Urge the children to make a short poem about one of the words they have suggested, either by themselves or in small groups.

Tell the children that on the days that follow the teacher will share a different Kuskin poem each day, and at times they may want to write a poem as a follow-up. Urge them to be sure to tape each one so others can share their creativity.

FOLLOW-UP ACTIVITIES FOR TEACHER AND STUDENTS TO SHARE:

1. After sharing Kuskin's cat poems in *Near the Window Tree* (pp. 48–57) urge the children to bring pictures of a cat pet or draw a

picture of a cat they would like. Using the cat's name as a beginning, urge them to make a short cat poem for the bulletin board.

2. Read Kuskin's *Roar and More* to the group. Urge the children to make the appropriate animal sounds. Think of farm animals or others not used by Kuskin and identify the sound they make. As a class project create short poems about the activities of each. Illustrate and put together as Kuskin did, including poem, picture, and sound.

3. Share the riddle poems in Kuskin's *Any Me I Want to Be* with children guessing the riddles as each is read. As a follow-up children may want to go to the library and get easy-to-read riddle books such as *Bennett Cerf's Book of Animal Riddles* (Beginner Books, 1964). Children may want to read them in small groups, select those they enjoy most, make them into poetry form, and illustrate. They might also want to record them on tape for other classes to guess.

4. Read Kuskin's *James and the Rain* aloud to the class. Recall the animals and the games each played. Dramatize the story. Disregard the numerical sequence in order to have all the animals represented.

5. Read Kuskin's *The Philharmonic Gets Dressed* to the class. See how many instruments the children can identify in the illustrations near the end of the book. Use a book from the library to identify any the children do not know. If the school district has an orchestra, arrange with the music teacher for a field trip to a rehearsal. Ask that the children get to hear the sound each instrument makes. Record that portion so the children can hear it later and identify the instrument. If available listen to Benjamin Britten's sound recording *Young Person's Guide to the Orchestra* (Columbia, 1973, 1 s., disc MS 6368) in which children are introduced to various instruments.

   Call the children's attention to the fact that Marc Simont rather than Karla Kuskin made the illustrations. Show them Janice Udry's *A Tree Is Nice* (Harper & Row, 1956), for which he won the Caldecott Medal. Have a student committee check to see if the school library has any other books Simont illustrated.

6. On page 12 of *Dogs and Dragons, Trees and Dreams,* Karla Kuskin explains the importance of rhythm to poetry. Share aloud the poems on pages 12–19, asking the children to listen for the rhythm. Using one of the poems ahead of time make an overhead transparency so the entire class can read the poem aloud after you have done so, being careful to express rhythm as they read.

7. Ask the children if they had ever thought of a recipe for writing poetry. What ingredients would they list? On page 78 of *Dogs and Dragons, Trees and Dreams,* Kuskin lists the ingredients for a poetry recipe. List these ingredients on the board and compare

with those named by the children. Read some of Kuskin's poetry aloud, letting the children discuss the ingredients represented.

8. Besides illustrating her own works, Kuskin has illustrated Winn's *What Shall We Do and Allee Galloo!* As you share with the children from this book, have the children notice how she decorated some of the capital letters in each song. As an art experience have the children select letters of the alphabet to decorate for a blackboard border.

The Worldly Adventures of Bill Peet's Animals

STUDENT OBJECTIVES:

- Create a new ending for a story
- Engage in creative art activities inspired by books
- Compare two stories
- Make up a new verse for a song

RECOMMENDED READING:

Peet, Bill. *Big Bad Bruce.* Houghton Mifflin, 1977.
The witch changes the bear's size, but he still remains a bully.

———. *Buford the Little Bighorn.* Houghton Mifflin, 1967.
Buford's horns make him awkward but finally cause him to be the star of the winter resort.

———. *Chester the Worldly Pig.* Houghton Mifflin, 1965.
Chester wants to be a star, and after many adventures he gets his wish in a surprising way.

———. *Cowardly Clyde.* Houghton Mifflin, 1979.
Clyde, the great warhorse of Sir Galavant, was not brave until he had to save his mother from the giant ogre.

———. *Eli.* Houghton Mifflin, 1978.
The lion rescues a vulture and she in turn saves his life.

———. *Encore for Eleanor.* Houghton Mifflin, 1981.
A retired circus elephant becomes a star as a zoo artist.

———. *Jennifer and Josephine.* Houghton Mifflin, 1967.
Josephine, a scrawny cat, makes an old touring car called Jennifer her home until a frenzied trip nets warm safety.

———. *The Luckiest One of All.* Houghton Mifflin, 1982.
A little boy who wishes to be a bird discovers that being a boy has advantages.

———. *No Such Things.* Houghton Mifflin, 1983.
Fifteen new and unusual characters are introduced, including a blue-snouted Twump, a spooky-tailed Tizzy, and a snickering Snoof.

———. *The Whingdingdilly.* Houghton Mifflin, 1970.
Wishing to be a horse causes Scamp many problems before he finally becomes a dog again.

BIOGRAPHICAL SOURCES:

For more information on Bill Peet, see *Something about the Author,* 2:201–03; *Third Book of Junior Authors,* 222–23; *Twentieth-Century Children's Writers,* 987–88; *Twentieth-Century Children's Writers,* 2d ed., 612–13.

GROUP INTRODUCTORY ACTIVITY:

Introduce Bill Peet by telling the children that animals were always of special interest to him. He recalls that on his first visit to the Cincinnati Zoo he spent all his savings from selling newspapers to buy film for a box camera so he could take a picture of every animal. None of the pictures turned out. From then on he took his sketch pad and drew the animals. After he was married and his two sons grew too old for the bedtime stories he used to make up for them, he began to write children's books as a hobby.[8]

Read *The Whingdingdilly* to the class. Note the dedication "In memory of a wonderful dog." After sharing the story, guess what the name of the wonderful dog might have been. Why might a family name a dog "Scamp"?

Talk about what the whingdingdilly looked like. Think of other animals that could have been combined in a humorous way. Urge the children to create their own whingdingdillys from clay, using collage, or with crayon.

FOLLOW-UP ACTIVITIES FOR TEACHER AND STUDENTS TO SHARE:

1. Read Peet's *Buford the Little Bighorn* to the class. Have children pretend to be sports announcers and describe a race in which Buford is a contestant. They may want to work together on the script or each record one separately on tape and share them with each other.
2. Read Peet's *Chester the Worldly Pig* to the class. Think of other acts Chester might have learned to do.

   Have each child draw a pig and create a new marking that would have made him famous. With the new markings, what would the pig have been named? Label each one and place on a CHESTER bulletin board.
3. Read Peet's *Big Bad Bruce* to the class. Talk about the ending. Did Bruce change? Think of a new ending in which Bruce's personality shows improvement. If he changed, did he deserve to be back in the forest again? How might that be accomplished?
4. Read Peet's *Eli* to the class. Sing the vulture's "Leo's a jolly good fellow" song. Make up new lines they could sing at the end of the story.

   Suggest that small groups read Brian Wildsmith's *The Lion and the Rat* (Watts, 1963), then discuss how the stories are alike.
5. Read Peet's *Encore for Eleanor.* Discuss some of the friends Eleanor may have made at the circus. Using charcoal or black crayon have children draw circus pictures that Eleanor might have drawn. Perhaps soon Eleanor will be drawing zoo animals. What might she enjoy drawing?
6. Read *The Luckiest One of All.* Let children think of people or objects they might like to be. Then, as a class create four-line poems about the difficulties each has.

   Make a list of advantages of being a child.
7. *Jennifer and Josephine* recounts a frightening ride with Mr. Frenzy. After reading the story aloud, have the children repeat the events of the story in sequential order while you list them on the bulletin board. Some may want to illustrate a favorite scene to share later and describe for the class. Let children discuss why Mr. Frenzy was given that name by Bill Peet. What other names might have been appropriate?
8. The title *No Such Things* indicates that these are nonsense characters from Bill Peet's imagination. After reading the book, have children guess what might have inspired him to create each character. To carry their imagination one step further, let children pretend each character is real. On the blackboard or a transparency write the following questions: If this character were real, what sounds would it make? What sights would it see? What scents would it enjoy smelling? What feelings would it

have? Ask the children to think of a character and answer each of the questions for the class.

9. After sharing Peet's *No Such Things* follow with an art and poetry experience in which the children create their own non-sense character from an everyday object. To complement the artwork, suggest they write a two- to four-line rhyme describing their character, just as Bill Peet did.

10. *Cowardly Clyde* introduces to the children the brave Sir Gala-vant and the cowardly warhorse Clyde. After sharing the story aloud discuss the two terms "brave" and "coward." Use this occasion to introduce a thesaurus such as *In Other Words: A Beginning Thesaurus* by Andrew Schiller and William Jenkins (Scott, Foresman, 1982). Have the children make a list of words that have meanings similar to "brave" and use each word cor-rectly in a sentence or story.

   A follow-up might be to have a new word contest each week. For example, instead of "brave," use the term "gallant." Each time that word is heard in classroom conversation, record on a blackboard tally.

Understanding Nature with Carol and Donald Carrick

STUDENT OBJECTIVES:

- Recall information about a number of sea animals
- Locate information in the card catalog
- Use science books for research on a selected topic
- Research and share information on sea animals
- Paint a mural of sea animals

RECOMMENDED READING:

Carrick, Carol. *Ben and the Porcupine.* Illustrated by Donald Carrick. Houghton Mifflin, 1981.
   Ben's dog suffers with porcupine quills in his nose, but Ben devises a plan to prevent the same situation from happening again.

―――. *The Crocodiles Still Wait.* Illustrated by Donald Carrick. Houghton Mifflin, 1980.
Factual information is given about the life of a female crocodile living during the age of dinosaurs.

―――. *Lost in the Storm.* Illustrated by Donald Carrick. Clarion, 1982.
Christopher must wait out a long, fretful night before searching for his dog, lost during an island storm.

―――. *Octopus.* Illustrated by Donald Carrick. Houghton Mifflin, 1978.
Illustrations and text depict the life cycle of a female octopus, including hatching her young.

―――. *Paul's Christmas Birthday.* Illustrated by Donald Carrick. Greenwillow, 1978.
Paul grumbles because his birthday was the day before Christmas, but someone from outer space makes his party special.

―――. *Sand Tiger Shark.* Illustrated by Donald Carrick. Houghton Mifflin, 1976.
The life of a male sand tiger shark is followed from birth to death in the jaws of a great white shark.

Carrick, Donald. *Morgan and the Artist.* Clarion, 1985.
A tiny man whom Frederick, the artist, painted helps him with his landscape art.

BIOGRAPHICAL SOURCES:

For more information on Carol and Donald Carrick, see *Fourth Book of Junior Authors & Illustrators,* 69–72; *Something about the Author,* 7:39–40.

GROUP INTRODUCTORY ACTIVITY:

Share with the children the Carricks' early love of nature. Carol says she grew up in a place surrounded by woods, fields, and a pond. This stimulated her interest in nature. She spent hours identifying wild flowers and seeking information on how to care for baby turtles. Her other love was reading. She remembers that when she got her first library card she had two ambitions: reading every book and copying the dictionary into a notebook.

Carol's husband Donald spent his early life near the hundreds of acres of farmland and woods bordering Henry Ford's estate in Michigan. He learned to appreciate trees and flowers, but the rivers never appealed to him because the factories made them "like mustard flowing through black banks."[9]

Read the book *Octopus* aloud to the class. Have the group identify in sequence important events in the life cycle of the octopus. Tell the class that Donald Carrick, who made the illustrations for the book, is the author's husband. The two have collaborated on over a dozen books for children. In the winter they live in Martha's Vineyard and they spend the summer in the Vermont woods. The love of nature they share with their sons is reflected in their books. Talk about the different sea animals mentioned in *The Octopus.* Perhaps some children will want to find out information about those animals to share with the class.

FOLLOW-UP ACTIVITIES FOR TEACHER AND STUDENTS TO SHARE:

1. Have a small group go to the library to find books by other husband-and-wife illustrator and/or author teams who work or have worked together on children's books, i.e., Hader, D'Aulaire, Rey, Duvoisin and Fatio, Dillon, Emberly, Lobel, Provensen. Bring some of their books back to the classroom for the children to examine and read. Note whether one made the illustrations and the other the text or if both worked together on both. Discuss problems that might occur in a team arrangement. What would the advantages be?
2. Read Carol Carrick's *Ben and the Porcupine* aloud to the class. Discuss facts the story presents about porcupines. Why did Ben leave his bat and an apple under the tree? What else might he have done to help his dog? Select a small group to go to the library and find more information about porcupines, using such books as Berniece Freschets's *Porcupine Baby* (Putnam's, 1978). Have them report or tape facts they learned to the class so class members can share the information.
3. Read *Lost in the Storm* to the class. Remind the class that the Carricks live on the island of Martha's Vineyard and the ocean worked its way into this book. Again a small boy is worried about the welfare of his dog. Discuss what other treasure might wash up on the beach in a storm. A committee may want to read a book such as Alice Goudey's *Houses from the Sea* (Scribner's, 1959) and share illustrations of kinds of shells Christopher might have found. Perhaps some child might have a shell collection that could be brought from home to share.
4. Read Carol Carrick's *The Crocodiles Still Wait* to the class. List the items of information learned about crocodiles. A committee may want to see if the library has any other factual books about crocodiles such as Ruth Gross's *Alligators and Other Crocodilians* (Four Winds, 1976). Have the teacher read a por-

tion about crocodiles so additional information can be added to the list.

5. Read Carol Carrick's *Paul's Christmas Birthday* to the class. Let children make a crocodile sock or paper bag puppets. Then pretend they are at Paul's party and make the animals talk. Perhaps they will want to share some "Did you know" facts about crocodiles.

   Discuss ways in which Paul's birthday party was different from many children's parties.

6. Read Donald Carrick's *Morgan and the Artist* to the class. Let children recall the ways Morgan helped Frederic. Let them explore the meaning of "landscape artist." What might such an artist paint? Suggest that each child make a watercolor painting of a landscape they can see out the window or recall, putting into the picture a small animal or person that might step out of the picture for them.

7. Read aloud to the class Carol Carrick's *Sand Tiger Shark*. Have students list what they know about sharks. There are many myths about sharks which may appear on the list.

   Have a committee find information about sharks in books such as Millicent Selsam's *A First Look At Sharks* (Walker, 1979) or John Waters's *Hungry Sharks* (Crowell, 1973) to check the merit of the ideas listed. They can also report on new facts learned about sharks.

8. After sharing the books by Carol Carrick and doing other forms of research, carefully examine the watercolor illustrations of Donald Carrick. Have the class make a mural for the classroom or media center in watercolor showing the different sea creatures who live together and depend on each other for survival.

9. When the research is complete, play a "stump the experts" game. Let three children volunteer to be experts. Let each child prepare a question—and answer—which they will ask the experts and try to stump them.

Laughing with Bernard Waber

STUDENT OBJECTIVES:

- Identify humor as a form of writing
- Predict the outcome of a story
- Realize that many people share similar personal problems
- Recognize difference in point of view

RECOMMENDED READING:

Waber, Bernard. *An Anteater Named Arthur.* Houghton Mifflin, 1967.
Arthur is an anteater who is sometimes bored, messy, and forgetful but most often lovable.

———. *A Firefly Named Torchy.* Houghton Mifflin, 1970.
Torchy discovers that his brilliant flash is as important as a light that twinkles and glows.

———. *The House on East 88th Street.* Houghton Mifflin, 1962.
Lyle, the abandoned crocodile, is found by the Primms in a bathtub in their house on East 88th Street.

———. *I Was All Thumbs.* Houghton Mifflin, 1978.
Legs, the laboratory octopus, has difficulty learning to live in the ocean.

———. *Ira Sleeps Over.* Houghton Mifflin, 1972.
Ira is excited about spending the night with a friend until he learns he might have to sleep without his teddy bear.

———. *Lovable Lyle.* Houghton Mifflin, 1969.
Lyle rescues the little girl whose mother refused to let her play when Lyle was around.

———. *Lyle and the Birthday Party.* Houghton Mifflin, 1966.
Lyle becomes green with jealousy over Joshua's birthday party.

———. *Lyle Finds His Mother.* Houghton Mifflin, 1974.
Lyle goes on a tour with Hector P. Valenti in hopes of finding his mother.

———. *Lyle, Lyle, Crocodile.* Houghton Mifflin, 1965.
Lyle rescues Mr. Grump, the next door neighbor, from a fire and thus convinces him to let Lyle return to the Primms house on East 88th.

————. *You're A Little Kid With A Big Heart.* Houghton Mifflin, 1980.
The kite grants Octavia her wish but later regrets it.

BIOGRAPHICAL SOURCES:

For more information on Bernard Waber, see *Third Book of Junior Authors,* 293–95; *Twentieth-Century Children's Writers,* 1294–95; *Twentieth-Century Children's Writers,* 2d ed., 799–800.

GROUP INTRODUCTORY ACTIVITY:

Introduce Waber by telling the children that the family moved often when he was a child, and he always wanted to be sure there was a public library and movie theater within roller-skating distance of his house. He says he wore many hand-me-down clothes and is glad his brother also handed down his interest in drawing.

Waber became interested in picture books while reading aloud to his children. In fact, his children asked him once why he didn't look at grown-up books in the library instead of following them to the children's room. It embarrassed them to have their father sitting in a little chair absorbed in picture books. These picture book experiences started him writing and drawing books.[10]

Read *Ira Sleeps Over* to the class. Before completing the story, stop reading and ask the students to predict what will happen once the boys begin telling ghost stories. After several ideas have been given, continue with the story. After the story is over, discuss how Ira must have felt when his sister said that Reggie would laugh if Ira took his bear along. How did Ira's feelings change when Reggie reached for his teddy?

What did Reggie and Ira do for fun during the evening? What other things do kids do when they "sleep over"?

Ask children to bring favorite stuffed animals or toys they used to sleep with. Set up a display.

FOLLOW-UP ACTIVITIES FOR TEACHER AND STUDENTS TO SHARE:

1. Read *An Anteater Named Arthur* to the class. Discuss the problems that Arthur posed for his mother. Ask the children to think about problems adults sometimes pose for children. Think about the same situation from both the parent's and the child's point of view.

Make up a recipe Arthur's mother could have used to fix him brown ants. Think of other animals, their favorite food, and what they would be called if "eater" were in the title, i.e.: rabbit/carroteater.

When Arthur was in his "why" mood, he wanted to rename some of the animals. Rename all of the farm animals according to Arthur's description. Rename objects in the classroom as Arthur tried to do.

Think of a new problem for Arthur and how he and his mother might have solved it.

2. After sharing *A Firefly Named Torchy* and the appealing illustrations, ask the children to close their eyes and imagine a woodland scene of fireflies in which "they twinkled and glowed, and together made a thousand chandeliers in the woodland." Using sponge art and tempera paint have the children illustrate their own woodland scene.

Some of the lights Torchy saw were described as opposites (i.e., big/little; bright/dim) or in figurative language such as "dazzling" or "zooming." Ask the children to describe the kinds of lights Torchy might see if he visited their town.

Discuss what the owl meant when he told Torchy, "Be proud of your light—nobody's perfect."

3. Before reading *The House on East 88th Street* tell the class that Waber said that his walking tours along Manhattan's Upper East Side were very helpful while planning the book. After reading the book, let children discuss what ideas in illustrations and text may have been inspired by Waber's walks.

In *The House on East 88th Street* children first meet the crocodile Lyle and the Primm family. Have the children suppose they had just moved into a new house and heard "swish, swash, splash, swoosh" List things that could have caused the sound.

Check the price of caviar. Estimate what it would cost to keep Lyle.

Committees of children may want to illustrate posterboard-size pictures of Lyle doing his tricks as if he were coming to school to perform.

4. After meeting Lyle in *The House on East 88th Street,* read aloud Waber's *Lovable Lyle.* Recall the humorous things that happened to Lyle. What else might have happened to Lyle during Mrs. Hipple's visit? Think of a new ending. How else might Lyle have won Mrs. Hipple's favor?

5. Read Waber's *Lyle and the Birthday Party* to the class. Discuss how we sometimes describe our feelings with colors, such as Lyle's being green with jealousy. What incident might make one white with fear? Think of other colors, feelings, and situations.

Plan Lyle's party. What guests could be invited? Think of an appropriate invitation. Plan games and refreshments. If some invited guests called and asked for gift ideas, what might be suggested?

6. Share Waber's *Lyle Finds His Mother.* Ask the children to each bring a picture from home of their mothers when they were children. Put all of the pictures with identification names on the back on a bulletin board and let children see if they can guess whose mother is whose. Discuss where else Lyle might have found his mother.

7. Read Waber's *Lyle, Lyle Crocodile.* How else might the story have ended? Imagine Lyle lost from Mrs. Primm in a department store. What else might have happened?

8. Read Waber's *I Was All Thumbs* to the group. Talk with the children about what makes this story funny. The octopus is called "Legs" by Captain Pierre. This is a form of humor. Think of the captain's puns that are funny to story listeners but not to Legs. Talk about other kinds of humorous writings that the children enjoy. Let children look for books of jokes in the library. Read one each day.

9. Read Waber's *You're a Little Kid with a Big Heart* to the class. Discuss Octavia's wish to be grown. Ask the children what they would wish if they had the opportunity. If they suddenly grew up, what job would they like to have? Could they do that job without additional education?

Getting to Know Tomie de Paola

STUDENT OBJECTIVES:

- Search for and discuss dedications
- Identify a nonfiction book as one that gives facts
- Distinguish between fact and fiction
- List and define new words found in a nonfiction book
- Compare characters in two different stories

RECOMMENDED READING:

de Paola, Tomie. *Big Anthony and the Magic Ring.* Harcourt Brace
Jovanovich, 1979.
Big Anthony becomes handsome with the help of Strega Nona's
magic ring, but without Strega Nona's assistance he cannot
change himself back again.

———. *Charlie Needs a Cloak.* Prentice-Hall, 1973, o.p., Prentice-
Hall, paper, 1982.
A shepherd named Charlie goes through the steps of making a
cloak from sheep's wool.

———. *Fin Mc'Coul, The Giant of Knockmany Hill.* Holiday House,
1981.
The wife of the giant of Knockmany Hill helped him defeat his
rival Cucullin.

———. *Helga's Dowry: A Troll Love Story.* Harcourt Brace
Jovanovich, 1977.
Clever Helga uses her magic to earn a dowry for herself.

———. *The Knight and the Dragon.* Putnam's, 1980.
A humorous tale of a knight and a dragon who each read "how
to" books on techniques for fighting each other.

———. *The Mysterious Giant of Barletta.* Harcourt Brace Jovanovich,
1984.
Through a clever act the giant statue saves the town from an
army attack.

———. *Now One Foot, Now the Other.* Putnam's, 1981.
Bobbie's grandfather teaches him to walk; later, Bobbie is able to
do the same for his grandfather.

———. *The Popcorn Book.* Holiday House, 1977.
In cartoon style two children learn some of the history of
popcorn as well as fun ways of eating it.

———. *The Quicksand Book.* Holiday House, 1977.
Jungle Boy gives a step-by-step explanation of how to save one-
self from quicksand while Jungle Girl slowly sinks.

———. *Sing, Pierrot, Sing: A Picture Book in Mime.* Harcourt Brace
Jovanovich, 1983.
Only the love and friendship offered by the children can mend
the broken heart of Pierrot in this wordless picture book.

———. *Strega Nona.* Prentice-Hall, 1975.
The magic pasta pot causes a great deal of trouble for Big
Anthony as he attempts to show off his magic for the towns-
people.

————. *Strega Nona's Magic Lessons.* Harcourt Brace Jovanovich, 1982.

Big Anthony attempts to get magic lessons by disguising himself as a girl.

BIOGRAPHICAL SOURCES:

For more information on Tomie de Paola, see *Fifth Book of Junior Authors & Illustrators,* 98–100; *Something about the Author,* 11:68–71; *Twentieth-Century Children's Writers,* 2d ed., 237–39.

GROUP INTRODUCTORY ACTIVITY:

Introduce Tomie de Paola by showing his picture from the blurb of one of his books and talking about his early life. In an Oklahoma speech, he said that when he was young, he used to color on his bedsheets because he wasn't supposed to draw on the walls. The public librarian wouldn't allow him to check out books until he was in school and could read. This created in him a great desire to read, so after the first week in school he could read a few words. He took his book home that weekend and learned to read it. Then he went to the public library to get his own library card and books. He was truly disappointed to learn that he could only check out one book from a specific section. This and subsequent experiences led him to call the librarian "The Dragon."

Discuss with the children the use of the public library and their school library. Do they need a library card to check out books at either library? Why? How many children have a library card? If some don't, this may be an ideal time to plan a trip to the public library.

After introducing de Paola, read aloud to the class *The Knight and the Dragon.* The dragon and the knight are each depicted as reading "how to" books. Point out these titles to the children. Ask them to describe other situations in which a "how to" book would be useful. How could they locate a "how to" book in the media center? Several children may want to use the card catalog to find subjects in which they are interested, such as building or drawing.

FOLLOW-UP ACTIVITIES FOR TEACHER AND STUDENTS TO SHARE:

1. Read *Strega Nona* aloud to the class. After discussing Big Anthony's problems, allow the children to dramatize their favorite parts of the story.

2. Before reading de Paola's *Big Anthony and the Magic Ring,* ask the children to imagine what mischief Big Anthony will get into with a magic ring. Read the story aloud until the part where handsome Big Anthony gets to the dance. Stop reading and ask the children to predict what they think will happen. When all who wish to do so have had the opportunity to predict the outcome, finish the story.

3. After sharing de Paola's *Strega Nona's Magic Lessons* with the class, ask one of the older students in the school to perform magic tricks for the class and teach the students how to do a simple trick. If no one is available, introduce a magic book such as Rose Wyler's *Magic Secrets* (Harper & Row, 1967) or Robert Lopshire's *It's Magic* (Macmillan, 1969) and ask the students to read them and create magic in the classroom.

4. Read de Paola's *Fin M'Coul, The Giant of Knockmany Hill* to the class. While three children pantomime the action, read the portion of the story where the wife helps the giant defeat Cucullin.

5. Instead of reading de Paola's *Helga's Dowry* aloud to the class, ask a fourth- or fifth-grade reading group to act out the story. Helga repeats several rhymes in the story. Put these rhymes on large poster board so the entire class can join in part of the presentation.

   After watching the dramatization, ask the class to identify the similarities and differences between Helga and Fin McCoul's wife.

6. Share de Paola's *Sing, Pierrot, Sing* with a small group so each child can read the pictures and contribute to the telling of the story. Before sharing the book give them some background information on the art of mime to heighten appreciation of the story. If possible, invite a high school student or community theater participant to demonstrate mime to the class.

7. Introduce *The Quicksand Book* as one of Tomie de Paola's nonfiction books. Explain the meaning of nonfiction and note that it is classified in the 500s (pure sciences). Before reading the book reproduce the charts on transparencies so it will be easy for the entire class to see. Fears of quicksand may have been aroused in the children because of television programs or movies. After sharing the book discuss these fears or questions the children may have. At the end of the book directions are given for making quicksand. Have a group of children or a parent volunteer carry out this project and demonstrate to the class.

8. Read to the class de Paola's Italian folktale *The Mysterious Giant of Barletta.* Let the children recall how the mysterious giant saved the town from the soldiers. Why was he called mysterious? Let children discuss reasons why statues are placed in towns and harbors. See if they can recall specific statues they

have seen. Let them share what they know about the Statue of Liberty and its restoration.

9. Read de Paola's *The Popcorn Book* to the class. Note that it is also classified as nonfiction, but it is in the 600s (applied sciences). Let the children explore the reason why it is classified as home economics and family living (640s) rather than in the 500s (pure sciences) as *The Quicksand Book* was. After reading the book, find out how many different methods the children can think of that can be used for popping corn. Let the class pop corn, eat some, and use the rest to make popcorn art.

10. Read de Paola's *Charlie Needs a Cloak* to the class. Discuss ways that children today get cloaks or coats. If possible, have a resource person in the community come and demonstrate weaving. Share Ella Beskow's *Pelle's New Suit* (Harper & Row, 1929) with the class. Discuss the ways in which the two stories are alike/different. Let children examine the photographs in Kathryn Lasky's *The Weaver's Gift* (Warne, 1980) and try to identify the steps in weaving the blanket. Make a list of new words learned in the stories and write a definition of each. Some of the words are defined at the end of *Charlie Needs a Cloak*.

11. Read de Paola's *Now One Foot, Now the Other* to the class. Discuss how Bobby showed the love he had for his grandfather. Make up other stories Bobby might have told his grandfather.

Culminating Activities after Second Grade/Third Grade

Discuss with the entire class the literature experiences they have shared. What authors and illustrators do they recall? What books did each person named write or illustrate? What book characters do the students remember?

What literature activities did the students particularly enjoy? Do the students remember any facts about specific authors or illustrators?

Sing any songs and repeat any poems learned. See if the children can recall any figurative language from a book they shared.

What is a tall tale? How is it different from any other story? What stories do they remember that were humorous? What is a riddle? What are the characteristics of cartoon illustrations? What is landscape art? Name any husband and wife team who have worked together on a book. What books have they done?

Name any star groupings that can be seen in the night sky. Give the meaning of any space terms relating to time or distance. Give the meaning of any new words learned through literature sharing. What is the difference between fiction and nonfiction?

REFERENCES

1. Selma Lanes, *The Art of Maurice Sendak* (New York: Harry N. Abrams, 1980), p. 39.

2. D. Galvin, "Maurice Sendak Observes Children's Literature," *Harper's Bazaar* 106 (December 1972): 102–03.

3. Anne Commire, ed., *Something about the Author* (Detroit: Gale Research, 1975), vol. 7, p. 201.

4. D.L. Kirkpatrick, ed., *Twentieth-Century Children's Writers* (New York: St. Martins Press, 1983), p. 394.

5. Sally Holmes Holtze, ed., *Fifth Book of Junior Authors & Illustrators* (New York: H.W. Wilson, 1983), p. 303.

6. Doris de Montreville and Elizabeth D. Crawford, eds., *Fourth Book of Junior Authors & Illustrators* (New York: H.W. Wilson, 1978), p. 254.

7. Doris de Montreville and Donna Hill, eds., *Third Book of Junior Authors* (New York: H.W. Wilson, 1972), p. 168.

8. de Montreville and Hill, pp. 222–23.

9. de Montreville and Crawford, p. 71.

10. de Montreville and Hill, pp. 293–94.

Chapter 4
Third Grade/Fourth Grade

Byrd Baylor Introduces the Southwest

STUDENT OBJECTIVES:

- Gain a better understanding of the culture of the Southwest Indians
- Become aware of desert sights and sounds and be able to compare them with those in his/her own community
- Sharpen awareness of the beauty of nature and the importance of simple things
- Experience translating from verbal to visual or visual to verbal
- Realize why books concerning similar subjects may be found in so many sections of the media center

RECOMMENDED READING:

Baylor, Byrd. *Before You Came This Way.* Illustrated by Tom Bahti. Dutton, 1969.
   The rock pictures in a Southwest canyon record the way of life of an ancient people.

————. *The Desert Is Theirs.* Illustrated by Peter Parnall. Scribner's, 1975.
   Poetic text in content and format identifies the closeness of desert plants, animals, and people.

————. *Hawk, I'm Your Brother.* Illustrated by Peter Parnall. Scribner's, 1976.
Sensitive tale of Rudy Soto, who releases his caged hawk and becomes aware of the joy of flight.

————. *Moon Song.* Illustrated by Ronald Himler. Scribner's, 1982.
Pima Indian legend explaining the close bond between coyotes and the moon.

————. *They Put on Masks.* Illustrated by Jerry Ingram. Scribner's, 1974.
Through authentic illustrated masks and the actual chants used by the dancers, the author and artist capture the importance of the ceremonial rituals of the North American Indians.

————. *The Way to Start a Day.* Illustrated by Peter Parnall. Scribner's, 1978.
Brief text and powerful illustrations depict the unique ways people around the world throughout the ages have greeted the dawn.

————. *We Walk in Sandy Places.* Illustrated by Marilyn Schweitzer. Scribner's, 1976.
Through sensitive text and animal tracks, the reader shares the mood of the desert.

————. *When Clay Sings.* Illustrated by Tom Bahti. Scribner's, 1972.
Using designs from prehistoric Southwest Indian pottery, children imagine aspects of the culture of those ancient people.

Baylor, Byrd, and Parnall, Peter. *Desert Voices.* Scribner's, 1981.
Poetic description of the home and way of life of a human and nine animals that are desert inhabitants.

BIOGRAPHICAL SOURCES:

For more information on Byrd Baylor, see *Fourth Book of Junior Authors & Illustrators,* 31–32; *Something about the Author,* 16:33–35.

GROUP INTRODUCTORY ACTIVITY:

In introducing Byrd Baylor tell children that during much of her early life she lived on ranches in Texas and in the mining country of Arizona and New Mexico. All her memories are of the outdoors and are reflected in her books. She recalls that she even attended a school in Tucson where she was allowed to study outdoors under a mesquite tree. She feels she needs the sun and the mountains, and because she writes about what she herself enjoys, most of her books are about the Southwest. She goes to Indian ceremonials, looks for ancient ruins, and feels at home in the desert lands.[1]

Introduce the children to all of the Byrd Baylor books they will be using. Explain that most of Baylor's books are nonfiction and are located in many sections of the library because of the differences in content.

Show the students the call number on each book and explain its meaning. *Before You Came This Way* is classified in the 700s (the arts) because it identifies the meaning of the rock pictures in a canyon of the Southwest. *The Desert Is Theirs* and *We Walk in Sandy Places* are in the 500s (pure science) because they factually describe desert plants and animals. *Desert Voices* is an Anglo poem about desert inhabitants and is classified in the 800s (literature). *They Put On Masks* is in the 300s (social science) because it describes the costumes and ceremonial rituals of North American Indians. *The Way to Start a Day* is classified in the 200s (religion) because it is a personal blessing to the dawn as a way to greet the day. *When Clay Sings* is classified in the 970s (general history of North America) because it examines aspects of the life of the prehistoric Southwest Indians. Since *Hawk, I'm Your Brother* is a picture story of a boy releasing a captive hawk, it is in the E (easy) section.

Read *When Clay Sings* aloud to the class to help children understand that the pottery designs are the artist's way of communicating a message. After discussing this concept, examine the design on other Indian pottery, either using pictures or actual objects. Discuss as a class possible messages the artist was communicating in each.

If available, invite a local potter to speak to the group, sharing some finished creations. Ask the potter to discuss the process as well as the meaning of the designs used.

FOLLOW-UP ACTIVITIES FOR TEACHER AND STUDENTS TO SHARE:

1. Read Baylor's *They Put on Masks* to the group. Ask each child or small committees to select one of the Southwest Indian masks described and seek more information in the library media center about the tribe and its ceremonial dances. Share with the class.

   If there is a local college, Indian, or Boy Scout group that performs Indian dances, ask them to visit the class in costume and share them.
2. Read Baylor's *The Desert Is Theirs* to the class. Discuss with the class the reasons for the closeness of desert animals, plants, and people. Is the same closeness evident in the neighborhood where the children live? Why or why not? Notice the dedication. Surmise why the book was dedicated to Baylor Stanley.
3. Read Baylor's *The Way to Start a Day* to the class. Discuss with the children the different ways adults and children react to awakening at dawn and greeting the new day. Do any reflect a

joyous feeling? Why/Why not? Do people in their culture ever have sunrise services? On what occasions?

4. Read Baylor's *Before You Came This Way* to the class. Discuss the content of drawings that could be made to depict current United States culture. Plan with the children a mural they can make to record the year's activities in the school or community. Display the mural in the library media center so it can be shared by the entire school.

5. Read Baylor's *We Walk in Sandy Places* to the class. Discuss with the students the kinds of tracks that reflect life in their community. For example, what kinds of messages do various tire tracks leave? How do they reveal today's way of life? How are the tracks mentioned by the children different from those suggested by Baylor?

   The children may want to prepare illustrations of various tracks discussed with a brief statement of what each means for today's society. These could be placed into a book that becomes a commentary on children's views of today's way of life.

FOLLOW-UP ACTIVITIES FOR INDIVIDUALS OR SMALL GROUPS:

1. After sharing Baylor's *They Put on Masks* in class, design a personal mask and describe in a paragraph or on tape the message of the combination of designs and colors used.

2. After sharing Baylor's *Hawk, I'm Your Brother* in class, you may want to pretend you are the hawk and describe for Rudy in paragraph form or on tape the despair caused by captivity, the joy at being set free, or one of the many sights seen in flight.

3. Work with a small group of students and read aloud Baylor's *Hawk, I'm Your Brother.* Then rewrite as a "Rudy, I'm Your Brother" story from Hawk's point of view.

4. After sharing Baylor's *The Desert Is Theirs* in class, research further in the library media center one of the desert animals or plants described in the book. Then write a brief report and share with the class.

5. Read Baylor's *Desert Voices.* Then think of a desert animal not included, research it, and write a free-form poem about it.

6. After sharing Baylor's *Before You Came This Way* in class, research cave drawings in the library media center. If an authentic reproduction is available, you may want to recreate it on a transparency and share with the class.

7. Work with a committee to look up deserts in the library media center card catalog. Locate books from various areas in the library, and after examining the books, explain why each was assigned a specific Dewey classification in the 500s, 800s, etc.

8. After Baylor's *We Walk in Sandy Places* is read in class, you may want to research in the library media center the tracks made by other desert animals not illustrated by Baylor. Draw and label each and place on a class bulletin board.

9. Work with a group of class members who have read *Moon Song.* Pretend you are an older member of the Pima Indian tribe telling this legend to the children. Each of you record your version on tape and let the class listen and compare.

Exaggeration in the Stories of James Flora

STUDENT OBJECTIVES:

- Recognize humor in illustrations
- Identify exaggerated statements in stories
- Develop a cumulative exaggerated story
- Participate in a mural art activity depicting humorous characters
- Write a script and commercial for ghost television

RECOMMENDED READING:

Flora, James. *The Day the Cow Sneezed.* Harcourt Brace Jovanovich, 1957.
The sneeze of Floss the cow causes a chain of events involving animals crashing through town.

———. *Grandpa's Farm.* Harcourt Brace Jovanovich, 1965.
Grandpa tells his grandson four tall tales about the arrival of the big blue barn, a giant corn stalk, a winter so cold the fire in the stove froze, and a hen that could hatch anything.

———. *Grandpa's Ghost Stories.* Atheneum, 1982.
Grandpa recreates the scary adventure he had as a boy when he encountered the bag o' bones, the Warty Witch, and the ghastly ghost.

———. *Grandpa's Witched-Up Christmas.* Atheneum, 1982.
Grandpa tells about the time when three witches almost caused him to miss Christmas.

———. *The Great Green Turkey Creek Monster.* Atheneum, 1978.
The town of Turkey Creek is overrun by the Great Green Hooligan vine; Argie Bargle discovers a way to control it.

BIOGRAPHICAL SOURCES:

For more information on James Flora, see *Something about the Author,* 30:110–12; *Third Book of Junior Authors,* 87–89; *Twentieth-Century Children's Writers,* 465–66; *Twentieth-Century Children's Writers,* 2d ed., 295–96.

GROUP INTRODUCTORY ACTIVITY:

To introduce James Flora, tell the children that his ability to create humorous exaggerated tales is not surprising: His father and grandfather were excellent storytellers. He says, "They could whip up a story about anything from a one-eye wombat to a three-legged ice baby at the South Pole. I naturally tried to imitate them and practiced on my younger brothers and sisters."[2]
Read *The Great Green Turkey Creek Monster* aloud to the class. After reading the story discuss with the class what is funny or humorous about the story. Explore alternative endings. Which seem appropriate?
Note the illustrations. Does the location of the vine on the page heighten the suspense?
To help them recognize Flora's sources of humor and exaggeration in his stories, recreate a Hooligan vine in the media center. Ahead of time draw the head of a monster on oak tag. Cut out at least 30 leaves (or whatever shape seems appropriate). As the children recall exaggerated events or humorous names in the book, write them down on the leaves to add to the monster. Staple the leaves together to make a monster. In the days that follow the activity the children may come to the media center, share humor from other Flora books with the media specialist, and record it on a blank leaf to add to the monster.

FOLLOW-UP ACTIVITIES FOR TEACHER AND STUDENTS TO SHARE:

1. Share aloud Flora's *The Day the Cow Sneezed.* After reading, have children reconstruct how one funny situation caused another which in turn caused another. How did the illustrations add to the humor? Have the class make a mural of Flora's zoo

characters as the children imagine them to be after the steam roller goes through.

2. Share with the class each of Grandpa's tall tales in Flora's *Grandpa's Farm*. The book ends when Grandpa says that he'd love to tell about the snow of '44, but there are no more pages. Have the class tell the tale in a "string" story. Use a cassette recorder to tape the story as it grows around the room. One child begins with "I remember when ..." Each child then adds one line to the story.

3. Read Flora's *Grandpa's Ghost Stories* to the class. Be sure to share the illustrations as the story is read. Place the book near an art center where items such as egg cartons, oatmeal boxes, pipe cleaners, milk cartons, yarn, buttons, glue, and scissors have been placed. Urge children to create their own spiders and other creatures that can be found in the cave of the Warty Witch. With yarn and black construction paper, change a corner of the classroom or media center into the cave of the Warty Witch and set up the characters the students have made.

4. After sharing Flora's *Grandpa's Witched-Up Christmas* with the class, go back and share more closely some of the humorous detailed illustrations by James Flora. Reread the description of the Witch's house, "What a house it was. You knew right away that a witch had to live there...." Urge children to examine closely how Flora illustrated that description. Have on hand strips of green construction paper. Have children cut and glue the strips of paper on white or light-colored paper to create the witch's house. Urge them to create imagined creatures that lurked around the house using only black and green crayons.

FOLLOW-UP ACTIVITIES FOR INDIVIDUALS OR SMALL GROUPS:

1. After having shared Flora's *The Great Green Turkey Creek Monster* and discussed the humor as a class, work with a group to rename streets and stores around the school or the downtown area of the city. The telephone book may contain area maps with names of streets on them. These can be used to prepare large maps where the renamed streets and stores can be labeled and shared with the class.

2. After hearing Flora's *The Day the Cow Sneezed,* develop your own sequence of events of what happened after the cow sneezed. These can be expanded and recorded on tape for the class to share.

3. If the class recorded a string story after reading Flora's *Grandpa's Farm,* you may want to work with a group to select various parts of the story to illustrate for an overhead projector

story. Make the drawings in pencil and either trace the pictures on acetate using overhead projector pens or copy the pictures on acetate with a thermofax machine. The story can then be shown on the overhead projector as the recorded story is heard.

4. In Flora's *Grandpa's Ghost Stories,* the ghastly ghost watches ghost television on Channel 41/2. Work with a group to make a TV out of a large box, write the script, and illustrate your version of "The Open Grave Show." Commercials may be developed to go along with the show. Illustrations may be made on a roll of paper for a roll screen or prepared on individual poster boards to place on the screen from the top of the box.

   For the "Hairy Snuffler Comedy Hour," your group may want to draw pictures for the screen and ask ghoulish questions or tell ghoulish jokes. To help spark your imagination, you may want to refer to October issues of magazines such as *Cricket* to find jokes and riddles.

5. One of the television shows in Flora's *Grandpa's Ghost Stories* was "Feeding Phantom Faces." Work with a small group to create and demonstrate your own ghastly recipes for the class.

6. You may want to write and/or tape record your own versions of a Witched-Up Valentine's Day, Easter, Fourth of July, Birthday, or other holiday after hearing Flora's *Grandpa's Witched-Up Christmas.*

Caldecott Medal Books

STUDENT OBJECTIVES:

- Understand the meaning of the Caldecott Medal
- Examine illustrations to note small details overlooked at first glance
- Recognize to what extent illustrations convey the message in various books
- Engage in monochromatic and Styrofoam illustration activities
- Dramatize a story
- Prepare a bibliography of books by a specific illustrator

RECOMMENDED READING:

Emberley, Barbara, adaptor. *Drummer Hoff.* Illustrated by Ed Emberley. Prentice-Hall, 1967.
In a story told in rhyming verse, Drummer Hoff stands ready to fire the cannon when General Border gives the order.

Haley, Gail E. *A Story, A Story.* Atheneum, 1970.
The African folk hero Ananse the spider man outwits the Sky God and brings stories back to earth.

Hall, Donald. *Ox-Cart Man.* Illustrated by Barbara Cooney. Viking, 1979.
The story repeats itself year after year as the farmer goes to market in the fall to sell and trade his yearly products and return to his family to begin again.

Ness, Evaline. *Sam, Bangs and Moonshine.* Holt, Rinehart & Winston, 1966.
Samantha's exaggerated stories, called "moonshine" nearly cost the life of her only friend Thomas and her cat Bangs.

Provensen, Alice, and Provensen, Martin. *The Glorious Flight.* Viking, 1983.
Describes the early attempts of Louis Blériot to fly and his later successful flight across the English Channel in Blériot XI on July 25, 1909.

Van Allsburg, Chris. *Jumanji.* Houghton Mifflin, 1981.
Two children who find a game board watch and participate when the game comes to life with the first roll of the dice and ends only when one of them reaches the golden city of Jumanji.

Ward, Lynd. *The Biggest Bear.* Houghton Mifflin, 1952.
When Johnny Orchard goes hunting for a bearskin, he surprises his family by bringing home a bear cub instead.

Zemach, Harve. *Duffy and the Devil.* Illustrated by Margot Zemach. Farrar Straus & Giroux, 1973.
The predicament in which lazy Duffy finds herself when she can't do the knitting for the Squire is recounted in this Cornish tale.

GROUP INTRODUCTORY ACTIVITY:

Before introducing Emberley's Caldecott Medal winner, *Drummer Hoff,* and sending the group of books selected for unit activities to the classroom, explain the meaning of the award. The Randolph J. Caldecott Medal is named in honor of Randolph Caldecott, a nineteenth-century English illustrator. The Caldecott Medal was established in 1938 by Frederick Melcher and is awarded yearly to the illustrator of the most distinguished picture book for children published in the United States in the preceding year. The illustrator must be a citizen or resident of the United States. The selection of the winner is made by an award committee of the Children's Services Division of the American Library Association. The face of the Caldecott Medal has a reproduction of Caldecott's illustration of John Gilpin's ride from "The Diverting History of John Gilpin." The reverse side has an illustration of "Four and Twenty Blackbirds Baked in a Pie."

Explain to the students that Ed Emberley received the Caldecott Medal for *Drummer Hoff* in 1967. Read it aloud, calling attention to the vibrant colors in the woodcut illustrations. If available, follow with the 16mm film *Drummer Hoff* (Weston Woods, 1969, col., 5 min.). Talk about which medium best expresses the idea of the story. The soldiers ignored the flowers and grass, yet in the end, nature was more lasting than the cannon they desert.

Review the events of the story and dramatize. The repetition of the rhyme and the humorous names make it an enjoyable drama activity.

Read the titles of the Caldecott Medal books you are sending to the classroom for follow-up activities. Explain to the students that these are not all of the books awarded the Caldecott Medal since 1938, and that they should check for others in their school or public library. Urge them to try to find out the artist's medium and technique for each book. Patricia Cianciolo's *Illustrations in Children's Books*[3] is a helpful professional guide for media specialists and teachers.

FOLLOW-UP ACTIVITIES FOR TEACHER AND STUDENTS TO SHARE:

1. Recall that the illustrations for Emberley's *Drummer Hoff* were woodcut. To help children better understand the woodcut approach, set up an art project in which students make their own Styrofoam cuts using Styrofoam plates or meat packaging trays from the grocery store. Have the students draw a simple picture on the Styrofoam with a pencil, being sure the illustration is firmly indented into the Styrofoam. Using a brayer, roll India ink or paint evenly over the Styrofoam. Then place a sheet of colored construction paper on the Styrofoam to produce a print which will appear the reverse of what was drawn into the Styrofoam.

2. Before sharing with the class Evaline Ness's *Sam, Bangs and Moonshine,* which won the Caldecott Medal in 1967, share how she got the idea for the book. Previously Evaline Ness had drawn a picture of a ragged little girl. In the same portfolio were

drawings of fishing boats. She explains how these pictures combined with thoughts of her childhood to produce the idea for the book: "The shabby misplaced child of my drawing became Sam, who told lies. And what else could she be except a fisherman's daughter, with all those drawings of boats handy? I added a cat because I have a live one to draw from, and I decided to put Thomas under a racy bicyclist's cap I had seen in a photograph. The baby kangaroo got into the story because of a newspaper article."[4]

After sharing the book let the class retell the story by examining the line and wash drawings. Then talk about the story. Were the characters believable? Identify Sam's character traits. How did the illustrations help in that identification? Does the setting have any effect on the story? What is the central idea or theme of the story? Ask the children to relate Sam's situation to themselves. How would they feel if they hurt someone because of a lie? How would they feel if they were Thomas?

3. Read aloud Alice and Martin Provensen's *The Glorious Flight,* telling students that it won the Caldecott Medal in 1984. After reading the story, let the class re-examine the illustrations of the planes. As a group, identify the improvements that were made in each plane.

4. Read Gail Haley's *A Story, A Story* to the class. Note that it won the Caldecott Medal in 1971. Let children observe the woodcut illustrations carefully as the story progresses. After reading the story let children recall the tricks Ananse pulled to fool the Sky God. See if children can name other stories involving tricksters (such as Brer Rabbit and Coyote).

If available, share the filmstrip *Gail E. Haley: Wood and Linoleum Illustration* (Weston Woods, 1978, 72 fr., col., 17 min.), which discusses her use of wood to illustrate stories and demonstrates the source of some of her ideas for *A Story, A Story.*

Examine again the woodcuts done by Ed Emberley for *Drummer Hoff* and those by Marcia Brown for *Once a Mouse,* also a Caldecott Medal winner. How are the illustrations alike and different?

5. Read aloud the 1953 Caldecott winner, *The Biggest Bear* by Lynd Ward. Examine the illustrations again, asking children to notice how Ward foreshadowed the dramatic growth of the bear by illustrating the upset sap buckets, etc., without picturing the bear.

Lynd Ward did his illustrations in monochromatic sepia. Have children explore why Ward selected the brown tones to illustrate his story. If Robert McCloskey's stone lithography monochromatic illustrations in *Make Way for Ducklings* (Viking, 1941) are available, compare the two books for color tones and intensity of color.

For fun and to help students prepare for an art project using one color, let the children see the world through colored glasses. Cut out spectacles from oak tag for each student. Tape colored cellophane to the spectacles as lenses. While the children wear the glasses, set up a still life of fruit in a bowl for them to examine closely.

The next day have each child select a colored pencil and prepare a color chart by beginning at the top with a white square, then shading in the five squares below it with each square getting progressively darker. The last square should be the darkest that is possible with a colored pencil. Now have each child draw the still life with that colored pencil, referring to their color chart squares for shades and intensities.

6. Share aloud Harve Zemach's Cornish folktale *Duffy and the Devil,* illustrated by Margot Zemach, which won the Caldecott Medal in 1974, allowing the children to examine the illustrations as the book is read. After the story is read, ask the children if the line-and-wash illustrations are as humorous as the story. Let children discuss in what ways the illustrations extend the printed text. How do the soft hues affect the mood of the story?

   The type of art chosen for this book is called folk art. As Patricia Cianciolo explains in *Illustrations in Children's Books* folk art is seldom a true-to-life copy of the world. The illustrator simplifies and exaggerates but includes the style of figures and mood of that culture group.[5]

   Ask the children if they have heard another version of the same story. If some children recall the Grimm Brothers' *Rumpelstiltskin,* have them discuss differences in the two versions.

   If the English version of the story *Tom Tit Tot,* illustrated by Evaline Ness (Scribner's, 1965), is available, share that version of the story. This, too, is folk art. Talk about differences in language and illustrations.

7. In Van Allsburg's *Jumanji,* the game board is very simple but the directions are crucial. Share this story, illustrated by Chris Van Allsburg, who received the Caldecott Medal in 1982, allowing the children to pay particular attention to the realistic illustrations as the story is read. After the story is read discuss what could have happened if Judy had not rolled a 12 and the game had continued. What if the children had not read the directions and tried to quit part way through? Could the story be made into a video game?

   As a class, create a fantasy adventure that can be made into a gameboard. Formulate brief written directions for players to follow.

FOLLOW-UP ACTIVITIES FOR INDIVIDUALS AND SMALL GROUPS:

1. After sharing Ed Emberley's woodcut illustrations, you may want to try some of the simple illustrations he demonstrates in *Ed Emberley's Great Thumbprint Drawing Book* (Little, Brown, 1977) or *Ed Emberley's Drawing Book of Animals* (Little, Brown, 1970) if these or any of his other drawing books are available in the media center. Share your results or demonstrate the technique to the class. Notice that these books are classified in the 700s (the arts).

2. After sharing Ness's *Sam, Bangs and Moonshine,* go to the library media center or public library to see if other books illustrated by Evaline Ness are available. Prepare a bibliography of those books, being sure to include author, title, illustrator, publisher, and date.

3. After sharing *Sam, Bangs and Moonshine,* recall that Evaline Ness said she had thoughts of her childhood in mind when she wrote the book. If you have photographs at home taken on vacation or at a special event, see if you can use them to illustrate a story in which you use the event and then make up a story. Be sure you have a problem or conflict and think of a believable way in which it is solved. Write the story and share with your class.

4. After sharing the Provensens' *The Glorious Flight,* read Alice Dalgliesh's account of Lindbergh crossing the Atlantic in *Ride on the Wind* (Scribner's, 1956, o.p.) if it is available in the library media center. How were Blériot's and Lindbergh's flights alike and different? With a small group of children volunteer to find material on flight by using the card catalog and vertical file. These can be used by the class to prepare a time line on flight.

5. Read Donald Hall's *The Ox Cart Man,* illustrated by Barbara Cooney. How did Barbara Cooney's illustrations help you in understanding the story? Record your answer to the above question. Barbara Cooney had to do a great deal of research to make the illustrations. Write down why you think that research was necessary. Make a time line showing what items, what family members, and when each of the products were made ready for sale.

   Barbara Cooney also won the Caldecott Medal in 1959 for her scratchboard illustrations in *Chanticleer and the Fox* (Crowell, 1958). If the book is available in the school or public library, read this book, paying careful attention to the detailed illustrations. Share your favorite illustration with the class and point out one detail that is easy to miss unless you carefully study the picture.

6. To highlight the changes in style of illustrations and use of color evident as one examines winners through the decades, with a committee of children use the library media center card catalog and pull cards of all the previous winners you can locate. Questions for you to consider and speculate about after examining the books include:

Why have recent illustrators not used stone lithography as Ingri and Edgar Parin d'Aulaire did in their Caldecott Medal–winning 1939 edition of *Abraham Lincoln*? (Teacher note: When the d'Aulaires remade the illustrations for the 1957 edition, they used acetate because the printers found handling the stones a problem.)

Why are there no photograph illustrations among the Caldecott Medal books?

In what ways do the scratchboard illustrations of Barbara Cooney in *Chanticleer and The Fox* differ from the tempera-and-felt-tip illustrations of Nicolas Sidjakov for Ruth Robbins's *Bahoushka and the Three Kings* (Parnassus, 1960)?

Folk Literature Illustrated by Marcia Brown

STUDENT OBJECTIVES:

- Compare two versions of the same story
- Identify character traits, using text and illustrations to document opinions
- Design an end paper pattern for a story
- Dramatize a story
- Make a shadow puppet
- Deduce the moral of a fable

RECOMMENDED READING:

Asbjornsen, P.C. *The Three Billy Goats Gruff.* Illustrated by Marcia Brown. Harcourt Brace Jovanovich, 1957.
Norwegian folk tale of three goats that escape being eaten by a troll.

Brown, Marcia. *Blue Jackal.* Scribner's, 1977.
    Indian folktale of a jackal whose dyed blue coat gains him
    momentary power over the animals of the forest.
———. *Dick Whittington and His Cat.* Scribner's, 1950.
    A Caldecott honor book about a young man who gained a
    fortune when his cat went to sea.
———. *Once a Mouse.* Scribner's, 1961.
    A Caldecott Medal winner about a tiger that was changed into a
    mouse.
———. *Stone Soup.* Scribner's, 1947.
    A French folk tale of three soldiers who gain the praise of
    villagers for supposedly creating delicious soup from stones. A
    Caldecott honor book.
Perrault, Charles, *Cinderella.* Illustrated by Marcia Brown. Scribner's,
    1954.
    Caldecott Medal-winning version of the maiden who lost her
    glass slipper at the ball.
———. *Puss in Boots.* Illustrated by Marcia Brown. Scribner's, 1952.
    Caldecott Medal honor book of a cat who helps his master gain a
    fortune and the beautiful princess.

BIOGRAPHICAL SOURCES:

For more information on Marcia Brown, see *Books Are by People,* 27–31; *More Junior Authors,* 32–33; *Something about the Author,*
7:29–31.

GROUP INTRODUCTORY ACTIVITY:

Introduce Marcia Brown by telling the children that reading was
the main family entertainment when she was a child. The fairy tales
of Andersen, Perrault, and the Grimm Brothers were her favorites
then and still are. Her father painted one of their kitchen walls to
serve as a blackboard and she would draw for hours. By the time she
was 12, she was sure that someday she wanted to illustrate books.[6]
Introduce the folk literature illustrated by Marcia Brown. Explain
that these tales are classified 398.2 because they originated in oral
form. In contrast, because Hans Christian Andersen's tales originated
in written form, his single tales are classified as Fiction.
Read *The Three Billy Goats Gruff* aloud to the class. Note the
"snip, snap, snout" ending. This storyteller ending evidences the oral
tradition. Call attention to the crayon-and-gouache illustrations.
Have children recall the scenes and dramatize the story. Use
class members not needed for goats or troll to be the bridge. The

bridge chorus will create the sounds of each goat's hoofs on the bridge.

FOLLOW-UP ACTIVITIES FOR TEACHER AND STUDENTS TO SHARE:

1. Read Brown's *Stone Soup* aloud to the class. Identify major scenes. Prepare to dramatize the story by discussing narration appropriate for the reaction of several families as the soldiers arrive. Dramatize the story. At a later time the children may want to bring a pot and vegetables and dramatize the story for another class.
2. Read Brown's *Once a Mouse.* Note that the book, with woodcut illustrations, won the Caldecott Medal as the most distinguished American picturebook for children in 1962.

   Re-examine the illustrations carefully. Consider the addition of red to evidence danger as the story progresses. Only yellow and green are seen as the story ends after the tiger is changed back to a mouse.

   The story is a fable from India. Let the children try to determine the moral.
3. Read Brown's *Dick Whittington and His Cat.* Carefully examine the linoleum cuts. Do they make the story seem to be an older tale than if brightly colored paint had been used?

   Discuss the plot of the story. It has been suggested that the story could have been based on a true event. Do the children feel it could have happened?
4. Read Perrault's *Cinderella* illustrated by Marcia Brown to the class. Call attention to the delicate drawings in pen line and colored crayon. (The book won the Caldecott Medal in 1955.) What kind of mood do the illustrations create?

   Have children recall other versions of the story they have heard. What differences in the versions can they recall?

FOLLOW-UP ACTIVITIES FOR INDIVIDUALS OR SMALL GROUPS:

1. After sharing *The Three Billy Goats Gruff* in class, work with a committee to prepare small construction paper or thin cardboard cut-outs of the three billy goats and troll, and a bridge the size of the overhead projector stage. Attach the cut-outs to a wire or stick so they can be moved easily. Create a shadow puppet play by using the overhead projector. Share with the class and, possibly, other classes.

2. After sharing the Perrault version of *Cinderella* illustrated by Marcia Brown, read the Grimm Brothers version, illustrated by Nonny Hogrogian (Greenwillow, 1981). Make a list of the many ways in which the versions are different. Which ending do you prefer? Why? Notice the end papers for the Hogrogian illustrated version. Why are they appropriate? Would they have been appropriate for Marcia Brown's version? Using crayon, make an end-paper pattern that would be appropriate for the Perrault version.

3. After sharing *Once a Mouse,* read Brown's *The Blue Jackal.* Were there any ways in which the tiger and jackal were alike?

4. Read the version of *Puss in Boots* that Marcia Brown illustrated. Characterize Puss, using both illustrations and text to get ideas and to use as examples in giving your reason for each character trait you list. For example, Puss was brave because he was willing to face the ogre in order to help his master.

   Now read Perrault's *Puss in Boots* with illustrations by Paul Galdone (Seabury, 1976). Examine your list of traits. Do the Galdone illustrations give you the same feeling about the cat's character and appearance? Are there any differences in the text?

5. Read the Marcia Brown version of *Puss in Boots.* She does not illustrate the ogre except after it had turned into a lion. Draw a picture of the ogre as it looked when he first receives the cat.

   Why was Puss called Master Slyboots? Think of another name that would also be appropriate.

6. After sharing *Stone Soup,* make a recipe for stone soup that would serve 40 villagers, using all the ingredients called for by the soldiers.

Success Stories by Clyde Robert Bulla

STUDENT OBJECTIVES:

- Make a stick puppet to act out part of a story
- Compare two different stories
- Analyze why a story was an award winner
- Draw a picture to illustrate the end of a story
- Research people and places mentioned in a story

RECOMMENDED READING:

Bulla, Clyde Robert. *The Beast of Lor.* Illustrated by Ruth Sanderson. Crowell, 1977.
An elephant that escaped from the invading Roman army helps Lud, a boy from an ancient British tribe, find the far-off places of which he dreams.

———. *The Cardboard Crown.* Illustrated by Michelle Chessare. Crowell, 1984
Through Adam's efforts to help Olivia, the imaginary princess in the cardboard crown, Olivia succeeds in finding contentment on the farm.

———. *Daniel's Duck.* Illustrated by Joan Sandlin. Harper & Row, 1979.
A Tennessee mountain boy receives high praise from a respected woodcarver for his first carving effort.

———. *Dexter.* Illustrated by Glo Coalson. Crowell, 1973.
The faith Alex has in his friend Dave saves the life of Dave's pony Dexter, left for dead after a family tragedy.

———. *A Lion to Guard Us.* Illustrated by Michele Chessare. Crowell, 1981.
Three poor English children encounter many problems before reaching their father in Jamestown colony.

———. *My Friend the Monster.* Illustrated by Michele Chessare. Crowell, 1980.
Hal, the lonely prince, saves the life of Humbert the monster and finds a friend.

———. *The Poppy Seeds.* Illustrated by Jean Charlot. Crowell, 1953.
Because Pablo shares his seeds, the Mexican village receives the gift of water.

———. *Shoeshine Girl.* Illustrated by Leigh Grant. Crowell, 1975.
A denied allowance causes Sarah Ida to take a job, resulting in new consideration for others.

———. *The Sword in the Tree.* Illustrated by Paul Galdone. Crowell, 1956.
A young boy seeks the help of King Arthur to right the wrong suffered by his family.

Bulla, Clyde Robert, and Syson, Michael. *Conquista!* Illustrated by Ronald Himler. Crowell, 1978.
A lost horse from Coronado's expedition becomes the gift of the sun-god for a young Indian boy seeking manhood.

BIOGRAPHICAL SOURCES:

For more information on Clyde Robert Bulla, see *Books Are by People,* 32–33; *More Junior Authors,* 34; *Something about the Author,* 2:39–40; *Twentieth-Century Children's Writers,* 199–202; *Twentieth-Century Children's Writers,* 2d ed., 134–35.

GROUP INTRODUCTORY ACTIVITY:

Share with the children information about Bulla from the book *The Sword in the Tree.* He spent his early life on a farm near King City, Missouri, and attended a one-room country school. He recalls that when he was in the first grade the teacher asked each pupil what he or she would do with a thousand dollars. His reply that he would buy a table made the others laugh. What he really meant was that he wanted a desk or flat surface so he could write. He wrote his first stories and songs while he was in grade school. His first book was written while he was working for a Missouri newspaper. He has traveled widely and now lives in Los Angeles.[7]

Encourage the children to identify reasons why it is helpful to have information about the author given in the book you are reading.

Read the story *Conquista!* to the children. After telling them that the story was first an almost wordless film produced by the illustrator, discuss whether they feel they could get the full story's meaning in a film. What are the advantages of film? Of a book? Talk about whether they feel this story might really have happened. How do the black-and-white illustrations contribute to the story?

Let children suppose they were out alone and saw a strange animal. How would they react?

FOLLOW-UP ACTIVITIES FOR TEACHER AND STUDENTS TO SHARE:

1. Read Bulla's *The Beast of Lor* aloud to the class. Discuss the ending. Was it a surprise? Think back to the scene when Edric gave Lud the jewel. After knowing the ending let children contribute new insights into Edric's meaning when he said, "It was always...heavy."

   Compare the stories *Conquista!* and *The Beast of Lor.* In what ways are they alike?
2. Read Bulla's *The Sword in the Tree* aloud to the class. Was the last chapter a surprise to anyone? In what ways had Bulla foreshadowed that chapter?

   Have a committee of children go to the library media center

to see if they can find pictures or information about King Arthur, Gareth, and Sir Kay which they can share with the class.

3. Read aloud to the class Bulla's *A Lion to Guard Us.* In what way does the end of the story remind the children of *The Sword in the Tree*?

4. Urge a small group of children to individually read Bulla's *Shoeshine Girl.* Ask the library media specialist to discuss the book with the children, being sure to consider the theme, character development throughout the story, and the climax. Did the illustrations contribute to their enjoyment of the book? If so, how? If not, why not?

FOLLOW-UP ACTIVITIES FOR INDIVIDUALS OR SMALL GROUPS:

1. Read Bulla's *Daniel's Duck.* Suppose you were a Tennessee mountain boy spending the long winter evenings making something to take to the fair. What would you choose? Try making a soap carving, drawing, or some item you might display.

2. Read Bulla's *Daniel's Duck.* Continue the story. Write or tape what happened when Daniel and Mr. Peltigrew went back to the hall.

3. After hearing *A Lion to Guard Us,* research in the library media center how long it would take by boat and by airplane to go from London to Jamestown, Virginia, today. Compare this with the time taken for Amanda, Jemmy, and Meg to cross the ocean.

4. Read Bulla's *Dexter.* Make a picture of the last paragraph of the story which describes how Dave imagined Dexter's new life.

5. Read Bulla's *Shoeshine Girl.* Make a list of the reasons you think it won awards voted on by children in three states—Oklahoma, Arkansas, and South Carolina.

6. Read Bulla's *My Friend the Monster.* With a classmate, make stick puppets of Hal and Humbert and make a play of the scene in the Land Between on pages 53 and 54. Share with classmates.

7. Read Bulla's *My Friend the Monster.* Imagine one of the games Humbert might have taught Hal at the end of the story. Make up rules and teach the game to your class.

8. Read Bulla's *The Cardboard Crown.* Think about what might have happened to Olivia on her train trip to the city. Was it a good idea for her to go? Share your thoughts in a paragraph, on tape or for the class. If sharing with the class, see if they think your idea of what could have happened is realistic.

9. After hearing Bulla's *Conquista!* continue the story by writing a paragraph or taping what happened when Little Wolf got back to the village with the horse. How did the other members of the tribe react?

10. Read Bulla's *The Poppy Seeds*. Then read Barbara Cooney's *Miss Rumphius* (Viking, 1982). In what way were Pablo's and Miss Rumphius's purposes the same?
11. After hearing Bulla's *The Beast of Lor* reread the ending after the arrow has been removed from Lud's shoulder. With a committee of your classmates dramatize pages 53–54.

Exploring the Senses

STUDENT OBJECTIVES:

● Share messages through actions and facial expressions without words
● Make a group haiku poem
● Closely observe and describe a supposedly familiar object
● Touch an object and describe its properties without looking at it
● Consider occupations requiring acute senses

RECOMMENDED READING:

Brenner, Barbara. *Faces.* Illustrated by George Acona. Dutton, 1970
    Introduction to using the eyes, ears, nose, and mouth to help understand messages.

Brown, Marcia. *Listen to a Shape.* Watts, 1979.
    Color photographs and brief text invite the reader to find imaginative messages in the shapes of nature.

———. *Touch Will Tell.* Watts, 1979.
    Sensitive color photographs offer children ideas for exploring the world about them by touching.

———. *Walk with Your Eyes.* Watts, 1979
    Color photographs and perceptive text stimulate the reader to observe the beauties of nature so often overlooked.

Castle, Sue. *Face Talk, Hand Talk, Body Talk.* Illustrated by Frances McLaughlin-Gill. Doubleday, 1977.
    Black-and-white photographs demonstrate children communicating their feelings and messages without words.

Lewis, Richard. *In a Spring Garden.* Illustrated by Ezra Jack Keats. Dial, 1965.
Children are introduced to the unique beauty of a spring day through haiku poetry and stirring illustrations.

Yolen, Jane. *The Seeing Stick.* Illustrated by Remy Charlip and Demetra Maraslis. Crowell, 1977.
An old blind man uses the "seeing stick" to help the princess be happy.

GROUP INTRODUCTORY ACTIVITY:

Introduce this unit by asking children to name the five senses: touch, taste, sight, hearing, and smell. Say that you hope they will become more aware of the use of each sense in communicating messages and appreciating the world around them.

After sharing *Touch Will Tell* by Marcia Brown, call attention to her use of photographs to illustrate this book instead of woodcuts, crayon, linoleum cuts, or some other method. Why are photographs particularly appropriate for this message?

Discuss what properties of an object—shape, texture, etc.—one can use to identify an object merely by touching.

Pass around a large sack containing such items as a paper clip, spoon, piece of cotton, button, and cork. Have each child in turn reach into the sack and hold one item away from the rest but not withdraw it from the sack. Have them identify the object, describe it, and tell how they were able to name the object without seeing it.

FOLLOW-UP ACTIVITIES FOR TEACHER AND STUDENTS TO SHARE:

1. Before sharing Brown's *Walk with Your Eyes,* talk about the difference in meaning of such words as "glancing," "seeing," "observing," and "looking." Suggest that author Marcia Brown wants us to form a habit of carefully and imaginatively observing our surroundings, and she has again used photographs to help us.

   After sharing the book, ask children to try to recall anything they carefully observed on the way to school. Then give them a list of simple questions they might observe every day, such as "How may steps are there leading into the schoolhouse?" "How many steps lead up to the slippery slide?" "What is the major color in the painting in the hall?" After they try to answer, let them go and observe at an appropriate time.

   Ask the children to look at something in nature carefully

and imaginatively on the way home from school. Suggest they draw a picture of it and make a brief observation about it that they could not have made by merely glancing at it.

2. Before sharing Brown's *Listen to a Shape,* suggest to the children that Marcia Brown wants them to observe the shapes of nature imaginatively and thoroughly in order to find a message. She has used close-up photographs and meaningful, brief thoughts to get them started.

   Take a walk with the class around the neighborhood or schoolyard. If possible, divide the children into small groups and use an upper-grade child to accompany each group and record their observations.

   What shapes can the students see in the clouds? Look at the bare branches of a tree. What are they saying? Find a piece of wood. What message does that shape give? Let each group find a small object such as a leaf or pebble that they can bring back to the classroom. As a group let them decide upon an imaginative message that the shape inspires. Record the message on a folded 3″ X 5″ card and display with the object.

3. Introduce haiku, a Japanese verse form with 17 syllables in which the first and third lines contain five syllables and the second line seven. Usually the poem may be divided into two parts, the first describing some aspect of nature relating to the seasons, and the second expressing a mood or feeling.

   Share Lewis's *In a Spring Garden,* which makes poetic statements about the beauty of a spring day. As you share the haiku, let children have time to examine the illustrations by Ezra Jack Keats very carefully.

   After sharing *In a Spring Garden,* let children select one of the objects the committees brought in from the *Listen to a Shape* walk. Read the observation aloud and then as a class enlarge the observation into haiku form. If the class enjoys the activity, the other objects may be selected by small groups and written into haiku form with the assistance of the teacher or library media specialist.

FOLLOW-UP ACTIVITIES FOR INDIVIDUALS OR SMALL GROUPS:

1. Close your eyes and listen to the sounds. Record those you hear, such as a book dropping.
2. If available, read Lillian Quigley's *The Blind Man and the Elephant* (Scribner's 1959, o.p.). Write or audiotape a story about a witch who one day takes away a family's sense of smell, touch, hearing, or taste.

3. In a small group, share large pictures of animals or plants. Discuss what you could find out about each of these animals or plants in real life by using various senses. Record for class sharing the one in which the most senses could be used.
4. Make a list of items you should *not* touch. Identify why each is "off limits."
5. Make a list of places such as the library, music store, bakery, etc. Record which sense is the most valuable in each of these settings. How are each of the other senses valuable?
6. Record occupations that would be almost impossible for you if you did not have specific senses. Be sure you have at least one occupation example for each sense.
7. Read a biography of Helen Keller such as *Helen Keller, Toward the Light* by Stewart and Polly Anne Graff, illustrated by Paul Frame (Garrard, 1965) if any are available in the library media center. Report to the class her efforts to overcome her inability to use all of her senses.
8. As a small group read Barbara Brenner's *Faces* and Sue Castle's *Face Talk, Hand Talk, Body Talk.* Talk about the photos and how they show ways to express feelings or messages without words. Act out different messages for your classmates to interpret.
9. Read Yolen's *The Seeing Stick.* If you were to make a seeing stick, what stories would you wish to carve into the stick? What image could represent each story?

The World of Hans Christian Andersen

STUDENT OBJECTIVES:

- Visualize and create a mobile depicting scenes in a book
- Interpret and use specific examples of figurative language
- Discuss the effect of illustrations on the mood created by a story
- Illustrate a scene from a story in a way that creates the mood of that story
- Set up a display of objects important in the stories of an author
- Relate an author's work to life experiences of that person

RECOMMENDED READING:

Andersen, Hans Christian. *The Emperor's New Clothes.* Illustrated by Virginia Lee Burton. Houghton Mifflin, 1949.
Swindlers pretending to be tailors deceive the vain Emperor.

————. *The Fir Tree.* Illustrated by Nancy Ekholm Burkert. Harper & Row, 1970.
A little fir tree wishing for greatness doesn't appreciate the beauty of the forest until it is too late.

————. *The Little Match Girl.* Illustrated by Blair Lent. Houghton Mifflin, 1968.
A tiny child who is freezing to death has wonderful visions as she lights matches to keep warm.

————. *The Snow Queen.* Illustrated by Marcia Brown. Scribner's, 1972.
A young girl's courage and love enable her to rescue her friend from the icy grip of the Snow Queen.

————. *The Steadfast Tin Soldier.* Illustrated by Thomas Di Grazia. Prentice-Hall, 1981.
A tin soldier with only one leg falls in love with a toy ballerina doll.

————. *Thumbelina.* Illustrated by Susan Jeffers. Dial, 1979.
A wee girl flees on the wings of a swallow to find a land of little people.

————. *The Ugly Duckling.* Illustrated by Adrienne Adams. Scribner's, 1965.
An ugly "duckling" is despised and persecuted until it becomes a lovely swan.

————. *The Wild Swans.* Illustrated by Marcia Brown. Scribner's, 1963.
An evil spell which changed 11 brothers into wild swans can only be broken through the silence and suffering of little sister Elisa.

BIOGRAPHICAL SOURCES:

For more information on Hans Christian Andersen (deceased), see *The Junior Book of Authors,* 2d ed., 5–6; *Yesterday's Authors of Books for Children,* 23–47.

GROUP INTRODUCTORY ACTIVITY:

To introduce the unit on Hans Christian Andersen, read aloud *The Ugly Duckling.* After reading the story, discuss the feelings the duckling expressed about his early life. How did the duckling feel about being the laughingstock of the barnyard? What was his mother's reaction to him the first day? Was there a change later? What feelings did the duckling have when he saw the swans fly over? How did the duckling express his feeling when the older swans bowed to him? Discuss the sentence "It doesn't matter about being born in a duckyard, as long as you are hatched from a swan's egg."

After discussing the story tell the students about Hans Christian Andersen. Hans was called a queer, ugly child who lived in a dream world of his own. He made up plays, and the happiest times of his childhood were when his poor cobbler father would read to him. His father died when he was 11, and after his mother remarried, he was on his own. After working in a number of factories, he broke his savings pig at the age of 14 and went to Copenhagen to be an actor. At 30, when he needed the money, he wrote four fairy tales and published them. The children's stories were successful, so he continued to write them at times throughout his life.[8] *The Ugly Duckling* is often considered to be autobiographical. Discuss the meaning of the term. Urge children to compare facts about Andersen's appearance and life to that of the ugly duckling.

Illustrations affect the tone and mood of the story. Examine again a few of Adrienne Adams's illustrations. What feelings do they arouse in the reader? If the version of *The Ugly Duckling* illustrated by Toma Bogdanovic (Scroll Press, 1971) is available, examine those illustrations to see if the same feelings are aroused.

Note that *The Ugly Duckling* is classified as fiction rather than folk literature (398.2) because Andersen's tales were his creation and originated in written form.

FOLLOW-UP ACTIVITIES FOR TEACHER AND STUDENTS TO SHARE:

1. To reinforce the importance of each child's liking himself/herself even if some might be labeled "ugly ducklings," recall that the ugly duckling turned into a swan and Andersen became a famous storyteller. Then have each child draw a profile of a face and head. Inside the brain portion ask the children to draw and color small pictures of what they like best about themselves or things they like to do. Mount them on colored construction paper so they appear to be framed. Encourage the children to show their profiles to the class and share what they like best

about themselves. The profiles can then be displayed in the room.

2. There are seven parts to Andersen's story *The Snow Queen.* When appropriate, discuss each part after reading it to reinforce the mood created by the figurative language. When Kay reaches the Snow Queen's palace, the description of its cold, sparkling grandeur is particularly effective. Follow at this point with an art activity. Using white tempera paint with salt added for texture, let each child paint the Snow Queen's palace on dark blue construction paper. The salt gives the tempera an icy effect.

3. Read Andersen's story *The Emperor's New Clothes.* Characterize the emperor and the people of his court. Why did no adults speak up when the Emperor passed by in the parade? Some people believe that Andersen wrote this story as his reaction to the people he met when he told stories in the palaces of the kings and queens. What does it tell us of his feelings toward them? What was Andersen trying to tell his listeners when he created this story?

The Emperor was said to have a different suit for each hour of the day. Let children use the calculator and figure out how many suits he would have in one day, week, month, and year. Working together let them design a wardrobe for the king. Ask them to bring scraps of materials from home, and have such materials as wallpaper, doilies, lace, burlap, wool, felt, fake fur, etc. available for use. Set up an art area where scissors, glue, and the materials are located. When possible ask the art teacher or another talented person to draw a paper doll sized for the Emperor.

If available examine the version of *The Emperor's New Clothes* illustrated in collage by Birte Dietz (Van Nostrand Reinhold, 1968, o.p.). Study the collage illustrations. How many fabrics can the children recognize?

4. Read Andersen's *Thumbelina* aloud to the class, making sure that the full-color illustrations by Susan Jeffers are shown to the class as the particular scene is described in the text. Let children recall and describe the different places where Thumbelina lived. Divide children into small groups to make mobiles depicting Thumbelinia in different settings. One mobile might represent the butterflies, which had wings of gossamer.

5. Read Andersen's *The Steadfast Tin Soldier* aloud to the class. Have the children characterize the tin soldier and the dancer, identifying scenes in the story that prompted their suggestion of each character trait. Suppose Hans Christian Andersen were telling the children that story. After he finished, what reasons might the children give for liking the story? If he said, "Did my story have any special message for each of you?" what might they want to tell him?

6. After reading Andersen's *The Wild Swans* to the class and sharing the illustrations, have the class discuss the causes and effects found in the story. For example, when the little sister took the vow to remain silent, what were the various effects of that decision? If nettles or some kind of thorny bush is available, bring to class to heighten their sensitivity to the physical pain the sister suffered.

   Ask a few children to volunteer to remain silent for half of the day. Let them share their feelings and frustrations at the close of the experience.

FOLLOW-UP ACTIVITIES FOR INDIVIDUALS OR SMALL GROUPS:

1. After hearing Andersen's *The Snow Queen* and recalling that Kay's heart went cold when a splinter which entered his eye reached his heart, seek other examples of stories in which splinters played a role. If available in the library media center, read Ingri and Edgar Parin d'Aulaire's account of troll splinters in *D'Aulaire's Trolls* (Doubleday, 1972). Report to the class.
2. Read Andersen's *The Little Match Girl.* Draw and paint or color a picture of what you imagine the little girl saw when she lit the matches.
3. Read Andersen's *The Fir Tree.* Cut out a fir tree shape from two 9″ X 12″ sheets of green construction paper. Then cut a white sheet of the same shape and staple inside. Write a story or message on the white page that the fir tree might have told a bird to carry back to the trees in the forest.
4. After sharing Andersen's *Thumbelina,* go to the media center to see if you can find a story about Tom Thumb, Hop-o'-my Thumb, Thumbling, or One Inch Fellow. Read the story and list the ways it is like *Thumbelina.*
5. After sharing Andersen's *The Wild Swans,* try to find the Grimm Brothers stories "The Seven Ravens" or "The Six Swans" in the library media center. Read either story and list the ways it is like *The Wild Swans.*
6. After sharing Andersen's *The Emperor's New Clothes,* carefully examine Mitsumasa Anno's *Anno's Journey* (Collins, 1976) if it is available in the library media center. See if you can find Anno's illustrations of *The Emperor's New Clothes.* Share with the class.
7. After sharing *The Ugly Duckling,* as a small group listen and view, if available, the sound filmstrip *The Ugly Duckling* illustrated by Otto S. Svend (Weston Woods, 1977, 51 fr., col., 17 min). Compare the illustrations and the story with the Adrienne Adams's version shared in class.

8. After sharing the available Hans Christian Andersen stories a small group can set up a display of the inanimate objects Andersen used in his stories, such as a box of matches, a walnut shell, etc. Arrange in the classroom or library media center, labeling objects and story.
9. If an index to fairy tales is available in the library media center, see how many references are made to swans in other stories besides *The Ugly Duckling.* Examine the Hans Christian Andersen stories you have shared. How many references to swans can you find? Write down what you think swans symbolized for Hans Christian Andersen.

Aileen Fisher's Poetic View of Nature

STUDENT OBJECTIVES:

- Discuss the influence of an author's home environment on his/her books
- Express poetry through choral reading
- Compose a group poem
- Listen for figurative language and discuss unusual descriptions of the same aspect of nature
- Find a favorite poem to illustrate and share

RECOMMENDED READING:

Fisher, Aileen. *All on a Mountain Day.* Illustrated by Gardell Christensen. Rod & Staff, 1956.
Figurative language highlights this story of the interaction of animals during a day in the mountains.

———. *Animal Houses.* Illustrated by Jan Wills. Bowmar-Noble, 1973.
Brief text and illustrations share the concept of animal homes that are round rather than square.

———. *Going Barefoot.* Illustrated by Symeon Shimin. Crowell, 1964.
As the child waits for June he thinks of the feelings of animals that have no shoes to restrict them.

————. *Like Nothing at All.* Illustrated by Leonard Weisgard. Harper
& Row, 1979.
Poetic descriptions of animals making use of protective coloring
to escape detection.

————. *Listen, Rabbit.* Illustrated by Symeon Shimin. Crowell, 1964.
A sensitive narrative poem of a small boy who attempts to make
friends with a rabbit.

————. *Out in the Dark and the Daylight.* Illustrated by Gail Owens.
Harper & Row, 1980.
One hundred forty brief poems loosely arranged by season.

————. *Rabbits, Rabbits.* Illustrated by Gail Niemann. Harper & Row,
1983.
Twenty-one imaginative illustrated poems about rabbits, utilizing
figurative language within the child's realm of experience.

BIOGRAPHICAL SOURCES:

For more information on Aileen Fisher, see *Books Are by People,*
74–77; *More Junior Authors;* 85–86; *Something about the Author,*
25:108–10; *Twentieth-Century Children's Writers,* 451–55; *Twentieth-
Century Children's Writers,* 2d ed., 286–88.

GROUP INTRODUCTORY ACTIVITY:

Introduce Aileen Fisher by explaining that she uses both observation and research in writing her children's books. As a child in
Michigan she walked four miles to school, and as an adult she takes
long walks daily near her Colorado mountain home and imaginatively
records her observations of animals.[9]

Before sharing poems from *Out in the Dark and Daylight,* note
that it is classified 811.5, meaning that it is poetry. Point out that
section of the media center collection.

Read "Speaking of Leaves," p. 3. Urge children to think of
another kind of leaf and have the class think of how some insect or
animal might use it.

Share "Raindrops," p. 36. Let children answer Fisher's poetic
question about what they'd do if they saw raindrops as big as they
are. Notice Fisher's rhymed couplet form. Write some group poems
in that form to answer her question.

Read "Thanksgiving Dinner," p. 74. Have children think of ideas
of how the poem would be different if it were before Christmas
Dinner.

Read "There Goes Winter," p. 109. Note the two three-line
verses with the last line of the two verses rhyming. Have children

think of the poem that would come next ("There Goes Spring"). Urge children to share ideas to make a group poem with the same form and rhyme scheme entitled "There Goes Spring." Make similar group poems for "There Goes Summer" and "There Goes Fall."

Note Gail Owen's black-and-white illustrations of some of the poems. Tell children that *Out in the Dark and Daylight* will be on the reading table in their room. Urge them to select a poem they like that is not illustrated, copy and illustrate it, and share with the class. Display the illustrated poems on an Aileen Fisher classroom or library media center bulletin board.

FOLLOW-UP ACTIVITIES FOR TEACHER AND STUDENTS TO SHARE:

1. Read Fisher's *Listen, Rabbit* aloud to the class. Let children think of advantages of two antenna ears like the rabbit has. In what ways would they be an inconvenience?

   Discuss how the boy tried to make friends with the rabbit. What else might he have done?

   Talk about the rhyming narrative. Do the children feel they enjoyed it more than if the text had been in nonrhyming paragraph form?

2. Read Fisher's *All on a Mountain Day* aloud to the class, one chapter at a time. Before reading Chapter 1, "The Snowshoe Rabbit Meets the Test," ask the children to listen for Aileen Fisher's figurative language about what the sound of the aspen leaves was like, what the sunlight did, and how the breeze went down the mountainside. After reading the chapter, have the children recall the figurative language and suggest what less descriptive words they might have used. Discuss the facts about the snowshoe rabbit that they learned—that the babies were fully furred and had eyes wide open when they were born, for example.

   Recall facts the library media specialist has shared about Aileen Fisher's life. Why was Fisher able to write these observations about the mountain animals?

   As each succeeding chapter is read, use a similar pattern for discussion. In Chapter 2, "The Little Grouse Sees the World," what was the little grouse like as he tumbled down the snowbank? What word did Fisher use to describe how it reacted when the warning caused an instant stop? When the coyote's paw almost knocked the mother grouse off balance, how did she react?

   Read each chapter. At the close of the book, let the class plot the interaction of the animals on that one day.

3. Read Fisher's *Like Nothing at All* to the class. Stop reading after the question, "Do you know what it was?" each time and let children identify the described animal. Have them share the clues that made them recognize the animal.

   After completing the book, allowing the children to identify each animal and to document the clues, discuss other animals that try to look like nothing at all. Perhaps children will want to research additional facts about each animal, such as the chameleon, that they name.

   Note the illustrations by Leonard Weisgard. How do they contribute to the text?

FOLLOW-UP ACTIVITIES FOR INDIVIDUALS OR SMALL GROUPS:

1. Read Fisher's *Going Barefoot.* Make a picture of a kangaroo or some other animal wearing shoes.
2. Read Fisher's *Going Barefoot.* Working with a committee, think of the styles of feet found in the woods and barnyard that go barefoot all year. Make a mural of those feet and label each. You will want to find illustrations of animals in magazines such as *Ranger Rick* and books about animals in the library media center in order to make realistic pictures of hoofs, padded paws, webbed feet, etc.
3. After sharing Fisher's *Like Nothing at All,* look for other books illustrated by Leonard Weisgard in the library media center. How many are books relating to nature? Are the illustrations similar to those in *Like Nothing at All?*
4. After sharing Fisher's *All on a Mountain Day* in class, select a favorite chapter. Draw pictures to highlight the action and add a brief paragraph to each in order to retell that animal's story.
5. Read Fisher's *Animal Houses.* Make a list of animals identified by Fisher that have round homes. Think of other animals that have round homes. Research in the library media center as needed. Make illustrations of those not named by Fisher, describe briefly, and share with the class.
6. Read Fisher's *Animal Houses.* Think of other houses not named by Fisher for domesticated animals, pets, and people that are more square than round. Make pictures of each and write a brief description.
7. Using the index to Fisher's *Out in the Dark and Daylight,* find the poems "Winter Morning," "Early Snow," and "Sparkly Snow." List the three different objects that Fisher used to share what snow was like. Think of something else snow looks like and write a brief poem about it. Share with the class.

8. Read Fisher's *Rabbits, Rabbits.* Think carefully about "Color Blind" and "To A Lady Cottontail." Are rabbits color blind? How does a rabbit make a nest? Go to the library media center and see if you can find a book that tells about wild rabbits. See if you can verify the facts Fisher gave in the poems.
9. Read Fisher's *Rabbits, Rabbits.* What are rabbit tails like? Write down the answers. Check the poem "Cotton Balls" and record how Fisher describes them. Read "Do Rabbits Have Christmas"? Write down how Fisher said frost and snow decorated the tree. Think of something you could do to add to the decorations on the rabbit's tree.
10. Read Fisher's *Rabbits, Rabbits.* Think of an animal about which you would like to collect poems. Find poems about that animal in the library media center in collections of poems such as *The Golden Treasury of Poetry* selected by Louis Untermeyer (Golden Press, 1959). Copy, illustrate, and make into a book. Perhaps you would like to get a committee of classmates to work with you on the project.

Favorites from Glen Rounds

STUDENT OBJECTIVES:

- Recognize exaggeration as a form of humor
- Participate in making a class filmstrip and cassette
- Gain a better understanding of life on the frontier
- Compare facts about cowboys to myths about cowboys
- Share a hyperbole

RECOMMENDED READING:

Rounds, Glen. *The Blind Colt.* Holiday House, 1960.
    A blind colt, growing up in the South Dakota Badlands, is adopted by a 10-year-old boy.

———. *Blind Outlaw.* Holiday House, 1980.
    A boy who cannot talk tames a blind and frightened horse.

——. *The Cowboy Trade.* Holiday House, 1972.
A realistic portrayal of the life of the cowboy, including equipment used, perils caused by the weather, and the demanding task of the roundup.

——. *Mr. Yowder and the Giant Bull Snake.* Holiday House, 1978.
With the assistance of Xenon Zebulon Yowder, an ambitious little snake becomes famous as Knutes, the Giant Bull Snake.

——. *Mr. Yowder and the Steamboat.* Holiday House, 1977.
Mr. Yowder's quiet day for fishing is changed when he meets a card-playing steamboat captain.

——. *Mr. Yowder and the Train Robbers.* Holiday House, 1981.
With the help of 27 rattlesnakes, Mr. Yowder captures the train robbers, but he loses them in a dust cloud created by the posse.

——. *Ol' Paul, The Mighty Logger,* rev. ed. Holiday House, 1976.
Pen-and-ink sketches enhance the rollicking exploits of the logging hero Paul Bunyan and his incredible ox Babe.

——. *Stolen Pony.* Holiday House, 1948, 1969.
When thieves steal a blind pony, a loyal dog leads it home again.

——. *The Treeless Plains.* Holiday House, 1967.
Recounts how pioneers living on the plains learned to build houses without wood.

——. *Washday on Noah's Ark.* Holiday House, 1985.
Despite the lack of a clothesline, Mrs. Noah figures out how to dry her wash on the clear forty-first day.

——. *Wild Appaloosa.* Holiday House, 1983.
A handsome Appaloosa eludes the wild horse hunters and ends up in the pasture to be trained and loved by Bert.

Schwartz, Alvin. *Whoppers: Tall Tales and Other Lies.* Illustrated by Glen Rounds. Lippincott, 1975.
A pack of "gallyfloppers, or preposterous stories, about the frustrations and hardships experienced by pioneers—from being chased by bears to ordeals caused by unpredictable weather.

BIOGRAPHICAL SOURCES:

For more information on Glen Rounds, see *The Junior Book of Authors,* 2d ed., 261–62; *Something about the Author,* 8:171–73; *Twentieth-Century Children's Writers,* 1073–76; *Twentieth-Century Children's Writers,* 2d ed., 668–70.

GROUP INTRODUCTORY ACTIVITY:

Before introducing Glen Rounds and his books, decorate the library media center or classroom with painted signs such as "4 Good Books C Your Library, signed XZY" and "Glen Rounds Writes Good Books, signed XZY." Be sure to sign each one "XZY" for Xenon Zebulon Yowder. When the class comes to the library media center, let them ask questions and try to figure out why the signs are up. Introduce Mr. Yowder, the sign painter, by reading aloud *Mr. Yowder and the Train Robbers.*

After sharing the book with the class, introduce a real sign painter, illustrator and author Glen Rounds. Rounds was born in the Badlands of South Dakota and spent his boyhood on a ranch in Montana. He later prowled the country as a muleskinner, cowboy, sign painter, railroad section hand, baker, carnival medicine man, and textile designer. He began experimenting with etching and painting and later wrote stories to accompany his drawings.[10]

After sharing facts about Glen Rounds, explore with the students how his life has affected his stories and illustrations.

FOLLOW-UP ACTIVITIES FOR TEACHER AND STUDENTS TO SHARE:

1. To follow up the introduction to Glen Rounds and Xenon Zebulon Yowder, read aloud to the class *Mr. Yowder and the Giant Bull Snake* in which Mr. Yowder is famous as "The World's Bestest and Fastest Sign Painter." After reading the story, discuss with the students what is humorous in the story. What statements exaggerate the story? How do the illustrations add to the humor? To help students recognize the humor in exaggeration, suggest that they write hyperboles. Give them examples, such as "I've told you a hundred times to shut the door" or "I'm so hungry I could eat a horse." To help students get started suggest their hyperboles answer such questions as how big the snake was or how powerful the steamboat was.
2. Continue sharing the antics of Mr. Yowder by reading Rounds's *Mr. Yowder and the Steamboat* to the class. Have prepared ahead of time a large laminated map of the United States with an outline of states only. After reading the story, have the children aid in tracking the travels of Mr. Yowder on the map.
3. Read aloud to the class, Rounds's *The Stolen Pony,* which describes the journey of a loyal dog and a blind pony back to the corral. After discussing moving scenes in the story, urge individual students or small committees to create dioramas of favorite scenes.

4. Patience, courage, and understanding are values demonstrated by the boy in Rounds's *Blind Outlaw.* After sharing the book aloud, have the class discuss the qualities of character found in the boy and document incidents that evidence those traits. Because of their disabilities, what adjustments did the boy and his horse have to make?

   After sharing aloud Rounds's *Stolen Pony* and *Blind Outlaw,* both involving a blind horse, invite someone who works with farm animals, such as a veterinarian or rancher, to talk about animal care and training.

5. Glen Rounds's line drawings realistically depict the settings he vividly describes in *The Treeless Plains.* Read aloud chapters one and two to a small group of students so all can easily see the illustrations. Then explain that the students are now going to share the story by studying the illustrations and telling the story from the pictures. Allow the children time to study the illustrations while the words on the page are covered by a card. Let children share the story page by page. If important facts are left out, read or tell that information. Read aloud some of the descriptions to help them visualize more fully life on the frontier.

   To help emphasize the bleakness of the prairie homes, have the children bring newspaper from home and decorate one corner of the classroom, as described on pages 73–74.

   The only light the pioneers had after dark was that from lanterns. If possible, bring a kerosene lamp or lantern to the classroom. With the lights turned off and blinds pulled, use only the light from the lantern for a few minutes so children can begin to imagine the problems families faced at night.

6. Before sharing Rounds's *The Cowboy Trade* with the class, have the students write down at least three things they know about cowboys. After reading the book to the class, let children discuss any of their recorded ideas that were included in Rounds's work. What myths did he identify that are believed by many people? Where else could they turn for more information about cowboys? Suggest that some students may want to seek out additional information not identified by Rounds and share it with the class.

7. Rounds's illustrations give humorous insights into the tall tales collected by Alvin Schwartz in *Whoppers.* Many of the tales resulted from hardships faced by frontier people. According to Schwartz, the larger the problems, the bigger the tales that were told. Select a few whoppers to share aloud. Ask the children to imagine why each might have been told. What might each actual situation have been?

   After sharing information about how big mosquitoes are, let children identify true size. Children may want to create their own brief whoppers.

FOLLOW-UP ACTIVITIES FOR INDIVIDUALS OR SMALL GROUPS:

1. After sharing Rounds's Mr. Yowder books, create other signs Mr. Yowder could have drawn. These can be drawn on paper or transparencies, with a cassette tape added to describe the situation requiring the sign.
2. After hearing Rounds's *Blind Outlaw,* continue the story by speculating about what happened to the mute boy and the blind colt as they headed for Oklahoma at the end of the story.
3. Read Rounds's *Washday on Noah's Ark.* Since the forty-first day appeared to be a day for cleaning, write a humorous paragraph about how Mr. Noah used certain animals to help clean the ark.
4. After sharing Rounds's *The Treeless Plains,* research tools and furniture used on the frontier, using such books as Edwin Tunis's *Frontier Living* (Crowell, 1976). With blank filmstrip and marking pencils work with your classmates to draw one item on a frame and record a description of that frontier item on a cassette. When the filmstrip is completed and an appropriate title frame added, the sound filmstrip can be shared by the class as a whole.
5. After sharing Rounds's *Blind Outlaw,* read *The Blind Colt.* After several children have read the book, the teacher or media specialist may want to lead a discussion in which you compare the settings in the two stories, character traits of the boy in each story, and events in each story.
6. After Schwartz's *Whoppers* is introduced, examine the line drawings of Glen Rounds, select a favorite story, and illustrate it more fully with pencil or pen only.
7. Examine the classification given to each of Rounds's books, as a group reach a consensus on why each was assigned, and discuss the conclusions with the media specialist for verification.
8. Read Rounds's *Ol' Paul, The Mighty Logger,* select a favorite story, make transparencies to aid in telling the story, and share it with your own or other classes.
9. Read Rounds's *Wild Appaloosa.* Write or tape an incident that might have happened if Bert and the Appaloosa had met the horse hunters again after Bert had tamed the Appaloosa and was riding her.

Beverly Cleary's Book Friends

STUDENT OBJECTIVES:

- Analyze characters and support the analysis with incidents from the text
- Compose poetry as a class and individually
- Create a new ending for a story
- Dramatize a humorous scene from a story
- Relate past costs identified in a story to current prices

RECOMMENDED READING:

Cleary, Beverly. *Beezus and Ramona.* Illustrated by Louis Darling. Morrow, 1955.
   The amazing activities of four-year-old Ramona are very embarrassing to her older sister Beezus.
      Some other books about Ramona:
      Ramona and Her Father. Morrow, 1977.
      Ramona and Her Mother. Morrow, 1980.
      Ramona Forever. Morrow, 1984.
      Ramona Quimby, Age 8. Morrow, 1982.
      Ramona the Brave. Morrow, 1975.
      Ramona the Pest. Morrow, 1968.

——. *Dear Mr. Henshaw.* Illustrated by Paul Zelinsky. Morrow, 1983.
   Through writing to an author and in his diary Leigh begins to cope with the divorce of his parents and his loneliness at school.

——. *Henry Huggins.* Illustrated by Louis Darling. Morrow, 1950.
   From filling his mother's fruit jars with guppies to going fishing with his dog Ribsy, unexpected developments always seem to complicate Henry's life.
      Some other books about Henry:
      Henry and Beezus. Morrow, 1952
      Henry and Ribsy. Morrow, 1954.
      Henry and the Clubhouse. Morrow, 1962.
      Henry and the Paper Route. Morrow, 1957.
      Ribsy. Morrow, 1964.

————. *The Mouse and the Motorcycle.* Illustrated by Louis Darling. Morrow, 1965.

Keith's friendship with the mouse Ralph proves worthwhile when illness disrupts the family's stay in an old hotel.

Some other books about Ralph:

Ralph S. Mouse. Morrow, 1982.

Runaway Ralph. Morrow, 1970.

BIOGRAPHICAL SOURCES:

For more information on Beverly Cleary, see *More Books by More People,* 88–94; *More Junior Authors,* 49–50; *Something about the Author,* 2:62–63; *Twentieth-Century Children's Writers,* 272–74; *Twentieth-Century Children's Writers,* 2d ed., 182–84.

GROUP INTRODUCTORY ACTIVITY:

Introduce Beverly Cleary's books by telling the children that when she was a child in Oregon, a teacher-librarian told her that she should become a children's author when she grew up. She decided that was a good idea, and began reading very critically. When she was 10 years old, she won two dollars in an essay contest, perhaps because no one else entered, but her first children's book was written years later, after she and her husband had moved to Berkeley, California. She found a stack of paper in a closet and told her husband that she should write a book but she never seemed to have sharp pencils. The next day he brought her a pencil sharpener, and Henry Huggins was the result of his action.[11]

Introduce *Beezus and Ramona* to the class after explaining to the class that Beezus was often embarrassed by Ramona's actions. Tell them that Ramona loved books about steam shovels and wanted them read over and over. Then read the students the scene in which Beezus must take the marked-up *Littlest Steam Shovel* back to the library (pp. 29–37). Let children volunteer to be Mother, Beezus, Ramona, and Miss Evans. Dramatize the scene. Urge the children to read the rest of the book and others about Ramona and her friends.

FOLLOW-UP ACTIVITIES FOR TEACHER AND STUDENTS TO SHARE:

1. Read Cleary's *Ramona the Pest* to the class. After reading the story, make a Ramona alphabet bulletin board using Ramona's idea for making pictures out of initials (just as Ramona made a cat out of a "Q").

After reading the story, have the children characterize Ramona, suggesting incidents that gave them the idea for each of the traits. List each trait and a brief statement of an action that documents each on a large sheet of paper, leaving space for added statements that indicate each trait. As they read additional books about Ramona, urge the children to add statements about scenes in other books that also indicate her character. Add traits as found. The list of traits added should show ways Ramona changed as she grew older.

2. Introduce Cleary's *Henry Huggins* by reading the chapter "Gallons of Guppies" aloud. It is often included in collections of humorous stories. After reading the chapter, let children choose to be Mr. Pennycuff, Henry, and his father and have them dramatize the scene when Henry took the guppies back to the store.

Note the cost of a fish tank, heater, and thermostat when the book was written. Select a child to check with a store and find out what those items would cost today.

3. Before reading Cleary's *The Mouse and the Motorcycle* to the class, share with them the origin of the idea for the book.

> This book came about after several years of wondering how I could write a book about motorcycles that eight-year-old boys would enjoy. One night in England, our son got a sudden fever; we were staying in a spooky, old hotel and did not have an aspirin and could not buy any at night. The next day, along with the aspirin tablets, we bought him some miniature cars and a miniature motorcycle for him to play with. When we returned home, a neighbor showed me a mouse that had fallen into a bucket in her garden. The thought crossed my mind that the mouse was the right size to ride the little motorcycle my son had brought home. That was the beginning of the book.[12]

After reading *The Mouse and the Motorcycle* aloud, have each class member write or tape the composition Keith might have written about Ralph getting him the aspirin. Suggest also that each student state what the teacher would say after sharing the composition.

4. Before reading Cleary's *Dear Mr. Henshaw* aloud, tell the class that Beverly Cleary was awarded the Newbery Medal in 1984; this book was selected as the most distinguished contribution to American literature published in 1983.

After hearing the story ask each child to write down the name of his or her favorite author and three questions that each might like to ask the author. Then write down three questions the author might like to ask. Some children may want to write to their favorite author after checking with the library media

specialist to see if that person is still alive. The letter can be sent to the author in care of the publisher.
5. Suggest that a reading group or several children may want to read all the Cleary books about Henry Huggins. Then they may want to select a favorite scene and dramatize it for the class.
6. Suggest that another group read Cleary's *Runaway Ralph* and *Ralph S. Mouse*. After they have read the stories, have them think of other middle initials for Ralph, the word it stands for based on his actions in some scene in one of the books, and a poem or paragraph about that scene. Share with the class.

FOLLOW-UP ACTIVITIES FOR INDIVIDUALS OR SMALL GROUPS:

1. Read Cleary's *Ribsy*. Think about your pet or a pet you would like to have. Suppose it was lost. Make an ad for the newspaper that you might run in order to locate your pet. If the advertisement cost 20 cents per word, what would you have to pay for the ad?
2. Read Cleary's *Henry and the Paper Route*. Think of another ending. How else might Henry have kept Ramona from picking up the papers he had delivered? Write or tape the ending you create.
3. Read Cleary's *Henry and Ribsy*. Write or tape a commercial about Wolfie's Dog Food and share it with the class.
4. Read Cleary's *Ramona and Her Father*. Make up and decorate some signs Ramona and Beezus might have placed around the house to remind their father to quit smoking.
5. Read Cleary's *Henry and the Clubhouse*. Make a list of reasons you think clubs should be only for boys or girls or reasons that you feel they should be integrated.
6. Read Cleary's *Ramona and Her Father*. Recall the long picture they made about the sights of Oregon. Make a long picture about your state. Perhaps you will want to describe the scene to the class and get volunteers to help you.
7. Read Cleary's *Ramona Forever*. Write a brief story telling what happened to Ramona's shoes after they were tied to the truck.
8. Read Cleary's *Ramona Forever*. Have you or one of your friends ever had siblingitis? What caused it? How was it cured?
9. Read Cleary's *Ramona and Her Mother*. Describe Ramona's mother in a paragraph. Would you like having her for your mother? Why or why not?
10. Read Cleary's *Ramona the Brave*. Think of something that could frighten you as you walked to school. Describe a spunky way you could avoid harm and get to school.

11. Read Cleary's *Ramona Quimby, Age 8.* Write a TV commercial book report for the book.
12. Read Cleary's *Henry and Beezus.* Pretend you went to a grand opening of a supermarket. List 10 samples you would enjoy eating and describe the prize you would like to win.

Culminating Activities after Third Grade/Fourth Grade

Discuss with the entire class the literature experiences they have shared. What authors and illustrators do they recall? What books did each person named write or illustrate? What book characters do the students remember?

What literature activities did the students particularly enjoy? Do the students remember any facts about specific authors or illustrators?

Discuss the meaning of the word "see." Talk about the specific meaning of other words related to the use of the eyes in perceiving an object. What other senses might one use in recognizing the properties of an object? In what instance might a sense other than sight be more useful for identification of an object?

Talk about the kinds of books found in different Dewey Decimal classifications in the library media center.

What is haiku? What might be an appropriate subject for a haiku poem? Recall any poetry shared.

What is a fable? What does exaggeration mean? In what type of books is it often used effectively? Give the theme for a story the class has shared.

What Caldecott Medal books do they remember? Who illustrated each? What styles of illustrations do they recall?

REFERENCES

1. Doris de Montreville and Elizabeth D. Crawford, eds. *Fourth Book of Junior Authors & Illustrators* (New York: H.W. Wilson, 1978), p. 31.

2. Doris de Montreville and Donna Hill, eds., *Third Book of Junior Authors* (New York: H.W. Wilson, 1972), p. 87.

3. Patricia Cianciolo, *Illustrations in Children's Books,* 2d ed. (Dubuque, IA: William C. Brown, 1976), pp. 28–93.

4. Anne Commire, ed., *Something about the Author* (Detroit: Gale Research, 1982), vol. 26, p. 152.

5. Cianciolo, p. 45.

6. Muriel Fuller, ed., *More Junior Authors* (New York: H.W. Wilson, 1963), p. 32.

7. Fuller, p. 34.

8. Stanley J. Kunitz and Howard Haycraft, eds., *The Junior Book of Authors,* 2d ed. (New York: H.W. Wilson, 1951), pp. 5–6.

9. D.L. Kirkpatrick, ed., *Twentieth-Century Children's Writers* (New York: St. Martin's Press, 1983), p. 454.

10. Commire, p. 17.

11. Lee Bennett Hopkins, *More Books by More People* (New York: Harcourt Brace Jovanovich, 1974), pp. 89–90.

12. Hopkins, p. 91.

Chapter 5
Fourth Grade/Fifth Grade

Let's Share Sid Fleischman's Strange Characters

STUDENT OBJECTIVES:

- Dramatize scenes from a story
- Record exaggerations found in tall tales
- Map the travels of characters in a book
- Illustrate new ideas for some of the stories
- Define some colloquial words
- Anticipate the ending of a story

RECOMMENDED READING:

Fleischman, Sid. *Chancy and the Grand Rascal.* Illustrated by Eric
   von Schmidt. Little, Brown, 1963.
   Chancy's chances of finding his brother and sisters after the Civil
   War are heightened when he comes across his fast-talking Uncle
   Will.

———. *The Ghost on Saturday Night.* Illustrated by Eric von Schmidt.
   Little, Brown, 1974.
   Opie's skill in guiding people through the dense fog pays off
   when he captures bank robbers.

———. *The Hey Hey Man.* Illustrated by Nadine Bernard Westcott.
   Little, Brown, 1979.
   Through the efforts of the wood sprite who fails the robber, the
   amazed farmer sees his gold being shed from his dogs like fleas.

———. *Humbug Mountain.* Illustrated by Eric von Schmidt. Little, Brown, 1978.
An itinerant newspaper publisher's family outwits the rascals and saves grandpa's town of Sunrise.

———. *Jim Bridger's Alarm Clock.* Illustrated by Eric von Schmidt. Dutton, 1978.
Three tall tales about a mountain echo that saves Jim from freezing, provides fiddle music for the dance, and helps capture the bank robbers.

———. *Jingo Django.* Illustrated by Eric von Schmidt. Little, Brown, 1971.
A boy escapes the chimney sweep master and with the surprising Mr. Peacock sees the treasure hunters get their just dues.

———. *McBroom Tells the Truth.* Illustrated by Walter Lorraine. Little, Brown, 1981.
First published in 1966 by Norton, this reissue introduces the reader to the swindler's land deal that backfired and netted McBroom the acre of fertile land that plays an important role in the McBroom stories that follow.
Other McBroom stories include:
McBroom and the Beanstalk. Little, Brown, 1978.
McBroom and the Big Wind. Little, Brown, 1982.
McBroom and the Great Race. Little, Brown, 1980.
McBroom Tells a Lie. Little, Brown, 1976.
McBroom the Rainmaker. Little, Brown, 1982.
McBroom's Almanac. Little, Brown, 1984.
McBroom's Ear. Little, Brown, 1982.
McBroom's Ghost. Little, Brown, 1981.
McBroom's Zoo. Little, Brown, 1982.

———. *Mr. Mysterious' Secrets of Magic.* Illustrated by Eric von Schmidt. Little, Brown, 1975.
Simple, carefully illustrated magic tricks are presented in an appealing style to inspire young readers to try their hand.

BIOGRAPHICAL SOURCES:

For more information on Sid Fleischman, see *Something about the Author,* 8:61–63; *Third Book of Junior Authors* 86–87; *Twentieth-Century Children's Writers,* 463–65; *Twentieth-Century Children's Writers,* 2d ed., 294–95.

GROUP INTRODUCTORY ACTIVITY:

Before introducing McBroom as one of Sid Fleischman's characters, tell the students about Sid Fleischman. He was born in Brooklyn in 1920, graduated from San Diego State College, served in the United States Naval Reserve, was a magician in vaudeville and night clubs, and was a newspaper reporter. Sid Fleischman says of himself that although he seldom uses direct personal experiences in his books, he sees glimpses of himself on nearly every page. His stories show his love of humorous situations, his joy in adventure, his fascination with frontier life and the colloquial language of that time. He says that because he doesn't plot his stories before beginning, the experience of writing a book is for him much like reading one. He seldom knows what will happen next and has to sit at the typewriter to find out. His starting point may be the setting, as was the gold rush to California in *By The Great Horn Spoon!* (Little, Brown, 1963). Sometimes he begins with a character such as Pa in *Mr. Mysterious and Company* (Little, Brown, 1962) or McBroom, who spins tall tales.[1]

Before reading *McBroom Tells the Truth* talk to the children about exaggeration as the basis for the tall tale and urge them to listen for all the improbable elements in the story.

After sharing the story start a list of McBroom Exaggerations on a roll of white butcher paper. After children think of all they can, they may want to read the story at a later time and add to the list. If time does not allow you to read the entire story, carry out the activities after reading chapters 1 and 2 and let the teacher read the remainder of the story aloud later in the classroom.

Talk about the way McBroom calls his children. Does that combination of names add to the humor? Let some children with several brothers and sisters verbalize how their family names would sound if combined as one word.

If the 1966 edition of the story illustrated by Kurt Werth is available, compare the illustrations. Which reveal McBroom as a more humorous character?

Urge children to read other McBroom stories and add to the McBroom Exaggerations list.

FOLLOW-UP ACTIVITIES FOR TEACHER AND STUDENTS TO SHARE:

1. Before reading the first tall tale in Fleischman's *Jim Bridger's Alarm Clock,* see if any children can think of a way the Jim Bridger tall tales are different from those about McBroom. Some child should recall that Jim Bridger actually lived, while McBroom was created from Fleischman's imagination.

Urge children to listen for exaggerations as you read the first story, "Jim Bridger's Alarm Clock." After reading, have them recall all they can remember.

Read the titles of the other two stories: "The Fiddler Who Wouldn't Fiddle" and "The Fifth of July." After telling them that the echo is involved, see if anyone can guess the plot of either of the two stories. After hearing a number of ideas, urge them to read the stories to see if anyone was right.

2. Introduce Fleischman's *Humbug Mountain* by telling the children that it is about a poor family whose father is a newspaper man on the frontier. They move from one small town to another trying to set up a newspaper office. Finally they decide to go to grandpa's town of Sunrise near Humbug Mountain. Read the scene where Pa, with little money, tries to find a steamboat that will take them up the river (last paragraph of p. 22 through p. 26). After sharing the scene select three students to dramatize it.

   If time allows, read the scene in which Jim Chitwood tries to take away Grandpa's claim to Sunrise (pp. 120–22). Select characters and dramatize.

   Talk about the title of the book *Humbug Mountain.* See if children can guess why Humbug Mountain was given that name. Urge the children to read the story and find out if anyone was right. The book would also make a good "class read-aloud" if time allows.

3. Read Fleischman's *The Ghost on Saturday Night.* Stop at the bottom of page 41 and let each student write or tape what was in the box and how the story ended. After letting the class listen to each of the endings, share the end of Fleischman's story.

FOLLOW-UP ACTIVITIES FOR INDIVIDUALS OR SMALL GROUPS:

1. Read the other two tall tales in *Jim Bridger's Alarm Clock.* Make a list of all the places Fleischman mentions in the three stories and locate them on the map. In the first story it says that "in time they named a fort and a forest after him, and a pass and a creek and a mountain or two." Use the atlas and other reference sources to make a list of towns, rivers, etc., named after Jim Bridger. If possible, locate them on a blank map.

2. After reading Fleischman's *Jim Bridger's Alarm Clock,* see if William Steele's *Daniel Boone's Echo* (Harcourt Brace Jovanovich, 1957, o.p.) is available in the school library media center or public library. If so, read the book. Then make a list of any ways in which the two stories are alike. Share the William Steele story with your classmates. Perhaps they can help you add to the list.

3. After reading "The Fiddler Who Wouldn't Fiddle" from Fleischman's *Jim Bridger's Alarm Clock,* see if the library media center or music teacher has a record of "Turkey in the Straw" or any other songs the fiddler played. Listen to see if a fiddle can be heard in the song. Ask your teacher if the music teacher, an old timer in the community, or someone from a square dance club might teach the class one of the dances that might have the caller's opening remarks: "Grab your partners, make a square/Music's comin' from I don't know where."

4. Read Fleischman's *Humbug Mountain.* With the assistance of a group of classmates who have also read or heard the book, make up the stories that might fill the issue of *The Humbug Mountain Hurrah* that would come out at the end of the story. Lay out the front page of the paper.

5. Read Fleischman's *The Hey Hey Man.* What funny thing might the wood spirit have done to the thief instead of starting a fire when he was chilled to the bone?

6. Read Fleischman's *Jingo Django.* Did you expect the search for the treasure to end in that way? Write or tape another way that the treasure part of the story might have ended. Think of another place the treasure might have been buried. Make a map that could guide the finder to the spot.

7. After reading Fleischman's *Jingo Django,* read James Giblin's *Chimney Sweeps: Yesterday and Today* (Crowell, 1982) if it is available in the school library media center or public library. Find out if children in the nineteenth century who were chimney sweeps were treated as Fleischman describes. How has the occupation of chimney sweeping changed today? Report your findings to the class.

8. Read Fleischman's *McBroom's Ear.* Think of another way the McBroom family could have disguised the ear of corn to get it to the fair. Draw a picture identifying your plan or write a paragraph about it.

9. Read Fleischman's *McBroom and the Beanstalk.* Find the words "lickety-toot," "flamdoodle," "golly-whopper," "splendiferous, " "rambunctious," and "gumption." How is each used or what does each describe? Write your own definition for each.

10. Read Fleischman's *McBroom Tells a Lie.* Examine the illustration of the popcornmobile. Identify the parts the children used. List others that were probably a part of that jim-dandy machine.

11. Read Fleischman's *McBroom and the Big Wind.* Think of other games the children could have played with the wind. Illustrate and/or write a description of each.

12. Read Fleischman's *McBroom's Ghost.* Make a list of all the unusual things that happened that made McBroom know it was going to be a dreadfully cold winter. Be sure also to add these to the class McBroom Exaggeration list.

13. Read Fleischman's *Chancy and the Grand Rascal.* Map the route followed by Chancy and his uncle in finding his brother and sisters. Record one event that happened in each place. List the modes of transportation they used.
14. Read Fleischman's *McBroom's Zoo.* Name, illustrate, and write a short description of the appearance and habits of another animal McBroom's family could have found for the zoo.
15. Read Fleischman's *Mr. Mysterious' Secrets of Magic.* Practice one of the tricks until you can do it well and share it with the class. Perhaps a classmate will work with you and you can present a magic show for the class or school.
16. Read Fleischman's *McBroom the Rainmaker.* List the disadvantages of vegetable timepieces. Choose a favorite vegetable, decide on its time growth pattern, and illustrate it as a 10-minute timepiece.
17. Read Fleischman's *McBroom the Rainmaker.* Write down Fleischman's description of a gallinipper. Then write your definition. Think of another way Heck Jones could have protected himself. Draw him using your idea for protection.
18. Read Fleischman's *McBroom's Almanac.* Write and illustrate two McProverbs and an ad for a sale item from McBroom's Wonderful One-Acre Farm. With eight other classmates prepare a school September–May Almanac, with each responsible for a story, recipe, proverb, for one month.

Peculiar Possibilities with Jack Prelutsky's Poetry

STUDENT OBJECTIVES:

- Illustrate an animal poem
- Create nonsense poetry
- Record poetry after selecting appropriate sound effects for the background
- Write a play
- Memorize and share a favorite poem
- Recognize alliteration in poetry

RECOMMENDED READING:

Prelutsky, Jack. *The Baby Uggs Are Hatching.* Illustrated by James Stevenson. Greenwillow, 1982.
Colorful descriptive words are coined to create 12 new creatures in poetic form with illustrations that stir the imagination.

———. *The Headless Horseman Rides Tonight; More Poems To Trouble Your Sleep.* Illustrated by Arnold Lobel. Greenwillow, 1980.
With fiendish rhymed delight a banshee, zombie, poltergeist, and others streak through pages decorated with cross-hatched black-and-white illustrations.

———. *The New Kid On The Block.* Illustrated by James Stevenson. Greenwillow, 1984.
This collection of over 100 poems includes such peculiar characters as the Cuckoodoctopus, Henrietta Snetter, and the Yubbazubbies.

———. *Nightmares: Poems To Trouble Your Sleep.* Illustrated by Arnold Lobel. Greenwillow, 1976.
Nightmarish creatures from ghouls to trolls come to life in the black-and-white illustrations and diabolical rhyme.

———. *The Queen of Eene: Poems.* Illustrated by Victoria Chess. Greenwillow, 1978.
Introduces 14 zany, poetic characters who do such things as collect pancakes and eat automobiles.

———. *The Random House Book of Poetry for Children.* Illustrated by Arnold Lobel. Random House, 1983.
Over 500 poems selected and arranged in 14 thematic sections with a new Prelutsky poem introducing each.

———. *Rolling Harvey down the Hill.* Illustrated by Victoria Chess. Greenwillow, 1980.
Five young rascals are humorously depicted in 15 poems.

———. *The Sheriff of Rottenshot.* Illustrated by Victoria Chess. Greenwillow, 1982.
Sixteen absurd but humorous characters are delightfully described in rhymed verse with eccentric illustrations.

———. *The Snopp on the Sidewalk and Other Poems.* Illustrated by Byron Barton. Greenwillow, 1977.
Twelve imaginary creatures are shared through nonsense words, rhymed verses, and other poetic devices.

———. *Zoo Doings.* Illustrated by Paul Zelinsky. Greenwillow, 1983.
A humorous collection of animal poems · such as "The Multilingual Mynah Bird," "The Turtle," and "Toucans Two."

BIOGRAPHICAL SOURCES:

For more information on Jack Prelutsky, see *Fifth Book of Junior Authors & Illustrators,* 251–52; *Something about the Author,* 22:195–97; *Twentieth-Century Children's Writers,* 2d ed., 627–29.

GROUP INTRODUCTORY ACTIVITY:

To introduce Jack Prelutsky, tell children that he spends several months each year visiting schools and sharing poetry to his guitar accompaniment. He tries to help children see that poetry is not boring. He says, "It is one way a human being can tell another human being what's going on inside. Kids memorize pop songs; they don't think of that music as apart from what they do. Poetry is the music of language."[2] Let children discuss what they think he means by "Poetry is the music of language."

Before sharing *Zoo Doings,* let the class suggest what they feel will be included in the collection. Check to see how many were selected by Prelutsky to write about. Since these are poems, see if anyone can recall in which area the book is classified.

Prelutsky once said that his poem "The Turtle" describes his feelings. After reading the poem, let children discuss what he meant by that statement. Share several of the poems. Then let children think of animals and funny descriptions or actions they would write about if they were writing a zoo poem.

Urge interested students to select one favorite poem from *Zoo Doings* to memorize and recite to the class. Have each of those students write out the poem chosen on a piece of construction paper and illustrate it. As the poems are being recited at a later date, collect their illustrated pages and add a title page to the collection of Favorite Prelutsky Zoo Doings. By punching holes in the pages and placing them in a ring binder, the student book can remain in the library media center to be shared while Prelutsky's book circulates.

FOLLOW-UP ACTIVITIES FOR TEACHER AND STUDENTS TO SHARE:

1. Share Prelutsky's poem "The Snopp On the Sidewalk," from the book of the same name, while holding a handmade Snopp. (It can be made with gray acrylic or other large-strand yarn. Refer to Bryan Barton's illustration of the Snopp to get the idea, beginning it as you would a large pom-pom with one end tied off instead of the center.) Encourage children to make their own

Snopps and display them in the library media center or class-room.

2. Read aloud "Herbert Glerbert: from Prelutsky's *The Queen of Eene.* As an art and listening activity reread the three stanzas, then have the students draw or make a collage picture of what they think Herbert Glerbert has become.

3. Read aloud the poem "Sadie Snott" from Prelutsky's *The Sheriff of Rottenshot.* Ask the class to write their own stanzas about what Sadie Snott ate, using the names of foods eaten in the school cafeteria, such as pigs-in-a-blanket or other made-up names of foods. To help students get started, make a list of the foods mentioned. As the poem is being composed collectively by the students, write it out on butcher paper for all to see. When the stanzas are completed, post them in the classroom or library media center.

4. Read to the students "The Ghostly Grocer of Grumble Grove" from Prelutsky's *The Sheriff of Rottenshot* as an example of humor in poetry through the use of alliteration. Suggest that the students find stanzas from other poems by Jack Prelutsky which use alliteration. After they copy and illustrate the stanza selected, being sure to also identify the title of the poem, let them arrange a bulletin board entitled Poetry's Peculiar Possibilities.

5. After reading such poems as "The Ghoul," "The Troll," and "The Ogre" from Prelutsky's *Nightmares,* ask the children to list some things that used to scare them. Have them describe the creatures listed and the sounds they might make.

6. Plan a frightful storytelling hour with the students. Use Prelutsky's *Nightmares, The Headless Horseman Rides Tonight* and Alvin Schwartz's *Scary Stories To Tell in the Dark* (Lippincott, 1981) as sources for stories and poems to share. Following the suggestions on how to tell stories that are found in Schwartz's book, have interested students select either a poem to read aloud or a story to tell. Share with another class.

FOLLOW-UP ACTIVITIES FOR INDIVIDUALS OR SMALL GROUPS:

1. Many of the poems in Prelutsky's *The Queen Of Eene* are eating poems. Select one to read, then list all of the foods and/or items eaten. Figure out how much it would cost to eat those items.

2. Read the poems in Prelutsky's *Rolling Harvey down the Hill.* Use any of the friends or situations mentioned and write a short play about it. Working with a committee of classmates share it with the class.

3. Research some of the fiendish creatures and mythical beasts mentioned in Prelutsky's poetry. Make a picture dictionary which defines and describes each.

4. Read and record on tape one of the poems from Prelutsky's *Nightmares.* Select appropriate music or sound effects to use for the background. You may want to have another student create original sound effects to use as you read.

5. *The Random House Book of Poetry for Children* is a collection of other people's poetry that Prelutsky has selected. Each section is introduced with a poem by Prelutsky. Before reading the section "Nature Is," list 10 poetic ideas you would include in defining nature. See if Prelutsky chose any of those you listed. Read the poems he included in this section. If you had been choosing poems for this section and could only choose three, which would they be? List the names of the three and tell why you would select each.

6. Read "Saucy Little Ocelot" from Prelutsky's *The Sheriff of Rottenshot.* Select someone else from the class to read the poem with you, with that person reading every third line—either "Ocelot" or "Saucy Little Ocelot." Share with the class.

7. Read "I've Got An Incredible Headache" in Prelutsky's *The New Kid on the Block.* Make a commercial to read to the class telling how to get rid of a headache that feels like an elephant.

8. Read "The Lurpp is on the Loose" from Prelutsky's *The Snopp on the Sidewalk.* Pretend the Lurpp is on the loose in your school. Write one more verse for the poem, describing its actions.

9. Read "The Gibble" from Prelutsky's *The Snopp on the Sidewalk.* Make up an imaginary animal and describe it, tell where it lives and what it eats in poetry form. Illustrate it and share your poem with the class.

10. Read the poem "Wrimples" in Prelutsky's *The Snopp on the Sidewalk.* Make a list of the things the Wrimples do at your house.

11. Read "The Quossible" from Prelutsky's *The Baby Uggs Are Hatching.* Since the Quossible is described as "big and blundery" and "its face is weird and withery," use scraps and leftovers to make your version of a Quossible. Egg and milk cartons, cereal boxes, toilet paper or plastic wrap rolls, etc. can be used to help create whatever you imagine.

12. Read the poem "The Baby Uggs Are Hatching" from Prelutsky's book of the same title. After each stanza, Prelutsky repeats a rhyme about the baby uggs. Read the rhyme aloud several times, listening for the rhythm, and then write your own rhyme describing the baby uggs to go with the poem.

13. Read either "The Wozzit" from Prelutsky's *The Snopp on the Sidewalk* or "The Snatchits" from *The Baby Uggs Are Hatching.* Think of all the things you have lost mysteriously to a snatchit

or a wozzit; then make a collage picture illustrating what has disappeared.

14. Read "Lumpy Is My Friend" from Prelutsky's *Rolling Harvey down the Hill.* After enjoying the friendship of these two boys, write an initial poem about a good friend of yours. To begin initial poetry, use the three initials of your friend, such as "K.A.R." In three columns write down as many words or phrases that begin with those letters that you can think of that reminds you of that person. For example:

K	A	R
Kindly Katy	Amateur acrobat	Rolls down the hill
Keeping her pet safe	Always smiling	Ribbons flowing from her hair
Kitten showered with love	Artfully walks alone	Rock and rolling

Now select your favorite, most poetic line from each column to combine into a poem.

K	A	R
Kindly Katy	Always smiling	Ribbons flowing from her hair

15. "Philbert Phlurk" in Prelutsky's *The Sheriff of Rottenshot* is an excellent example of using rhyming words in poetry. After reading the poem either select your own or write down the following pairs of rhyming words: day/weigh, write/light, seat/heat, shop/mop, hands/bands. Compete with a friend to see who can think of the most rhyming words for each pair in an amount of time you determine. Have a classmate time you. For additional fun see how many nonsense rhyming words you can create to rhyme with above words, such as phlurk-play to rhyme with day.

16. After reading "The Dance of the Thirteen Skeletons" from Prelutsky's *Nightmares,* put on a shadow show for the class. Use the overhead projector. Cut out a graveyard scene and 13 skeletons from any type of paper, as it becomes opaque on the projector. Ask someone to read the poem for you as you move the skeletons on the projector. Make copies of the refrain "And they'll dance in their bones...." and have your classmates join in the refrain.

Respect for Dogs

STUDENT OBJECTIVES:

- Draw a picture of a favorite dog
- Recall the names of other dogs shared in stories at some earlier time
- Share in writing a class poem about a dog
- Find facts about how to select and care for a dog
- Make a bibliography of dog stories found in the fiction section of the school library media center or public library

RECOMMENDED READING:

Ames, Lee J. *Draw 50 Dogs.* Doubleday, 1981.
    Starting with simple shapes that help develop an eye for proportion, the artist sketches six simple steps for drawing each of the dogs.

Curtis, Patricia. *Cindy, A Hearing Ear Dog.* Illustrated by David Cupp. Dutton, 1981.
    Describes how a dog can be taken from an animal shelter and trained as companion and ear for its deaf owner.

Gardiner, John Reynolds. *Stone Fox.* Illustrated by Marcia Sewall. Crowell, 1980.
    Ten-year-old Willie and his dog Searchlight save Grandpa's farm through a desperate dog race.

Garfield, Leon. *Fair's Fair.* Illustrated by S.D. Schindler. Doubleday, 1983.
    A huge dog lures two orphans from the London streets to an empty mansion where they have the opportunity to prove their worth.

Hess, Lilo. *A Puppy for You.* Scribner's, 1976.
    Appealing photographs capture the reader's attention in this brief but well-written discussion of how to select, care for, and train a puppy.

Hopkins, Lee Bennett. *A Dog's Life.* Illustrated by Linda Rochester Richards. Harcourt Brace Jovanovich, 1983.
    Large black-and-white illustrations help capture the spirit of each of the 23 carefully selected poems about one's "best friend."

Pinkwater, Jill, and Pinkwater, D. Manus. *Superpuppy.* Clarion Books, 1977.

A readable reference to all aspects of selecting, training, caring for, and enjoying a dog.

Stolz, Mary S. *A Dog on Barkham Street.* Illustrated by Leonard Shortall. Harper & Row, 1960.

The bully next door and the longing for a dog are serious problems partially solved for Edward by an absent-minded uncle.

Thomas, Jane Resh. *The Comeback Dog.* Houghton Mifflin, 1981.

The dog Daniel rescued showed no gratitude or affection, but all went well the second time around.

Wallace, Bill. *A Dog Called Kitty.* Holiday House, 1980.

Ricky is afraid of dogs but is almost forced to care for a starving, homeless stray that arrives on the family farm.

GROUP INTRODUCTORY ACTIVITY:

Before reading Leon Garfield's *Fair's Fair,* share with the class the information about him found on the book jacket. It is important that they know he is an English author who lives in London, that he enjoys secrets and mysteries, and that he is fascinated with the England of the eighteenth and nineteenth centuries.

Talk about what the title might mean. Explain that the story is about two orphan children who never had the chance to go to school—so they occasionally use ungrammatical English. See if they hear any incorrect English as the story is read.

Read the story aloud, then talk again about the title. Let children explore more ideas about its meaning. Think of incidents in the story that showed that Jackson believed in the title.

Think about the life of Leon Garfield. What made him able to write this story? Did this take place in modern England? What things in the story or illustrations show them that it took place a long time ago?

Reread the last paragraph of the first page. Talk about the meaning of "Dreadful weather, as hard and bitter as a quarrel." How would they describe the weather? How does it make them feel to read "with snowflakes fighting in the wind"?

Have them try to remember the description of the dog. How big was it? What were its jaws and eyes like? After the class tries to recall Garfield's figurative language, reread the first line of page 3, "Huge: as big as a donkey, nearly, with eyes like streetlamps and jaws like an oven door."

See if the children can recall the dog's name. Was it appropriate? What else might the dog have been named? What were the five character traits that Mr. Chamber wanted in children? What made him sure they had each one? What other character traits can the class think of that the children possessed? Have them document from the story what made them suggest each trait.

FOLLOW-UP ACTIVITIES FOR TEACHER AND STUDENTS TO SHARE:

1. Before reading Gardiner's *Stone Fox,* explain to the class that it is based on a Rocky Mountain legend that was told to the author while he was drinking a cup of coffee at a cafe in Idaho Falls, Idaho.

   After sharing the story, talk about the ending. If the story had another chapter, what might the plot of that chapter be?

   Talk about the title. Why do the children think John Gardiner named it *Stone Fox* instead of *Searchlight* or some other title? What other title might have been used?

   Examine the illustrations. Ask the children why they think the illustrations were in black-and-white rather than color. What ideas and mood does the lack of color help to convey?

   Ask the children to recall the name of the dog in *Fair's Fair.* Now they have two dog friends from books—Growler and Searchlight. See if they can recall others from picture books read in earlier grades (i.e. Angus, Pinkerton, etc.) Suggest that they go to the school library media center and get the books about the dogs they have named so they can recall how each looked. Then, as a class, make a Dog Friends from Books mural, coloring and naming each dog. As they read other dog stories during the unit, add to the mural. If they have problems drawing a certain breed of dog, they may want to examine Ames's *Draw 50 Dogs* to get ideas about body shape.

2. Share poems from Hopkins's *A Dog's Life* with the class. Read "Dog" by Valerie Worth, p. 24, without sharing the illustration. Can anyone guess what breed of dog it is? What clues are given?

   Before sharing "The Ambiguous Dog," by Arthur Guiterman, p. 17, see if anyone can define "ambiguous." Read the poem. Are there more ideas about the meaning of the word? After identifying the meaning, discuss why the poet said the dog was ambiguous. Can anyone think of another action of some dog that could be called ambiguous?

   Read Robert Tyler's "Puppy," p. 16, without revealing the title. Then ask if the poet is describing the action of a young or old dog. Let each child document the reason for his/her decision. Show the illustration. How did the poet describe the garden hose? Why is cobra a wise choice of word?

   Read McLeod's "Lone Dog" and Kuskin's "Full of the Moon." Discuss how the poets' choices of words created two different moods. Which dog would be more fun to play with?

Can any one describe what the early life of "Lone Dog" might have been like?

Share David McCord's "Gone." How did the owner feel? What other things might have happened to the dog? Let someone in the class share an incident in which his or her dog was missing—or think of a way in which a dog might be lost. Using three-line verses with the rhyme scheme McCord used, let the children write a class poem about the lost dog they described.

3. Introduce Stolz's *A Dog on Barkham Street* by reading chapter 4. As a preface, explain to the class that Edward Frost had two problems. The first was the bully, Martin Hastings, who lived next door, and the second was that he wanted a dog but his parents didn't think he was old enough to accept the responsibility.

Read the chapter. Let children characterize Martin. Would they like to be his friend? How might Edward handle him?

Recall one of the scenes in the chapter and let children dramatize it, or already have prepared a scene in play form and let members of the class volunteer to read the scene.

FOLLOW-UP ACTIVITIES FOR INDIVIDUALS OR SMALL GROUPS:

1. Read Stolz's *A Dog on Barkham Street.* Select a short scene, rewrite it in play form and, with the aid of other classmates, read aloud to the class.
2. Read Stolz's *A Dog on Barkham Street.* If Mary Stolz's *The Bully of Barkham Street* (Harper & Row, 1963) is available in your school or public library, read that book also. Try to justify to the class why Martin acted as he did in the chapter read aloud to the class.
3. Read Wallace's *A Dog Called Kitty.* What do you think Ricky will name the new dog? Tell why you selected that name.
4. Read Wallace's *A Dog Called Kitty.* Illustrate your favorite scene. Describe it to the class as you share your illustration.
5. Make a list of all the reasons one might want a dog. Then read Curtis's *Cindy, A Hearing Ear Dog.* Do you now have more ideas to add to the list? If so, place a check by those that *Cindy* made you think of.
6. Read *Cindy, A Hearing Ear Dog.* List the advantages of getting the dog from the animal shelter instead of some other source. What skills was Cindy taught? What is a disadvantage of being a trainer?
7. Use the index of the Pinkwaters' *Superpuppy* and find the answers to the following questions:

- What is a puppy mill? What is wrong with them?
- Why would one want to give a puppy the five-part test?
- What house plants are dangerous for young puppies?
- What is kibble?
- Why was the Doberman pinscher given that name?
- Notice that the book is classified in the 300s. Why?

8. Use Ames's *Draw 50 Dogs* to find a favorite breed of dog and draw a picture of it. Write a paragraph about an adventure you had with this dog. Notice that the book is classified in the 700s. Why?
9. Read Hess's *A Puppy for You.* Make a list of 10 facts you learned about caring for a young dog.
10. Read Hess's *A Puppy for You.* Think of 10 questions you would still like to know about caring for a puppy. Arrange with your teacher or parents to visit a veterinarian and get answers to your questions. Perhaps you can take a tape recorder along so you can play the interview back for your class.
11. Read Thomas's *The Comeback Dog.* Why was the book given that name? Did you blame Daniel for being angry at Lady? Why or why not? What made Daniel change his feelings toward her?
12. Make a bibliography of the fiction books about dogs in the school library media center or public library. Be sure to list author, title, name and location of publisher, and copyright date for each. Select a book from your list to read. Give a book talk about it for the class.
13. Suppose you were editor of a magazine called *All about Dogs.* Make an imaginary table of contents to show what one issue would have in it. Look at *Ranger Rick* and other magazines in the library media center to get ideas.

Enjoy History with Jean Fritz

STUDENT OBJECTIVES:

- Differentiate between biography and fiction
- Interpret what the Bill of Rights meant to our forefathers and what it means today
- Select a President and find interesting facts about him

- Recognize the qualities of people that contributed to their greatness
- Collect facts and stories about his or her own family tree

RECOMMENDED READING:

Fritz, Jean. *And Then What Happened, Paul Revere?* Illustrated by Margot Tomes. Coward, 1973.
An honest, humorous portrayal of Revere's busy life as a silversmith, father, leader of the Sons of Liberty, and secret agent.

———. *The Cabin Faced West.* Illustrated by Feodor Rojankovsky. Coward, McCann & Geoghegan, 1958.
A young pioneer, Ann Hamilton, who learns how to work hard and have fun in the western Pennsylvania wilderness, entertains George Washington.

———. *China Homecoming.* Putnam's, 1985.
Fritz describes her return to China as an adult.

———. *The Double Life Of Pocahontas.* Illustrated by Ed Young. Putnam's, 1983.
The presentation of the roles Pocahontas was forced to play in two different cultures dispels many misconceptions about her.

———. *George Washington's Breakfast.* Illustrated by Paul Galdone. Coward, McCann & Geoghegan, 1969.
George Washington Allen knew many interesting facts about his namesake, President George Washington, but his curiosity led him to find out even more.

———. *Homesick: My Own Story.* Illustrated by Margot Tomes. Putnam's, 1982.
A fictionalized biography of Fritz's childhood in China.

———. *The Man Who Loved Books.* Illustrated by Trina Schart Hyman. Putnam's, 1981.
Through legend and truth, St. Columbia's humble life and devotion to books is depicted.

———. *Stonewall.* Illustrated by Stephen Gammell. Putnam's, 1979.
The conflicting aspects of Jackson's personality from his birth to his death as a Civil War heroic leader are presented.

———. *What's the Big Idea, Ben Franklin?* Illustrated by Margot Tomes. Coward, McCann & Geoghegan, 1976.
Franklin is depicted as a man with a keen and curious mind whose approach to life was based on practicality.

———. *Where Was Patrick Henry on the 29th of May?* Illustrated by Margot Tomes. Coward, McCann & Geoghegan, 1975.
Recounts Henry's growth from a boy who displayed no useful talents to an outstanding orator.

————. *Will You Sign Here, John Hancock?* Illustrated by Trina
Schart Hyman. Coward, McCann & Geoghegan, 1976.
Hancock, one of the richest men in New England, is presented as
a flamboyant show-off who made important contributions to
early history.

BIOGRAPHICAL SOURCES:

For more information on Jean Fritz, see *More Books by More
People,* 172–78; *Something about the Author,* 29:79–84; *Third Book of
Junior Authors,* 94–95; *Twentieth-Century Children's Writers,* 478–80;
Twentieth-Century Children's Writers, 2d ed., 303–04.

GROUP INTRODUCTORY ACTIVITY:

Introduce Jean Fritz as an author who has written both true
accounts of people's lives, classified in the library media center as
biography, and stories based on actual events but classified as fiction.
Share with children the fact that she was born in 1915 in Hankow,
China, where her parents were missionaries. Fritz says that when she
was a child she spent more time with story characters than she did
with actual people. She learned that words could help her go anywhere, but especially to America. In addition to reading, she created
twin imaginary characters, Sue and Margery, who did all the American things she longed to do, like shooting off firecrackers on the
Fourth of July and going to grandma's for Thanksgiving. The family
returned to America when Jean was 13.[3] Show the children the book
Homesick: My Own Story, which tells about her early life in China.
Suggest that someone may want to read it and share with the class
interesting events in Fritz's early life.

Tell the children that in Fritz's biographies, she tries to make the
person she writes about be a real person with many character traits,
both good and bad, with whom we can identify. Never is someone's
life presented as a series of factual events from birth to death,
although many events that happened in that person's life are described.

Show the children the Fritz biographies in which the title is a
question. Have them explore ideas of why that approach to a title
may have been used.

Read aloud *What's the Big Idea, Ben Franklin?.* Call the children's attention to the classification for biography on the spine of the
book. Let the children identify the big ideas Franklin had. What
effects did some of those ideas have upon the lives of people then
and now?

Ask the children if anyone has read another biography about Benjamin Franklin or some other famous person. How was that biography different in the way it was written from this one by Fritz?

Using *Bartlett's Familiar Quotations* or some other proverb source, read several of Franklin's quotes that became famous. Before reading, see if any of the children can remember one they may have heard, such as "Early to bed and early to rise makes a man healthy, wealthy and wise"; "He that riseth late must trot all day"; and "Necessity never made a good bargain." As each proverb is shared, let the children discuss the meaning and explore ideas of what might have made Franklin write that particular proverb.

FOLLOW-UP ACTIVITIES FOR TEACHER AND STUDENTS TO SHARE:

1. Read aloud Fritz's *Where Was Patrick Henry on the 29th of May?* to the class. Let them discuss Henry's contribution to our country. Call attention to the fact that he opposed the proposed constitution of the United States because the freedoms and rights of the individual were not even mentioned. As a result of his passionate concern and that of others, the Bill of Rights was added to the Constitution. Display a copy of the Bill of Rights in the classroom. The first eight amendments address the rights and freedoms of every citizen. Divide the class into groups and have each study one of the eight amendments and write down what that freedom means to them. What specific things does it allow them to do? One person from each group can present their report for the whole class to discuss.

2. Read aloud Fritz's *George Washington's Breakfast*. Let the children suggest why this book is classified as fiction instead of biography. Even though Jean Fritz has created a fictional character, she has given interesting facts in the book about the real George Washington. Let the children discuss the facts that George Washington Allen knew about his namesake. Suggest that each child choose a President to research. Using the library media center card catalog, have them try to locate a biography on that President. If none is available, they can use the encyclopedia to find information. After reading the account, have them list three to five interesting facts about the life of each President selected. As a culminating activity, cook the breakfast that George Washington ate regularly if equipment is available. After eating, each child can share his/her presidential information.

3. Read aloud Fritz's *The Man Who Loved Books*. Let the children discuss evidence that supported the title. St. Columbia was ecstatic to see the new book from Rome. In it he saw highly

decorated capital letters with margins spilling over with designs. As a class project, have the children select a letter of the alphabet or their initials and create their own fancy design. They may want to refer to *The Man Who Loved Books* again to study ideas used by Hyman in preparation for their own imaginative design.

FOLLOW-UP ACTIVITIES FOR INDIVIDUALS AND SMALL GROUPS:

1. After reading Fritz's *And Then What Happened Paul Revere?* pretend you are Paul Revere and record five entries in his imaginary diary as he might have written them. Let the entries show some trait in his character.
2. After reading one of the biographies by Jean Fritz with a question title answer the following:
   Describe the appearance of the main character.
   Describe an action or event that showed the hero's character.
   What was one change that occurred in the attitude or action of the hero to cause him to take his place in history?
   Why was the book given that particular title?
3. After reading Fritz's *What's The Big Idea, Ben Franklin?* refer to *Famous First Facts* (4th ed. H.W. Wilson, 1981) or the *World Almanac and Book of Facts* and make a list or time line of famous, first events that occurred during Franklin's lifetime (1706–90). Were any of those you listed mentioned in Fritz's book?
4. After reading Fritz's *And Then What Happened Paul Revere?* list the things he did to make money. For example, he made picture frames. Be ambitious like Paul Revere and design a cardboard picture frame in which to place your school picture.
5. After reading Fritz's *And Then What Happened Paul Revere?* pretend you are a member of the Sons of Liberty. Write and tape record or read to the class a radio news broadcast as if you were there for the Boston Tea Party.
6. After reading Fritz's biographies about Ben Franklin or Paul Revere, make a mobile illustrating activities from their lives.
7. Read Fritz's *China Homecoming.* Make a list of five problems Fritz encountered on her return to China. List three specific changes she found. What do you feel was the most exciting adventure she had? What made you decide on that particular incident as the most exciting?
8. Read Fritz's *The Double Life of Pocahontas* and Ingri and Edgar Parin d'Aulaire's *Pocahontas* (Doubleday, 1946). Record any differences in fact or characterization evident in the two works.

9. After reading *Where Was Patrick Henry on the 29th of May?* locate on the map the city where he made his famous speech on March 23, 1775. Research in the library media center to find out why he made that speech. What famous line did it contain?

10. Read Fritz's *Homesick: My Own Story.* Tell the class about her problems with the song "God Save The King" and how her family helped her with the solution. Share any other event in her life which you think the class would enjoy.

11. Read Fritz's *Where Was Patrick Henry on the 29th of May?* What made May 29 an important date for him? Select one calendar date and list five memorable events or enjoyable activities that have happened to you on that date.

12. Read Fritz's *Will You Sign Here, John Hancock?* What made his signature on the Declaration of Independence famous? Using a calligraphy pen, if available, practice signing your name in a fancy manner.

13. Read *The Cabin Faced West,* which Jean Fritz wrote after researching the story of her great-great-grandmother, Ann Hamilton. She feels, however, that much of the story is really about her own feelings. Why do you think the book was classified as fiction instead of biography? What famous visitor did Ann have? If you could select someone to visit you today, who would it be? Why?

    Do you know where your great-great-grandparents lived, their names, and their occupations? Be a researcher like Jean Fritz and collect stories or facts about your ancestors. Share an interesting one with the class. If you are interested in further research about your ancestors, refer to Suzanne Hilton's *Who Do You Think You Are? Digging for Your Family Roots.* (Westminster Press, 1976).

14. After reading Fritz's *The Cabin Faced West* imagine that through a time machine you and your family have just gone back in time to when the events of the story took place. Using the book for ideas describe in detail where you are living and tasks that members of the family must do.

15. After reading Fritz's *Stonewall,* think about what you would have done if you had already promised to sell a fish you caught for 50 cents and then someone offered you a dollar for it. Do you agree with Stonewall's decision? Why? Later, as a teacher he wrote, "A man of words and not of deeds is like a garden full of weeds." Describe how this quote can be applied to his life. How does the last paragraph of the book show his men's feelings toward him?

16. Copy and illustrate one of the quotes or proverbs of Benjamin Franklin that was not shared in class.

What Bird Is That?

STUDENT OBJECTIVES:

- Identify some common birds, their nests, and their calls
- Analyze and predict ways the lives of birds can be made more pleasant
- Explain why some books used in the unit are classified in the 500s while others are in the 600s, 700s, and 800s
- Illustrate realistically and find facts about a favorite bird
- Write or participate in writing a bird poem
- Make a bird feeder and prepare appropriate food

RECOMMENDED READING:

Baskin, Tobias. *Hosie's Aviary.* Illustrated by Leonard Baskin. Viking, 1979.
Brief poetic text and watercolor illustrations of a variety of birds.

Brady, Irene. *Owlet, The Great Horned Owl.* Houghton Mifflin, 1974.
Sensitive black-and-white illustrations enhance the details of the life of the great horned owl.

Conklin, Gladys. *If I Were a Bird.* Illustrated by Artur Marokvia. Holiday House, 1965.
Briefly acquaints readers with 27 birds, including their calls and notations of calls.

Crook, Beverly Courtney. *Invite a Bird to Dinner.* Illustrated by Tom Huffman. Lothrop, 1978.
Gives ideas for many types of easy-to-make feeders with titles such as "Lunch in a Bag" and "Egg Carton Cafeteria" as well as recipes for a peanut butter meal, ideas for a summer picnic, and other tasty treats.

Freedman, Russell. *How Birds Fly.* Illustrated by Lorence F. Bjorklund. Holiday House, 1977.
Includes anatomical drawings to help identify how birds fly, including stages of flight.

Gans, Roma. *Bird Talk.* Illustrated by Jo Polseno. Crowell, 1971.
Simple identification of the sound and meaning of a variety of bird calls.

Heilman, Joan Rattner. *Bluebird Rescue.* Lothrop, 1982.
> In addition to describing the nesting and feeding habits of blue-birds, the author describes and illustrates how a nesting box and jug house can be made to encourage the return of this endangered species.

Henry, Marguerite. *Birds at Home.* Illustrated by Jacob Bates Abbott. Hubbard Press, 1972.
> Figurative language and colored illustrations add to the appeal of the factual descriptions of the family life of 21 familiar birds.

Kuskin, Karla. *Dogs and Dragons, Trees and Dreams.* Harper & Row, 1980.
> A collection of poems that give "more word sounds to read aloud, taste, [and] listen to."

McGowen, Tom. *Album of Birds.* Illustrated by Rod Ruth. Rand McNally, 1982.
> Discusses the unique way of life of many birds, including nest building, care of baby birds, and migration.

Zim, Herbert S., and Gabrielson, Ira N. *Birds,* rev. ed. Golden Press, 1956.
> A Golden Nature guide to over 125 American birds, with full-color illustrations and facts about nests, eggs, and habits to aid in identification.

GROUP INTRODUCTORY ACTIVITY:

Introduce the variety of books that will be used in the unit. Explain that those such as Herbert Zim's *Birds* whose primary concern is birds in their natural surroundings are classified in the 500s, or (pure science); those such as Joan Heilman's *Bluebird Rescue* which are concerned with how we can help to save an endangered species are in the 600s (applied science); those that describe how to make bird houses and prepare food, such as Beverly Crook's *Invite a Bird to Dinner,* are in the 700s (the arts); and poems about birds in books such as Karla Kuskin's *Dogs and Dragons, Trees and Dreams* are in the 800s (literature).

Read Baskin's *Hosie's Aviary,* taking time for children to enjoy the full-page watercolor illustrations that extend the brief, haiku-like text. After sharing the book, ask children to recall the bird and the message of the text they like best. Ahead of time, print the hummingbird text on a transparency. Let the children make the sound of a chorus of hummingbirds.

Share again the illustration and text for the egret. As a class, make a similar-style text in which the egret's legs are highlighted.

Talk about the meaning of the brief caption-like text "Freedom's eagle" for Eagle I. What message was Baskin giving?

Show the children illustrations of other birds not included in *Hosie's Aviary*. As a class prepare the kind of text for each that Tobias Baskin might have made. Children may want to follow up by individually writing others.

FOLLOW-UP ACTIVITIES FOR TEACHER AND STUDENTS TO SHARE:

1. Introduce Marguerite Henry's *Birds at Home*. Tell children that this is the same author that wrote *Misty of Chincoteague* and other horse stories for young people. Read the introduction to give the class an idea of the way the author prepared herself to write this book.

   After reading Chapter 1, "Birds to the Rescue," ask children to list all the good things birds do for people. Suggest they start a class list of good things people can do for birds. Add to either list later as they get more ideas during the unit. Someone may want to use the calculator to find out how many insects six million birds can destroy in a year.

   Read Chapter 2, "The Sparrow." Have children make a list of the five most interesting or unusual facts they learned about the sparrow.

   Ask the children to select a favorite bird from the chapters that follow and, without naming the bird, list five interesting or unusual facts about that bird. Entitle the list "What Am I" and after all have prepared their sheet, let them each read theirs aloud and see if others can guess.

   After sharing they may want to replace "Who Am I" with the bird's name, illustrate the page, and make a class book, *Facts about Our Favorite Birds*.
2. Read Conklin's *If I Were a Bird* aloud. Using the notation let the class make the sound for each bird as the brief text is shared. Talk about kinds of feathers. Extend the activity by using a segment of Gans's *Bird Talk* to imagine how some of the calls would sound if the bird were happy, sad, or afraid.

   If available, listen to a few of the birds on the record *Birds on a May Morning* (Droll Yankees, 1963, disc DY-14) or another recording of bird songs. If your community has a local birdwatcher's club, they may be able to share information about bird calls, as well as introduce the pleasures of birdwatching and our responsibility in protecting endangered species.
3. Share "If I Were A..." and "I Have a Lion" from *Dogs and Dragons, Trees and Dreams*. Share the poem "Write about a Radish." As a class, make a new poem "Write about a Bird." Use Kuskin's first verse, substituting "bird" for "radish." Kuskin said her poem seemed to write itself and was very surprising.

When the children finish the bird poem, see if they think it was surprising.

Read "Bugs," p. 2. Let children think of two lines that could follow "I am very fond of birds," and make their own very simple poems. If available, share a portion of the sound film-strip *Poetry Explained by Karla Kuskin,* (Weston Woods, 1980, 43 fr., col., 16 min.) in which she reads poetry from *Dogs and Dragons, Trees and Dreams.*

If available share "The Woodpecker," "The Blackbird" and "Chickadee" from May Hill Arbuthnot's *Time for Poetry* (3d ed., Scott, Foresman, 1968, o.p.). Do not reveal the titles and sub-stitute "little bird" instead of the name in each poem. See if the children can guess the kind of bird read about.

FOLLOW-UP ACTIVITIES FOR INDIVIDUALS OR SMALL GROUPS:

1. After sharing Conklin's *If I Were a Bird,* read *Bird Talk.* Make a list of five birds, write the sound of one call each bird makes, and describe the meaning of each sound listed.
2. Using Zim's *Birds* and/or any other available sources, make a numbered collage of birds' nest illustrations you have drawn and the suitable eggs for each. Try to be as accurate in your illustrations as possible. Give a key to your collage to the teacher. Place the picture on the bulletin board with a list of numbered blanks below it. Let classmates try to fill in the numbered blanks with the appropriate bird for each nest.
3. Read McGowen's *Album of Birds.* Write a paper telling about the differences in the ways various birds care for their young.
4. Read Freedman's *How Birds Fly.* Collect bird feathers, using suggestions found in the book and in Conklin's *If I Were a Bird.* Label each.
5. Read Heilman's *Bluebird Rescue.* Make a bluebird jug house. Share with your class ideas about how they can help to attract bluebirds to your neighborhood and protect birds from being disturbed.
6. Read Brady's *Owlet, The Great Horned Owl.* Share with your class Brady's description of an owlet just after hatching and when he was eight weeks old. Describe for them two dangers owlet faced.
7. Read Crook's *Invite a Bird to Dinner.* Make other "Did You Know That" tips about birds and their eating habits that Crook might have used. Illustrate your list with the wise old owl similar to Huffman's illustration. Share on the bulletin board.

8. Enlist a group of classmates to help you have a bird dinner party like one suggested by Crook in *Invite a Bird to Dinner.* Make the bird feeder as well as preparing the meal for the birds.

Gerald McDermott, The Visual Storyteller

STUDENT OBJECTIVES:

- Tell a story to the class
- "Read" the illustrations in textless pages
- Tape the ending to a story after examining the pictures
- Compare two different versions of a story
- Generalize why some books in the unit are classified in the 200s while others are in the 300s

RECOMMENDED READING:

McDermott, Gerald. *Anansi the Spider.* Holt, Rinehart & Winston, 1972, o.p.
Geometric shapes enhance this tale from the Ashanti of how the Moon appeared in the sky.

———. *Arrow to the Sun.* Viking, 1974.
Caldecott Award–winning Pueblo Indian tale of how the Lord of the Sun sent his spirit to the earth.

———. *Daughter of Earth.* Delacorte, 1984.
Retelling of the Roman myth of Pluto's abduction of Prosperpina.

———. *The Magic Tree.* Holt, Rinehart & Winston, 1973. o.p. Penguin, 1977, pap.
Congo tale of Mavungu, who lost his home and loved ones by breaking his pledge of silence.

———. *The Stonecutter.* Viking, 1975.
Japanese folk tale of Tasaku, the lonely stonecutter whose desire for power makes his wishes unsatisfying.

———. *Sun Flight.* Four Winds, 1980.
Dramatic illustrations highlight the Greek myth of the escape of
Daedalus and Icarus from the Labyrinth, which ends in disaster
after Icarus ignores his father's warning.

BIOGRAPHICAL SOURCES:

For more information on Gerald McDermott, see *Fifth Book of
Junior Authors & Illustrators,* 207–09; *Something about the Author,*
16:199–202.

GROUP INTRODUCTORY ACTIVITY:

Introduce the Japanese folk tale *The Stonecutter* by explaining
that McDermott first created the story as an animated film, then
adapted it to book form. McDermott feels that all his mythical
stories, no matter from what culture they were drawn, have the
common theme of a hero quest in which victory is gained over a
supernatural force and fellow humans are aided.[4] Call attention to the
398.2 classification, indicating the tale was first shared in oral rather
than written form.
Explain to young people that McDermott is very interested in
young people developing visual literacy, enabling them to examine
and understand the meaning of illustrations. Before reading the story,
urge the class to examine the illustrations closely as the story progresses, looking for in-depth meaning in the color and graphic symbols of the book.
After completing the story, ask children to share any concepts or
symbolism they saw in the illustrations. To help them understand the
meanings that one can derive from the illustrations, share the sound
filmstrip *Evolution of a Graphic Concept: The Stonecutter* (Weston
Woods, 1976, 33 fr., col., 7 min.) narrated by the author, in which he
explains how the illustrations evolved.
After sharing the sound filmstrip let the children discuss the new
insights they gained about the message of the illustrations. Re-
examine the illustrations as needed for the discussion.

FOLLOW-UP ACTIVITIES FOR TEACHER AND STUDENTS TO SHARE:

1. Before reading McDermott's *Anansi, The Spider* tell the students
   that this is an Ashanti folktale. Ask if anyone can tell what the
   classification number for the book is, for it too began in the oral

tradition. After establishing the 398.2 classification, discuss the need to examine the illustrations carefully as the story is read to understand the symbolism of the gouache and ink illustrations.

After reading the story ask the students to share their observations from "reading" the illustrations. If the students have problems finding meaning in the geometric shapes, re-examine the illustrations of the six sons. How is each body symbol appropriate for each son's name?

2. Before reading McDermott's *Arrow to the Sun,* call attention to the 398.2 classification. What does that indicate to the students? *Arrow to the Sun* won the Caldecott Medal. Have the students recall the meaning of the medal and name other books that have won the same honor. (See "Caldecott Medal Books" in Chapter 4.)

   Read *Arrow to the Sun* aloud. Urge the children to participate in reading the textless pages signifying the boy's four trials to prove himself. Discuss how color and geometric shapes make the illustrations particularly appropriate for this Pueblo Indian tale.

3. Share McDermott's *Sun Flight* with a small group. Explain that it is a Greek myth, classified in the 200s (religion) because it represents religious mythology. Read the story of Daedalus and Icarus to the textless ending after Daedalus has warned his son not to fly too fast, too high, or too low. Ask each student to examine separately the textless ending and tape their version of that ending.

   Come together as a group and read the ending that Ian Serraillier recorded in *A Fall from the Sky* (Walck, 1965) or some other version of the story. Play the recorded taped endings and discuss how well the illustrations were "read."

FOLLOW-UP ACTIVITIES FOR INDIVIDUALS OR SMALL GROUPS:

1. After sharing McDermott's *The Stonecutter,* find a version of Grimm's *The Fisherman and His Wife* in a collection of Grimm's tales or the version illustrated by Monika Laimgruber (Greenwillow, 1978). Compare the fisherman's wife and Tasaku. In what ways are they alike? Are the endings comparable?
2. After sharing McDermott's *Anansi, The Spider* make new designs that you feel would be appropriate for each of the six sons.
3. After sharing McDermott's *Anansi, The Spider,* go to the library media center and try to find another story about Anansi. If one such as Philip Sherlock's *Anansi, The Spider Man* (Crowell, 1954) is available, read a story and share it with the class.

4. If available, share the sound filmstrip *Anansi, The Spider* (Weston Woods, 1973, 43 fr., col., 10 min.) and *Arrow to the Sun* (Weston Woods, 1975, 36 fr., col., 8:40 min.). Do you prefer the stories in book or sound filmstrip form? Why?

5. Read McDermott's *The Magic Tree,* which was adapted from an animated film. Write a paragraph giving words to the last four illustrated pages with no text which describe Mavungu's reaction to breaking his pledge and his return to his home.

6. Read McDermott's *The Magic Tree.* Describe the meaning of the sentence "His words became as silence."

7. Read McDermott's *The Magic Tree.* List the clues in the text and illustrations that made you know it is a tale of the Congo.

8. Read McDermott's Roman myth, *Daughter of Earth.* Then read *Persephone and the Springtime* by Margaret Hodges (Little, Brown, 1973) or another Greek version of the myth found in the library media center. Make a list of the likenesses and differences in the Roman and Greek versions.

9. Read McDermott's *Daughter of Earth.* Examine the illustrations carefully and write a paragraph describing how they contribute to the telling of the myth.

10. Read McDermott's *Daughter of Earth.* Why was the pomegranate chosen as the fruit to tempt Proserpina? Check in the library media center to find out more about the pomegranate—where it grows, its size and color, and how it is eaten. Check with your grocery store manager to see if pomegranates are ever for sale there.

Friendship

STUDENT OBJECTIVES:

- Enjoy vicariously friendships developed by book characters
- Share feelings about the meaning of friendship
- Role-play situations portraying character development
- Write a follow-up chapter to a book
- Illustrate a scene from a book that depicts friendship
- Dramatize a scene from a book

RECOMMENDED READING:

Billington, Elizabeth. *Part-Time Boy.* Illustrated by Diane De Groat. Warne, 1980.
Through his friendship with Mattie Swenson, Jamie learns many things about himself as well as about the animals he helps Mattie care for.

Doty, Jean Slaughter. *Can I Get There by Candlelight?* Illustrated by Ted Lewin. Macmillan, 1980.
A rusted gate opens the path for an unusual friendship between two girls from different centuries.

Erickson, Russell E. *A Toad for Tuesday.* Illustrated by Lawrence Di Flori. Lothrop, 1974.
When Warton the toad sets out for a winter visit, he is captured by an owl and has until Tuesday to find a way to escape.

Lowry, Lois. *Anastasia at Your Service.* Illustrated by Diane De Groat. Houghton Mifflin, 1982.
Humiliating is the only way to describe Anastasia's situation when she becomes a maid instead of a companion to a very wealthy elderly woman.

Peck, Robert Newton. *Soup.* Illustrated by Charles C. Gehm. Knopf, 1974.
Despite the fact that he plays tricks on his friend Rob, Soup is still the kind of person one wants for a friend.

Shura, Mary Francis. *Chester.* Illustrated by Susan Swan. Dodd, Mead, 1980.
In one short week, Chester, with his unmatched socks, freckles, and unusual family, manages to make new friends and change a neighborhood.

Smith, Doris Buchanan. *Last Was Lloyd.* Viking, 1981.
Even though Lloyd wants to have everyone like him and to have a special friend, he goes out of his way to act dumb and to avoid his classmates.

———. *A Taste of Blackberries.* Illustrated by Charles Robinson. Harper & Row, 1973.
A young boy whose best friend dies suddenly must overcome the sense of loss and guilt he feels.

White, E.B. *Charlotte's Web.* Illustrated by Garth Williams. Harper & Row, 1952.
A beautiful friendship develops between Wilbur the pig and Charlotte, the spider that saves Wilbur's life.

GROUP INTRODUCTORY ACTIVITY:

Before introducing the unit on friendship, make bookmarks for each student in the class with Richard Wilbur's poem "The Opposite of Two" in Jack Prelutsky's *The Random House Book of Poetry for Children.* (Random House, 1983, p. 167) typed on them.

The Opposite of Two
by Richard Wilbur

What is the opposite of two?
A lonely me, a lonely you.

Add to the bookmark the names of book friends that have become the friends of the students in past years, such as George and Martha (in James Marshall's books), Peter and Archie (in the books of Ezra Jack Keats) and Frog and Toad (in books by Arnold Lobel).

Begin the class sharing by giving each student a bookmark. Read the poem and let students discuss its meaning. Ask the students to try to recall who created each of the book friends listed on the bookmark and the name of the book or books in which each can be found. Ask them to recall scenes involving these characters that demonstrated their friendship. Suggest they try to locate the creator of any of those listed that no one could recall.

See if the students can think of other book characters who were friends that could have been included on the bookmark. Perhaps the students may want to find another poem about friendship and make a bookmark listing other book character friends. The bookmarks can be displayed on the class or library media center bulletin board.

Introduce Chester (in *Chester* by Mary Frances Shura) as a book friend they might like to know. Give a book talk identifying key events leading up to page 58 when Chester begins his explanation of why he was late for class. Read aloud pages 58–64, concluding with a statement such as "Discover how Chester's goat helps him become a hero by reading *Chester* by Mary Francis Shura."

After the book talk ask students if they think they would have wanted to be Chester's friend. Why/why not? Can they identify any of Chester's character traits from your talk?

FOLLOW-UP ACTIVITIES FOR TEACHER AND STUDENTS TO SHARE:

1. Read aloud E.B. White's *Charlotte's Web* to the class. As you finish reading each day, urge the students to discuss the traits of the main characters, suggesting scenes or lines from the book that document their decisions.

   Near the end of the book (p. 164) Wilbur asks Charlotte,

"Why did you do all this for me?... I don't deserve it. I've never done anything for you." Let students discuss Charlotte's reply. As a follow-up have the students write a paragraph explaining what friendship means to them.

2. Read aloud *Last Was Lloyd* by Doris Smith to the class. As the reading progresses, allow time for students to discuss such questions as: Why was Lloyd always chosen last? What could he do to change? How did the new girl, Ancil, probably feel when Lloyd ridiculed her? Why does Kirby befriend Lloyd? How was Lloyd's character changed by the end of the story?

   After the story is completed, suggest that students role-play certain scenes so they can experience the feelings of another person. Ask students to recreate certain situations in the story. Chapters 1, 3, 8, 12, and 15 offer excellent situations for role-playing.

FOLLOW-UP ACTIVITIES FOR INDIVIDUALS OR SMALL GROUPS:

1. Read *Soup* by Robert Newton Peck. With the help of as many classmates as are needed, select an incident to dramatize for the class. After sharing the incident let the class discuss whether, based on that scene, they would like Soup for a friend.

2. Read Russell Erickson's *A Toad for Tuesday*. Think about the unique friendship that Warton and George developed. Consider George's statement on page 62, "and I thought that perhaps having a friend might not be too bad. I mean . . . I don't need any friends, of course . . . but . . ." Now write your version of what Warton will tell his brother Morton about his adventure and his new friend George.

3. Read Lois Lowry's *Anastasia at Your Service*. Write a résumé explaining Anastasia's qualifications for the job she desired. The résumé should include her name, address, age, education, work experience, if any, and why she feels she is qualified for this job. Now think of summer employment you would like. Prepare your résumé.

4. Go to the library media center and, using the card catalog, make a bibliography of books you think you might enjoy under the subject heading Friendship. For each book you select, list the author's last name, first name, title, publisher, and date of publication. For example, your bibliography might contain:

   Coutant, Helen. *The Gift.* Knopf, 1983.
   Doty, Jean. *Can I Get There by Candlelight.* Macmillan, 1980.
   Hahn, Mary Downing. *Daphne's Book.* Clarion Books, 1983.

   Select one of the books and read it. Give a book talk about

this book to your classmates emphasizing how the main characters became friends or an incident that shows their friendship.

5. Read *Part-Time Boy* by Elizabeth Billington. Jamie is described as a loner. After reading his story, list five adventures he and Mattie Swenson had as their friendship developed and illustrate what you think would be Jamie's happiest memory of his summer as a part-time boy.

6. Read *Can I Get There by Candlelight?* by Jean Doty. Make a diary entry that Gail might have recorded when the friendship with Hilary, the girl from another century, had to end. Be sure it expresses the loneliness she experienced.

7. Read *Can I Get There by Candlelight?* by Jean Doty. Using your own imagination and pictures from magazines or your own drawings, make a scrapbook that Gail could have made depicting her summer in both worlds.

8. Read Smith's *A Taste of Blackberries*. Losing his friend caused Jamie many guilt feelings as well as sadness and loneliness. Finally, Jamie went out to pick fresh blackberries. Write a paragraph explaining how this helped Jamie.

9. Read Smith's *A Taste of Blackberries*. Write a paragraph explaining the meaning of the title and giving the reason you feel it was chosen for this book. Think of another title for the book. Write the reason you chose it.

10. Keeping in mind the quotation "A friend in need is a friend indeed," read one of the following books: *Part-Time Boy* by Elizabeth Billington, *Can I Get There by Candlelight?* by Jean Doty, or *A Toad for Tuesday* by Russell Erickson. Apply what you think this quote means to the relationship of the friends in the book you selected. Describe incidents in the story that illustrate the relationship of the quote to the book you read.

Meet A.A. Milne's Winnie-the-Pooh

STUDENT OBJECTIVES:

- Participate in the choral reading of poetry
- Reconstruct and dramatize a scene from a story
- Rewrite and demonstrate a game based on the original story
- Recite a favorite poem to the class
- Find, copy, and illustrate a song
- Define the difference between poetry and fiction

RECOMMENDED READING:

Milne, A.A. *The House at Pooh Corner.* Illustrated by Ernest H. Shepard. Dutton, 1961, c. 1928.
Pooh and Christopher Robin become acquainted with Tigger and continue their adventures with Rabbit and their other friends.

———. *Now We Are Six.* Illustrated by Ernest H. Shepard. Dutton, 1961, c.1927.
Poems about the thoughts and adventures of Christopher Robin, Pooh, and friends.

———. *Pooh's Alphabet Book.* Illustrated by Ernest H. Shepard. Dutton, 1975.
The alphabet is derived from 26 illustrated quotes from *Winnie-the-Pooh* and *The House at Pooh Corner.*

———. *The Pooh Story Book.* Illustrated by Ernest H. Shepard. Dutton, 1965.
Three stories from *Winnie-the-Pooh* and *The House at Pooh Corner* with new full-color illustrations.

———. *When We Were Very Young.* Illustrated by Ernest H. Shepard. Dutton, 1961, c. 1924.
The 44 poems which Milne described as "friends" of Christopher Robin's include the familiar "Missing," "Buckingham Palace," and "The King's Breakfast."

———. *Winnie-the-Pooh.* Illustrated by Ernest H. Shepard. Dutton, 1974, c. 1926.
Pooh, Christopher Robin, and Piglet have many adventures with their friends Kanga, Baby Roo, and Eeyore.

BIOGRAPHICAL SOURCES:

For more information on A.A. Milne (deceased), see *The Junior Book of Authors,* 2d ed., 221–23; *Twentieth-Century Children's Writers,* 892–96; *Twentieth-Century Children's Writers,* 2d ed., 546–49; *Yesterday's Authors of Books for Children,* 174–81.

GROUP INTRODUCTORY ACTIVITY:

Before introducing the A.A. Milne books, share with the class that Milne was an English author and poet. His two poetry and two fiction books for children were published over a five-year period when his own son Christopher was small. Christopher and his toys—Pooh, Piglet, Tigger, Eeyore, Kanga and Roo—were Milne's inspiration.[5]

Read Chapter 2 of *Winnie-the-Pooh,* "In which Pooh Goes Visiting and Gets into a Tight Place" to the class. After reading, have the children reconstruct the events of the scene and then let three volunteers dramatize it. Have Pooh's tra-la-la humming song prepared on a transparency or large sheet of paper so the entire class can "sing-song" it as an introduction to the scene.

Tell the class that there is a *Pooh Song Book* (Dutton, 1961), but that it is out of print. Perhaps a copy can be located, but it would also be fun to make their own. One section of the song book is "The Hums of Pooh." If they would copy each of the hum poems from *Winnie-the-Pooh* and *The House at Pooh Corner* and illustrate them, they can use them as hum songs even if they do not have H. Fraser-Simon's music from the out-of-print song book.

See if the class can figure out the classification of a song book (700s, the arts). Tell them the class will also be sharing Milne's poetry books, which are classified 821 for English poetry. *Winnie-the-Pooh* and *The House at Pooh Corner* are classified as fiction. Have them recall the meaning of the word "fiction."

FOLLOW-UP ACTIVITIES FOR TEACHER AND STUDENTS TO SHARE:

1. Read Milne's *Winnie-the-Pooh* aloud to the class. After reading chapters such as "In Which Eeyore Looses a Tail and Pooh Finds One" and "Eeyore Has a Birthday," the students may want to recall the conversation and dramatize it. Urge the students to copy and illustrate Pooh's songs after the book is read.

2. Read aloud Milne's *The House at Pooh Corner.* After reading Chapter 2, "In Which Tigger Comes to the Forest and Has Breakfast" have the students recreate each of the scenes. Then, using different students for the characters in each scene, dramatize the search for an appropriate breakfast.

3. Introduce Milne's poetry collection, *When We Were Very Young.* Read "Shoes and Stockings" as a choral, dividing the class in half and having each say "Hammer, Hammer, Hammer" and "Chatter, Chatter, Chatter" as you point to the group at the appropriate time. Then share "Hoppity" as a choral with the same groups.

   Now share "Rice Pudding" as a choral. Be sure the two groups see that "What" is the emphasis for the first group and "is" for the second group's question.

   Read "Little Bo-Peep and Little Boy Blue" aloud. Then

have the class make some nursery rhyme poems together, beginning with such questions as: "What is that on your thumb, Little
Jack Horner?" and "Where are your children, Old Woman?."

Tell the class that you are placing both *When We Were
Very Young* and *Now We Are Six* on the reading table so they
can read other poems as they wish. They may want to share
their favorite with the class as time allows.

FOLLOW-UP ACTIVITIES FOR INDIVIDUALS OR SMALL GROUPS:

1. Read Milne's *The Pooh Story Book,* which includes three chapters from *Winnie-the-Pooh* and *The House at Pooh Corner.* After
   examining these books, select the three chapters you would use
   if making a Pooh Story Book and give the reason why you chose
   each.
2. Read *Pooh's Alphabet Book.* Get some classmates to help you
   make a new alphabet book, selecting other quotes from the
   Milne stories and poems to highlight the letters. Illustrate each
   page.
3. Dutton published *The Pooh Cook Book* by Virginia H. Ellison in
   1969, but it is now out of print. Check your school library
   media center to see if it is available. Look at the recipes. Since
   Pooh liked honey, get a group of your classmates to help find
   recipes using honey. Copy each on a sheet of paper, illustrate
   with Pooh eating or making the food, and quote a sentence or
   paragraph from one of the books in which honey is mentioned.
   Be sure to identify book and page, and let each recipe have a
   different quote. When the Pooh's Honey Recipe Book is finished, someone may want to make one of the recipes and share
   with the class.
4. Read "Forgiven" from *Now We Are Six* and "Missing" from
   When We Were Very Young. List the ways the two poems are
   alike. In what ways are they different?
5. Read "Happiness" from Milne's *When We Were Very Young.*
   Make up your own Happiness poem using the form of only one
   to three words to a line. End with "And that—(Said ———)
   Is—that."
6. With a few of your classmates, plan a Pooh party for the rest of
   the class. Make Pooh invitations, play appropriate games such as
   "Pin the Tail on the Donkey," or share scenes from the books.
   Perhaps one of the honey recipes from the Pooh Cook Book can
   be used to make refreshments. Dutton published *The Pooh Party
   Book* by Virginia E. Ellison in 1969, but it is now out of print.
   Check your school library media center to see if it is available
   for additional ideas.

7. A set of three Pooh posters were produced by Dutton in 1972–75. See if they are available in your school media center. If so, share them with the class. If not, perhaps you and some of your classmates would each like to draw and paint or color a large picture illustrating a favorite scene from one of the books. Display them in the classroom or media center.

8. After hearing Milne's *Winnie-the-Pooh* and *The House at Pooh Corner,* make a large map or ask your classmates to help you make a mural map locating houses and spots where adventures took place. Draw a picture of each spot and label the location and adventure.

9. If available, listen to the record *When We Were Very Young,* (Caedmon, n.d., disc TC1356) read by Judith Anderson. Listen particularly for "The King's Breakfast." Was it more fun to hear her read it than to read it yourself? Give a reason for your answer.

10. Read "Sand-between-the-Toes" from Milne's *When We Were Very Young.* Add a verse about another experience they might have had such as picking up shells or building a castle of sand.

11. Read "Cherry Stones" from Milne's *Now We Are Six.* Play the seed game "Tinker Tailor, Soldier, Sailor, Rich Man, Poor Man, Ploughboy, Thief" with the seeds from an apple or orange by repeating each occupation in order as you count the seeds. What occupation was repeated for the last seed? As Milne did in the poem, make up eight new occupations. Now play the seed game again with another apple or orange, using the new occupations. What occupation was last this time?

Animal Books by Jack Denton Scott

STUDENT OBJECTIVES:

- Differentiate fact and fiction about common animals
- Increase vocabulary about animals
- Research class questions about specific animals
- Develop concern about endangered species of animals
- Recognize the value of photographs in gaining information about animals

RECOMMENDED READING:

Scott, Jack Denton. *The Book of the Goat.* Illustrated by Ozzie Sweet. Putnam's, 1979.
The goat, one of humankind's oldest animal friends, is presented as intelligent, proud, and friendly.

———. *The Book of the Pig.* Illustrated by Ozzie Sweet. Putnam's, 1981.
The pig is depicted through text and photographs as not only intelligent and adaptable but capable of affection for human beings.

———. *Canada Geese.* Illustrated by Ozzie Sweet. Putnam's, 1976.
The geese are shown beginning their migration in northern Canada, going South for survival, and returning to reproduce their young.

———. *Gulls of Smuttynose Island.* Illustrated by Ozzie Sweet. Putnam's, 1977.
Survival for the gulls is uppermost as they mate and raise their young.

———. *Island of Wild Horses.* Illustrated by Ozzie Sweet. Putnam's, 1977.
Tells about Assateague Island, home to the horses who arrived mysteriously years ago and have survived in the soggy marshes.

———. *Loggerhead Turtle, Survivor from the Sea.* Illustrated by Ozzie Sweet. Putnam's, 1974.
Observes the female loggerhead, who traverses hundreds of miles to lay her eggs on a strange beach.

———. *Moose.* Illustrated by Ozzie Sweet. Putnam's, 1981.
Photographs and text majestically present the moose as a master of its environment.

———. *The Submarine Bird.* Illustrated by Ozzie Sweet. Putnam's, 1980.
Examines the cormorant's survival through the ages.

BIOGRAPHICAL SOURCES:

For more information on Jack Denton Scott, see *Something about the Author,* 31:149–52.

GROUP INTRODUCTORY ACTIVITY:

Share with the children the concept that as Scott traveled around the world more than a dozen times, he developed a special respect for animals. He conveys this in each of his books through text and the photographs by Ozzie Sweet. He says that in *The Book of the Goat* he tried to make right some of the old negative misconceptions about the goat so that children would respect this useful animal.[6]

Before sharing Scott's *The Book of the Goat* introduce a goat puppet or stuffed animal. Arouse the children's curiosity by having them discuss what they know about goats. The goat puppet or stuffed goat can whisper facts to you or tell the class when false information or myth is given. Introduce *The Book of the Goat* as a factual book about goats. See if anyone in the class can tell why *The Book of the Goat* and *The Book of the Pig* are classified in the 600s (applied sciences), while *Moose, Canada Geese,* and others are classified in the 500s (pure sciences). Read *The Book of the Goat* aloud, being sure to share the photographs. Then have children share interesting facts they have learned. List each fact on butcher paper and suggest that some of the class may want to look up additional information about goats and add to the list. Let the children discuss why photographs were an appropriate medium for this informational book.

FOLLOW-UP ACTIVITIES FOR TEACHER AND STUDENTS TO SHARE:

1. Read Scott's *Loggerhead Turtle, Survivor from the Sea* to the class. Have them recall the five species of sea turtles: loggerheads, rudleys, hawksbills, green turtles, and leatherbacks. Divide the class into groups to do further research on these turtles to determine their location, the foods they eat, and facts about their life cycle. Then, after each group shares its findings, discuss how these turtles are alike and different.

2. Before sharing Scott's *The Book of the Pig* with the class, ask the students to give facts or myths about pigs. List these statements on the blackboard. As you read the book and share the photos, cross out any statements which the children identify as wrong. For example, someone may have said that pigs are dumb creatures; yet the book indicates that pigs are the smartest of all farm animals and are more intelligent than dogs. After the book is read, have children give facts they have learned about pigs to add to the blackboard list. If possible, follow up the session with a field trip to a pig farm or have a piglet visit the classroom.

3. Entice the class to do research on the deer family by sharing information and photos from Scott's *Moose*. Students should

enjoy the narration and photos on pages 12–17, showing the majestic moose in his natural environment. Pages 48–53 are also good to share. Let children discuss what they would like to know about the deer family. Then divide them into groups to research the questions they asked, being sure to include various members of the deer family and problems the deer have in obtaining food in the national parks during the winter. Let children share their research findings.

4. Read Scott's *Canada Geese* to the class. Then invite a ranger, wildlife conservationist, or someone interested in birdwatching and protecting endangered species to talk to the class.

FOLLOW-UP ACTIVITIES FOR INDIVIDUALS OR SMALL GROUPS:

1. Reread Scott's *The Book of the Goat* after the media specialist has shared it. List all the new words you found that describe the actions or personality of a goat. Include such words as "gambol," "caper," "aggressive," "submissive," "curious," and "placid." Define each word and use it correctly in a sentence or define the word and draw a picture of a goat that demonstrates the word defined.

2. Reread Scott's *Loggerhead Turtle, Survivor from the Sea.* Draw and label a diagram of a turtle's body.

3. Reread Scott's *Loggerhead Turtle, Survivor from the Sea.* Find 10 of the following words:

adroitly	genera
amiable	haphazard
antediluvian	omnivorous
carapace	pilgrimage
cavorting	precariously
disposition	pugnacious
enigmatic	survival

Define each word and copy the sentence in which each word was used.

4. Read Scott's *The Submarine Bird.* Write a comparison of the cormorant and the anhinga bird.

5. Read Scott's *The Submarine Bird.* Then try to find information on how the Chinese and Japanese trained the cormorant to fish for them. Share your findings with the class.

6. Read Scott's *The Submarine Bird.* Draw a map showing the areas where the cormorant can be found.

7. Read Scott's *The Submarine Bird.* Choose 10 of the following words from the book:

anhinga	ornithologists
elongate	permeable
fledglings	plumage
foraging	raucous
incubate	rookeries
intimidation	vascular

    Write a definition for each and copy the sentence in which Scott used each word.

8. Reread Scott's *Canada Geese* after the teacher has read it to the class. You learn that the geese use four flyways: the Atlantic, the Mississippi, the Central, and the Pacific. Draw a map or make a transparency showing each of these flyways. Share with the class.

9. Reread Scott's *Canada Geese* after the teacher has read it to the class. Choose 10 of the following words:

biological	precocial
contour	predator
gosling	preening
meteorologist	ritualistic
migration	tundra
navigator	vulnerable

    Write their definitions and copy the sentence in which Scott used each word.

10. After reading Scott's *Island of Wild Horses* list 15 facts you learned about the wild horses of Assateague.

11. Read Scott's *The Gulls of Smuttynose Island.* Choose 10 words Scott used that were new to you. Find and copy their definitions and give the sentence Scott used as an example of each.

Threes in Folktales

STUDENT OBJECTIVES:

- Read folktales from various countries and identify unique characteristics indicating their origin
- Compare two or more versions of the same tale
- Identify characteristic elements of a folktale
- Tell a folktale to the class
- Locate the section of the library media center where one can browse for folktales
- Recall folktales using the "three" motif

RECOMMENDED READING:

Afanas'ev, Aleksandr. "The Three Kingdoms" in *Russian Fairy Tales.* Illustrated by Alexander Alexeiff. Pantheon, 1975, c. 1945.
The youngest of three sons sent to find brides for themselves finds three kingdoms with a maiden in each.

Carew, Jon. *The Third Gift.* Illustrated by Leo and Diane Dillon. Little, Brown, 1974.
The Jubas had the gifts of work and beauty, but the best gift of all was the third—imagination.

Courlander, Harold. "Three Fast Men" in *The King's Drum and Other African Stories.* Illustrated by Enrico Arno. Harcourt Brace Jovanovich, 1962.
The feats of three men who have worked and hunted become highly exaggerated when their story is told.

Gag, Wanda. "The Three Feathers" in *Three Gay Tales from Grimm.* Coward, 1943.
The third and youngest son of the king completes three tasks with the help of Mother Toad, wins the hand of the fair maiden, and inherits the throne.

Grimm, Jakob, and Grimm, Wilhelm. *The Devil with the Three Golden Hairs.* Illustrated by Nonny Hogrogian. Knopf, 1983.
To regain his bride, a young man is sent to fetch three golden hairs from the devil.

Haviland, Virginia. "The Foolish Wife And Her Three Foolish Daughters" in *Favorite Fairy Tales Told in Greece.* Illustrated by Nonny Hogrogian. Little, Brown, 1970.
A priest who became impatient with the foolishness of his wife and daughters left home, only to find even more foolishness in the world.

———. "The Three Goslings" in *Favorite Fairy Tales Told in Italy.* Illustrated by Evaline Ness. Little, Brown, 1965.
Three goslings meet a big wolf as they set out on a journey into the world.

Jeffers, Susan. *Three Jovial Huntsmen.* Bradbury Press, 1973.
In this Mother Goose rhyme, three men go hunting all day long but can find nothing.

Minard, Rosemary. "Three Strong Women: A Tall Tale From Japan" in *Womenfolk and Fairy Tales.* Illustrated by Suzanna Klein. Houghton Mifflin, 1975.
A famous wrestler who called himself Forever-Mountain meets three strong women who make him reflect on what they think a strong man should be.

———. *The Three Wishes.* Illustrated by Paul Galdone. McGraw-Hill, 1961.
The old woodsman wastes the three wishes he receives for saving an oak tree.

GROUP INTRODUCTORY ACTIVITY:

Suggest to the class that the motif of number three is found in folklore around the world. Such ideas as three tasks or ordeals, three aspects of nature, three events, three objects, three magical elements, or three brothers or sisters are common.

Have the students recall the folktales they know that have the number three in the title or in aspects of the story. List the titles they recall on butcher paper. Suggest that as they think of more folktales that utilize the number three, they may add those titles to the list.

Ask the students if anyone can recall the section of the library media center in which the folktales they named are found. Reinforce that folklore, 398, is part of the larger category of social science, the 300 classification.

Read aloud the Grimm Brothers' tale *The Devil with the Three Golden Hairs,* illustrated by Nonny Hogrogian. Urge the students to look at the illustrations carefully as the story is read. After sharing the story, discuss the motif of the number three and other significant aspects of the tale through asking questions such as: How many and what tasks were performed? Was the number three introduced in any other way? What was the significance of the frogs and the toads introduced in the text and found in the illustrations? Were there other animals in the illustrations that had significance in the story?

Remind the class that as they read other folktales utilizing the number three, they should add them to the butcher paper list. Have the students guess how many titles they think the list will have at the end of the unit.

FOLLOW-UP ACTIVITIES FOR TEACHER AND STUDENTS TO SHARE:

1. Before reading to the class "The Three Feathers" in Gag's *Three Gay Tales from Grimm* suggest that all folktales have certain aspects in common. The introduction, giving setting, characters, and conflict, is always brief. A small number of incidents lead to the climax. The ending of the story comes soon after the climax. Urge the students to think of these characteristics as the story is read. After hearing the story, have the students discuss whether the setting, characters, and conflict were quickly introduced; whether there were few or many main incidents leading to the climax; and whether the story ended quickly or long after the climax. In what ways was the number three used in the story?
2. Read aloud the tall tale "Three Fast Men" in Courlander's *The King's Drum....* Let the children discuss whether the story followed the common characteristics of folktales identified in the discussion of "The Three Feathers." Were there any elements of the story that made the students know it was an African tale? Encourage the students to discuss what really happened and why each man exaggerated his story. Have the students identify the exaggerations in the story of each man that make it a tall tale.
3. After reading aloud "The Three Goslings" in Haviland's *Favorite Tales Told in Italy* see if the students can think of another story that is similar to this one. If someone suggests "The Three Pigs," have them identify things the two stories have in common. If available, read aloud the story "Old Sow and the Three Shoats" from Richard Chase's *Grandfather Tales* (Houghton Mifflin, 1948, p. 81–87). Have the students compare it with "The Three Goslings."
4. Before reading *The Three Wishes,* tell the class that it is classified as fiction but it is set in ancient Africa and draws on folklore themes. Read the story *The Three Wishes,* illustrated by Paul Galdone, to the class. Have the students recall how the old man used his wishes. Were the choices he made wise? Now have each student write down three wishes. Let them discuss what they wished for and why. Have them suggest better wishes they could have made. Read the poem "I Keep Three Wishes Ready"

by Annette Wynne in Nancy Larrick's *Piping down the Valleys Wild* (Delacorte Press, 1968). As a follow-up have the students write down the three wishes they would carry in their pocket.

5. After reading Carew's *The Third Gift* and sharing the illustrations, lead a discussion about the gifts the Jubas received. Involve the students by asking them to explain the significance of each gift and the role of the gift bearer. Why was the last gift of imagination so important to the tribe then and now? Turn back to the illustrations of Leo and Diane Dillon. What significance did the colors that indicated the gifts have?

6. After reading "The Three Kingdoms" in Afanes'ev's *Russian Fairy Tales* to the class, have the students identify any aspects that made them know it was a Russian tale. Discuss the quest on which the three sons were sent and the events that happened to each. In what ways was the motif of three evident? The ending involved forgiving the brothers for what they had done. Discuss what events the younger brother could have changed. How would these have changed the ending? Have the class think of other folktales whose endings involved forgiving brothers or sisters for wrongdoing toward one member of the family.

FOLLOW-UP ACTIVITIES FOR INDIVIDUALS OR SMALL GROUPS:

1. After reading "Three Strong Women" in Minard's *Womenfolk and Fairy Tales* record at least two exaggerations that show the strength of each of the three women. Identify how strong Forever Mountain became through the efforts of the three women. What things made you know the story came from Japan?

2. Read *Womenfolk and Fairy Tales*. Record the names of five other folktales besides "Three Strong Women" with strong female characters.

3. Read a folktale from three different countries. List one clue from each story that would help you identify the country from which each story came. Locate those countries on a map.

4. Read Susan Jeffers's version of *Three Jovial Huntsmen*. Nursery rhymes are part of the folklore of the world. Find another nursery rhyme involving the number three. Copy the rhyme, making an illustration for each line. Share your illustrations with the class.

5. Read Susan Jeffers's version of *Three Jovial Huntsmen*. Study the illustrations. Many animals are hidden. List the names of all the animals the huntsmen could have seen.

6. Reread Carew's *The Third Gift* after it has been shared by the class. Use your imagination now. What if you were sent to the

top of the Nameless Mountain? What gift would you find? What message could it bring to inspire the tribe?

7. Reread either "The Three Feathers" in Gag's *Three Gay Tales from Grimm* or "The Three Kingdoms" in Afanes'ev's *Russian Fairy Tales*. List all the times the number three occurred in either story.

8. After reading "The Foolish Wife and Her Three Foolish Daughters" in *Favorite Fairy Tales Told in Greece,* list the lessons that could be learned from the story.

9. Use the library media center card catalog to find a folktale with the number three in the title. Read and practice telling the story until you can tell the story to the class without the help of the book.

10. Use the library media center card catalog to find a folktale with the number three in the title. Read the story and see if it has the characteristics of folktales. Identify the setting, main characters, and conflict. Were these three elements introduced on the first page of the story? Record the incidents that led to the climax. What was the climax? Did the ending occur soon after the climax?

Culminating Activities after Fourth Grade/Fifth Grade

Discuss with the entire class the literature experiences they have shared. What authors and illustrators do they recall? What books did each person named write or illustrate? What book characters do the students remember?

What literature activities did the students particularly enjoy? Do the students remember any facts about specific authors or illustrators?

Have students recall the general Dewey Decimal classifications for myths, folklore, pure science, applied science, and poetry. Have available a group of books in these classifications. Tell the students each title and describe each book. See if they can identify in which hundred the book is classified.

Share poems that were memorized. What is meant by alliteration? What is meant by colloquial language? What are the characteristics of a tall tale? What is a myth?

Discuss new discoveries about the habits of animals gained through library media center research. What is meant by an endangered species?

REFERENCES

1. D.L. Kirkpatrick, ed., *Twentieth-Century Children's Writers* (New York: St. Martin's Press, 1978), pp. 463–65.

2. Sally Holmes Holtze, ed., *Fifth Book of Junior Authors & Illustrators* (New York: H.W. Wilson, 1983), p. 252.

3. Doris de Montreville and Donna Hill, eds., *Third Book of Junior Authors* (New York: H.W. Wilson, 1972), p. 95.

4. Holtze, p. 208.

5. Kirkpatrick, p. 895.

6. Anne Commire, ed., *Something about the Author* (Detroit: Gale Research, 1983), vol. 31, p. 152.

Chapter 6
Fifth Grade and Up

Observing Nature with Jean Craighead George

STUDENT OBJECTIVES:

- List information about Alaska discovered from reading a fiction book
- Create a diary account of the events that might follow the ending of a book
- Compare the plots and characters in books by the same author
- Discuss ecological problems introduced in a book
- Analyze why a specific title was given to a book
- Relate the experiences of an author to the plot and theme of his/her books
- Examine the impact of figurative language in establishing setting

RECOMMENDED READING:

George, Jean Craighead. *The Cry of the Crow.* Harper & Row, 1980.
As Mandy cares for a baby crow without telling her father of its existence, she develops an understanding of family love and responsibility.

———. *Hook a Fish, Catch a Mountain.* Dutton, 1975.
Thirteen-year-old Spinner accidentally catches a cutthroat trout and becomes involved with her cousin in an attempt to solve the mystery of its origin and survival.

————. *Julie of the Wolves.* Illustrated by John Schoenherr. Harper & Row, 1972.
A pack of Artic wolves help Julie, an Alaskan girl, survive in the Arctic wilderness. A 1973 Newbery Award winner.

————. *My Side of the Mountain.* Dutton, 1959.
The diary account of Sam Gribley's self-sufficient life in the Catskill Mountains with only animals for companions.

————. *One Day in the Alpine Tundra.* Illustrated by Walter Gaffney-Kessell. Crowell, 1984.
Recounts the reactions of animals, plants, and a boy to the arrival of a storm.

————. *One Day in the Desert.* Illustrated by Fred Brenner. Crowell, 1983.
Animals and a Papago Indian family survive the desert heat and storm.

————. *The Talking Earth.* Harper & Row, 1983.
Forced to live alone in the Florida Everglades because of a destructive fire, Billie Wind, a Seminole Indian girl, finds the meaning of the old legends about earth's messages.

————. *Who Really Killed Cock Robin?* Dutton, 1971.
An ecology-conscious town becomes widely concerned with the death of a family of robins; the solution to the mystery involves a study of the upset balance of nature.

————. *The Wild, Wild Cookbook.* Illustrated by Walter Kessell. Crowell, 1982.
Describes how to locate edible wild plants in each of the four seasons and gives simple recipes for preparing them.

————. *The Wounded Wolf.* Illustrated by John Schoenherr. Harper & Row, 1978.
Wounded young Roko thwarts death with the help of the leader wolf.

BIOGRAPHICAL SOURCES:

For more information on Jean Craighead George, see *More Books by More People,* 178–87; *More Junior Authors,* 99–100; *Something about the Author,* 2:112–14; *Twentieth-Century Children's Writers,* 507–10; *Twentieth-Century Children's Writers,* 2d ed., 318–20.

GROUP INTRODUCTORY ACTIVITY:

Introduce Jean Craighead George as an author who grew up being concerned about the balance of nature and the responsibility of people in not upsetting that balance. Her father was an entomologist for the Department of Agriculture in Washington, DC. With her brothers, who are now ecologists, she was introduced to wildlife through trips into the wilderness to study animals and plants in their natural habitats. Hiking trails, cooking wild plants, and paddling canoes are part of her childhood memories. Summers were enjoyed at the old family home in Craighead, Pennsylvania.[1]

As indicated in the Harper & Row brochure, *Jean Craighead George,* she was a reporter for *The Washington Post,* and as an author of magazine articles for *Reader's Digest,* she traveled extensively throughout the United States.

She and her three children have kept 173 pets, besides dogs and cats, in her present home in Chappaqua, New York. She says, "Most of these wild animals depart in the autumn when the sun changes their behavior and they feel the urge to migrate or go off alone. While they are with us, however, they become characters in my books, articles and stories." Information for *Julie of the Wolves,* a 1973 Newbery Medal Winner, and *The Wounded Wolf* was obtained when she and her son Luke spent time studying wolves and the tundra at the Arctic Laboratory at Barrow, Alaska.[2]

Read *The Wounded Wolf* to the class, being sure to share the black-and-white illustrations by John Schoenherr. At the close of the story, ask the students to describe the mood of the Alaskan tundra. How did they gain those feelings?

Reread the first page. Talk about the impact of figurative language such as "a massive spine of rocks and ice" and "dawn strikes the ridge" in setting the mood. Continue the story after asking the students to stop the rereading each time they hear poetic language that affects the mood.

FOLLOW-UP ACTIVITIES FOR TEACHER AND STUDENTS TO SHARE:

1. Before reading *Who Really Killed Cock Robin?* aloud to the class, share with them the author's note that the book was inspired by a little girl who brought a dying robin to Jean George's house to find out what was wrong with it. She became involved in discovering the robin's killer and modeled the setting of the story on an actual town with ecological problems. After reading the story, make a list of the positive advances Saddleboro made. Again, examine the local community. What could young people do? If possible, share Jean George with other upper-grade classes and organize a clean-up campaign in the schoolyard, park, etc. Ask a local person such as a county extension agent, high school science teacher, or college professor to discuss ecological balance with the class. Write a letter to the editor of the local paper enlisting community concern.

2. Before introducing *Julie of the Wolves,* recall with the students the information about Jean George shared by the library media specialist in the introductory activity. Continue with information about her by telling the students that her inspiration for *Julie of the Wolves* evolved from two specific events during the summer she spent studying wolves and the tundra at the Artic Research Laboratory of Barrow, Alaska: "One was a small girl walking the vast and lonesome tundra outside of Barrow; the other was a magnificent alpha male wolf, leader of a pack in Mount McKinley National Park.... They haunted me for a year or more as did the words of one of the scientists at the lab: "If there ever was any doubt in my mind that a man could live with the wolves, it is gone now." She describes the wolves as "truly gentlemen, highly social, and affectionate."[3] Before reading pages 5 through 13 of *Julie of the Wolves* to the class, ask them to listen for three things: information about Alaska, character traits of Julie, and figurative language such as that found in *The Wounded Wolf.* Discuss their findings after the excerpt is shared. Urge them to continue thinking of those three aspects as they continue reading the book. After several students have read the story, discuss the book with them.

3. Introduce George's *The Talking Earth* by reading the first chapter, "Lost Day Slough." Then discuss similarities and differences already revealed between the character of Billie Wind and Julie of *Julie of the Wolves.* In what ways does it appear the plots *may* have similarities? Anticipate some of the problems Billie Wind may have. Will she find the answer to her quest? How? Urge them to complete the book. After several students have read the story, continue with those children a group discussion of theme, characterization, and suspense which the story creates. Is the story believable?

FOLLOW-UP ACTIVITIES FOR INDIVIDUALS OR SMALL GROUPS:

1. Read George's *My Side of the Mountain.* Make a list of foods such as acorn pancakes that Sam prepared. Check for the recipes in *The Wild, Wild Cookbook.* Share one recipe that sounds good with the class and, if possible, prepare it.

2. Read George's *My Side of the Mountain.* Make a daily entry for the diary Sam kept after the family built their house on the Gribley land.

3. Read George's *Julie of the Wolves.* If you had been a member of the Newbery committee, would you have given it the award in 1973? Justify reasons for your decisions.

4. Read George's *Julie of the Wolves*. Write the letter Julie might have written to Amy after returning to Kapugen, recounting her adventures.

5. Read George's *Julie of the Wolves*. Seek additional information about lemmings in the library media center such as that found in James Newton's *The March of the Lemmings* (Crowell, 1976). Share information about their habits with the class.

6. After reading George's *Julie of the Wolves*, read Scott O'Dell's *Island of the Blue Dolphins* (Houghton Mifflin, 1960), also a Newbery winner. Record the ways Julie and Karana were alike and different. Justify each answer.

7. Read George's *The Cry of the Crow*. Were you expecting the ending? Were you satisfied with it? Why or why not? Think of another ending Jean George might have used.

8. Read George's *Hook a Fish, Catch a Mountain*. Write a paragraph discussing why the book was given that title. What else might it have been named? Is your title as catchy and meaningful as the actual title? Why or why not? What was the theme of the book?

9. Examine George's *The Wild, Wild Cookbook*. How many recipes use edible foods available in your area? Copy the recipes and make a display of the plants involved. If possible, cook one of the recipes as a class project.

10. Read George's *The Talking Earth*. With another classmate who has read the book, select a part of the scene with Oats Tiger to dramatize for the class.

11. Read George's *The Talking Earth*. Compare it with another survival story such as Armstrong Sperry's *Call It Courage* (Macmillan, 1940) or Scott O'Dell's *Island of the Blue Dolpins* (Houghton Mifflin, 1960). What character traits did the two protagonists have in common? Were any themes of the two stories the same?

12. Read George's *One Day in the Desert*. Make a list of all the animals and plants introduced, and give a sentence explanation for each on how they survived the heat.

13. Read George's *One Day in the Alpine Tundra*. Why did Jean George introduce a human character into this information book? Did it increase the suspense? What did the publishers mean in calling this book a "close-up view of nature"? Would you have preferred a factual account in encyclopedia style? Why or why not? How do you suppose George gathered the information needed to write this book?

14. Read George's *One Day in the Desert*. Select an animal about which you know little and find more information about it in the library media center or public library. Prepare a brief report and share with the class.

What It Takes to Survive

STUDENT OBJECTIVES:

- Experience vicariously the struggle to survive
- Analyze the type of conflict in which the main character engages
- Determine the effectiveness of figurative language in making the story more vivid for the reader
- Formulate a game based on conflicts a character experienced
- Recreate a specific historical time and place by making a report, preparing a model, or creating a display
- Prepare a map depicting the route characters followed

RECOMMENDED READING:

Anderson, Margaret J. *The Journey of the Shadow Bairns.* Knopf, 1980.
  Rather than be sent to an orphanage and separated from her brother, Elspeth decides that they should leave Scotland and journey to Canada to begin a new life.

Fife, Dale. *North of Danger.* Illustrated by Haakon Soether. Dutton, 1978.
  Two hundred miles of frozen wasteland lie between Arne and his father as Arne sets out on a nearly impossible journey to find him.

Fleischman, Paul. *The Half-A-Moon Inn.* Illustrated by Kathy Jacobi. Harper & Row, 1980.
  A mute boy, Aaron, leaves home in search of his mother, who he believes is lost in a snowstorm, and falls into the hands of wicked Miss Grackle.

Lasky, Kathryn. *The Night Journey.* Illustrated by Trina Schart Hyman. Warne, 1981.
  As Rachel listens, her great-grandmother tells her of the time when she was nine years old and her family was forced to flee czarist Russia.

Moeri, Louise. *Save Queen of Sheba.* Dutton, 1981.
  As the lone survivors of an Indian raid, King David must keep himself and his sister, Queen of Sheba, alive until they can find help and safety.

O'Dell, Scott. *Island of the Blue Dolphins.* Houghton Mifflin, 1968.
This account of a young girl, Karana, depicts her solitary life and struggle to survive on a deserted island.

Speare, Elizabeth George. *The Sign of the Beaver.* Houghton Mifflin, 1983.
Thirteen-year-old Matt learns the meaning of survival in pioneer Maine through the help of an Indian boy and his family.

Steele, William O. *The Magic Amulet.* Harcourt Brace Jovanovich, 1979.
Abandoned by his tribe and left to die, Tragg uses the magic amulet in his struggle to survive in a time when mammoth and mastodon herds roamed the earth.

Steig, William. *Abel's Island.* Farrar, Straus & Giroux, 1976.
Survival takes on a new meaning as Abel, a highly educated and sophisticated mouse, finds himself alone on a deserted island.

Taylor, Theodore. *The Cay.* Doubleday, 1969.
A shipwreck leaves 12-year-old Phillip stranded on an island in the Caribbean with his only chance of survival in the hands of an aging black man, Timothy.

GROUP INTRODUCTORY ACTIVITY:

Set up a display or prepare a bulletin board showing some of the books to be used in this unit. To catch the students' attention, use the caption "What Would You Have Done?" Prepare to discuss the caption by making a card for each book noting the situations which the characters must overcome in order to survive. Challenge students to read and find out what decisions the book characters made. Use the cards in individual or group discussions with the students, helping them to identify the decisions, hypothesize what they might have done in a similar situation, and relate the decision-making process to their own lives.

Do a book talk for the group describing Aaron's bleak situation at the hands of Miss Grackle in Paul Fleischman's *The Half-A-Moon Inn.* An excellent place to stop sharing in order to keep the students in suspense is at the point when Aaron discovers his mother has come and gone without even seeing his sign asking for help. At the close of the unit, bring the group back together and let a student who has read the book finish the story so all can cheer over the happy ending.

FOLLOW-UP ACTIVITIES FOR TEACHER AND STUDENTS TO SHARE:

1. Speare's *The Sign of the Beaver* is an excellent selection for reading aloud. It could be particularly useful in conjunction with a social studies unit on the 1700s. During the time in which the story is read aloud to the class, assist the students in setting up a display or preparing a bulletin board showing weapons, toys, household items, and clothing used by the settlers in the colonial period. Set up a similar display or bulletin board showing artifacts used by the Northeast Indians. Refer to Edwin Tunis's book *Colonial Living* (Crowell, 1976) for information on tools and items used during this period. In *The Sign of the Beaver,* Elizabeth George Speare develops two strong characters. The lives of Matt, the white boy, and Attean, the Indian boy, are developed to the degree that they can be termed "round" (fully developed) and "dynamic" (evidencing change in the story). At the close of appropriate segments required for the time allotted for reading aloud, lead the students in a discussion of how the characters become credible to the reader. How does the setting affect the character development? Give examples of what the author tells the reader about Matt's and Attean's character. What does each boy say and do that assist in making them round characters? Discuss what each boy was like in the beginning of the story. How did they change? Compare their life styles.

2. Read aloud *North of Danger* by Dale Fife. When Arne realized the danger his father was in, he made the decision to go in search of his father. Discuss with the class each decision Arne had to make to accomplish his goal. What would the students have done if they had faced each problem? To give students a better understanding of the setting for the story, locate Svalbard on a globe or map. Use an opaque projector to enlarge the map in *North of Danger* and, at the close of each reading session, have a student color in the distance Arne travels and add all illustrations depicting the problems he encounters.

3. Read aloud all or portions of *The Night Journey* by Kathryn Lasky, giving special emphasis to the flashbacks from the present to the past. In this unusual tale of survival, we meet Rachel's family of four generations. How many children can relate to Rachel's love and concern for her great-grandmother Nana Sashie? Be sure to read the section in the introduction where Rachel is scolded by all three generations. Discuss her wonderment. What feelings can the children share about their own families and ties with the past?

   Nine-year-old Sashie's plan to have the family escape disguised as Purim players saves the family in this book. Give several students an opportunity to find out more about the Purim festival and its meaning to Jews. The problem of carrying the gold was solved by baking it in special cakes called *hamantaschen*. If possible, serve these cakes to the class. What significance does the samovar have in Sashie's and Rachel's lives? In this dramatic escape, another figure comes vividly to life—Wolf Levinson, whose "eyes were frozen like pinpricks of terror in the pale yellowish irises" (p. 35). Lasky's careful description of Wolf dramatically sets the tone and mood of the escape. Discuss Wolf's effect on the family. To lighten the tone Lasky introduces Reuven Bloom, who played music that was "so hushed and fragile that Sashie thought of a world so silent that you could hear the sounds of flowers moving in the breeze." (p. 120) How does tone affect this story? How do Trina Schart Hyman's illustrations also help set the tone of this story? If the book is read in its entirety, ask the students to listen for other passages where the tone changes, as it adds dramatically to the telling of the story. If the book is introduced and children are urged to read it in order to participate in a discussion session, the students should be asked to watch for tone changes. To close a discussion on this book, ask an open-ended question such as "What else besides the lives of seven people survived as a result of Nana Sasha's escape from Russia?"

4. Read aloud the entire book or passages from *The Cay* by Theodore Taylor so that the students get a feeling for the relationship that develops between Phillip and Timothy in their struggle to survive. Several students may want to locate the islands mentioned on a globe or atlas. After reading the passages where Phillip finally gets a feeling for what their tiny island must look like (pp. 79–81), have the students use watercolors or another medium to draw the island visualized by Phillip's senses of touch, smell, taste, and hearing.

FOLLOW-UP ACTIVITIES FOR INDIVIDUALS OR SMALL GROUPS:

1. After reading or listening to Speare's *The Sign of the Beaver,* design a model of Matt's cabin or a model of Attean's village.
2. After hearing *North of Danger,* read Dale Fife's *Destination Unknown* (Dutton, 1981). Compare the conflicts that the main characters experience in each story. Which do you think required the greatest courage? Why? Select one of the characters and explain what you would have done in his situation.
3. After reading or listening to Lasky's *The Night Journey,* think about being forced to escape as Nana Sasha and her family were. If you were driven from your home, what one thing would

you choose to take with you that was no larger than a full-grown rooster? List each of your family members and decide upon one item you think each would take with them.

4. The dedication for Theodore Taylor's *The Cay* reads "To Dr. King's dream, which can come true if the very young know and understand." After reading or hearing *The Cay,* explain how this dedication comes to life in the relationship between Phillip and Timothy.

5. In Anderson's *The Journey of the Shadow Bairns,* it is 13-year-old Elspeth who becomes responsible for her life and the life of her brother when her parents die. After reading the book, identify at least three passages which show that Elspeth is a determined and courageous girl capable of surviving the long journey from Scotland. For example, when Elspeth learns at the train station that she and Bobbie are to be sent back to Scotland (pp. 76–80), Elspeth says, "We came on our own. We had tickets like everyone else. Anyway, I'm nearly fourteen. I'm too old for an orphanage. I want to get a job as a maid."

6. Read Anderson's *The Journey of the Shadow Bairns* and Moeri's *Save Queen of Sheba.* In what ways were Elspeth's and King David's problems alike? In what ways were they different?

7. Read Moeri's *Save Queen of Sheba.* Then, using reference books, locate a map of the Oregon Trail that David and Queen of Sheba traveled. Draw your own map showing present-day states that the Oregon Trail crossed. Mark an approximate location where the raid took place.

8. One of the wagons described in Moeri's *Save Queen of Sheba* was the Conestoga. After reading the book and doing research, draw and describe the Conestoga wagon in which King David and Queen of Sheba were riding. Using C.J. Maginley's book *Historic Models of Early America* (Harcourt Brace Jovanovich, 1947), build a scale model of the Conestoga wagon (pp. 28–33).

9. Moeri's *Save Queen of Sheba* ends with David and his sister being rescued by their father. After reading the story, write your own account of what you think might have happened to their pa and ma when they became separated *or* write a continuation of the ending describing what happened after they were found. Did the family stay at Fort Laramie or go on to Oregon?

10. After reading O'Dell's *Island of the Blue Dolphins,* list some of the skills Karana knew and those she had to learn that enabled her to survive. What traditions or taboos did she have to break? Even though Karana had been trained to live with nature, her struggle to survive depended on her ability to defend herself against nature. Locate and describe a passage where Karana is in direct conflict with nature. How did she overcome the problem?

11. After reading O'Dell's *Island of the Blue Dolphins,* reread the section describing the beautiful coastal island (p. 9). Build a model of Karana's island that makes visual her description.

12. Create a game and gameboard using conflicts in O'Dell's *Island of the Blue Dolphins* or another survival story you have read as problems encountered in the game.
13. Survival on the island is easier for Abel in Steig's *Abel's Island* after he discovers that the island abounds with edible plants, many of which he recognizes from illustrations in his encyclopedia (p. 29). After reading the book, use a reference book to make a list of plants edible for mice. Compare the list with a list of those Abel found. Were any on both lists?
14. After reading Steele's *The Magic Amulet,* make a list of the animals that Tragg encountered, either enemies or those hunted. Select one animal, such as a mastadon, mammoth, or saber-toothed tiger, and find out when it lived, whether it had a use to the Neanderthal or Cro-Magnon man, and when/why it ceased to exist. Share your information with your class.
15. Miss Grackle in Fleischman's *The Half-A-Moon Inn* is depicted as a gruesome character who looks like a mummy wrapped in a shawl. To make Miss Grackle's speech help identify her character, the author has her continually making comparisons between unlike things (similes) such as "Let me see 'em [the flames] hiss like snakes and snap their jaws like wolves!" (p. 35). After reading the book, examine her conversation for similes and other forms of descriptive language. List at least five statements using similes and explain what each makes you feel about her character. Select one scene that dramatically presents Aaron's struggle to survive Miss Grackle's evil ways and read it aloud to the class.
16. In *A Critical Handbook of Children's Literature* Rebecca Lukens says that there are four forms of plot conflict: self against self, self against another, self against society, and self against nature.[4] Select one of the survival books you have read and list the problems the main character had to overcome in order to survive. Identify which of the four forms of conflict each would be.
17. Working in a small group, devise a "Who Am I" game using the books any of you have read in this unit on survival. For each book, write five clues about their survival problems in question form. The first clues may be very general and the latter ones very specific. Answers should ask for title, author, or main character. Decide on the game rules and share with the class.

Pioneer Life with Laura Ingalls Wilder

STUDENT OBJECTIVES:

- Assess the problems of living on the frontier as revealed in fiction
- Contrast holidays in pioneer times with those of today
- Dramatize events enjoyed by pioneer families
- Illustrate favorite scenes from the books in the unit
- Map the travels of characters
- Compare schools of today with those in pioneer days

RECOMMENDED READING:

The Laura Ingalls Wilder Songbook. Edited by Eugenia Garson. Illustrated by Garth Williams. Harper & Row, 1968.
Includes words and music for 62 songs shared by the Ingalls family in the Little House series with introductory quotes to indicate pages and book in which each song is found.

Walker, Barbara Muhs. *The Little House Cookbook.* Illustrated by Garth Williams. Harper & Row, 1979.
In addition to recipes for food mentioned in the Little House books, the origins of these foods, how they were accessible on the frontier, and pioneer methods of preparation are discussed.

Wilder, Laura Ingalls. *By the Shores of Silver Lake.* Illustrated by Garth Williams. Harper & Row, 1953.
Pa gets a job at a Dakota Territory railroad camp and the Ingalls family leave Plum Creek so Pa can find a Dakota Territory homestead.

———. *Farmer Boy.* Illustrated by Garth Williams. Harper & Row, 1953.
Recounts the life of nine-year-old Almanzo Wilder growing up on a northern New York farm.

———. *The First Four Years.* Illustrated by Garth Williams. Harper & Row, 1971.
Describes the problems faced by Laura and Almanzo during their first years of marriage.

————. *Little House in the Big Woods.* Illustrated by Garth Williams. Harper & Row, 1953.
This first book of the Little House series recounts the experiences of Laura, Mary, baby Carrie, and their parents in a Wisconsin log cabin far from neighbors.

————. *Little House on the Prairie.* Illustrated by Garth Williams. Harper & Row, 1953.
The Ingalls family leaves Wisconsin, moves west, and builds a log house in Indian territory.

————. *Little Town on the Prairie.* Illustrated by Garth Williams. Harper & Row, 1953.
Recounts Laura's preparation to be a teacher while Mary leaves home to attend a college for the blind.

————. *Long Winter.* Illustrated by Garth Williams. Harper & Row, 1953.
The Ingalls family moves to a small Dakota Territory town and barely survive the horrible winter when lack of food and fuel threatens the lives of everyone.

————. *On the Banks of Plum Creek.* Illustrated by Garth Williams. Harper & Row, 1953.
After leavinig Indian territory, the Ingalls family travels to Minnesota, where they first live in a dugout and then in the wood house Pa built.

————. *On the Way Home.* Edited by Rose Wilder Lane. Harper & Row, 1962.
Provides a diary record of the trip of Laura, Almanzo, and their children from South Dakota to Mansfield, Missouri, in 1894 with introductory and final chapters by Rose Wilder Lane.

————. *These Happy Golden Years.* Illustrated by Garth Williams. Harper & Row, 1953.
Laura has her first experiences teaching school and marries Almanzo Wilder.

————. *West from Home.* Edited by Roger Lea MacBride. Harper & Row, 1974.
Made up of edited letters written to Almanzo during Laura's two-month visit with daughter Rose in San Francisco in 1915.

BIOGRAPHICAL SOURCES:

For more information on Laura Ingalls Wilder (deceased), see *The Junior Book of Authors,* 2d ed., 299–300; *Something about the Author,* 29:239–49; *Twentieth-Century Children's Writers,* 1341–44; *Twentieth-Century Children's Writers,* 2d ed., 827–29.

GROUP INTRODUCTORY ACTIVITY:

To introduce the Laura Ingalls Wilder Little House series, share with the class information about Wilder in Walker's *The Little House Cookbook* and *The Laura Ingalls Wilder Songbook* and other bibliographic information about Laura Ingalls Wilder. Be sure to tell the children that Laura was in her sixties when her daughter Rose urged her to write down her childhood memories of the Middle West as it was in the 1870s and 1880s. Instead of becoming an autobiography, her memories became a series of fiction books.[5]

Introduce *The Little House in the Big Woods,* the first in the series of the Little House books, by explaining that in this book, Laura turns five years old and lives with her parents, her older sister Mary, and baby sister Carrie in a log cabin in the Wisconsin woods. There were no close neighbors or stores, and the family raised or hunted for their food. There was no television, of course, and their source of music was the songs Pa sang while playing the fiddle.

Before sharing the description of Laura's fifth birthday, let the children guess what her gifts might be.

Share pages 96–99. Ahead of time, have the words to "Pop Goes the Weasel" on a transparency and, after sharing the birthday scene, let the children sing this song Pa sang to Laura, found on pages 72–73 in *The Laura Ingalls Wilder Songbook.*

FOLLOW-UP ACTIVITIES FOR TEACHER AND STUDENTS TO SHARE:

1. Read Wilder's book *Little House in the Big Woods* aloud to the children. Be sure to sing "Old Grimes" from *The Laura Ingalls Wilder Songbook* after the description of Ma making cheese, p. 192, is read. Let children dance the play party song of "Buffalo Gals" (pp. 58–59 in the songbook) after reading about the dance at Grandpa's. After reading the book, select children to use the index to Walker's *The Little House Cookbook* and read recipes of foods shared by the family in the book. Let each describe the recipes so the class can discuss how appetizing each sounds.

   After reading the book, ask the children to write a paragraph or make a list of reasons why they would have liked to live in the Big Woods over 100 years ago or why they preferred to live in their own community today. If the original edition of *Little House in the Big Woods* is available through the public library, let the children compare the illustrations by Helen Sewell and those by Garth Williams. Which do they enjoy more?

2. The next book Wilder wrote in the series was *Farmer Boy,* which describes the boyhood of her husband, Almanzo, on a

farm in northern New York. Introduce *Farmer Boy* by reading the first chapter to the class. Let the children discuss the differences between Almanzo's school in New York over a century ago and theirs. From that small introduction to Almanzo's early life, see if children can identify differences between his and Laura's early life. Which family had a harder time making a living? Suggest that a group of children read *Farmer Boy* and share with the class scenes that evidence those differences, such as "Christmas," "Sheep-Shearing," "Country Fair," and "Keeping House." In "Keeping House," the children make ice cream using white sugar bought at the store. Check out a description of the recipe used, pages 309–11, in *The Little House Cookbook.* Have the class discuss today's sources of ice cream.

3. Introduce Wilder's third book, *Little House on the Prairie,* in which the author returns to the Ingalls family as they leave their house in the Big Woods to go west. Read the chapter "Mr. Edwards Meets Santa Claus" aloud. Then discuss the children's joy over their gifts. The description of the cakes is on pages 200–01 in Walker's *The Little House Cookbook.*

   Introduce the title of the next chapter, "Scream in the Night." Let children imagine the content.

   Place an outline map of the United States on the bulletin board and let the children locate the setting of the first two books. Ask for volunteers to read this book and trace the travels of the Ingallses from Wisconsin to Kansas. Ask them to describe for the class exciting scenes such as "Fire in the Chimney," "Prairie Fire," and "Scream in the Night." Perhaps they will want to dramatize pages 201–04 of the "Fire in the Chimney" chapter. The volunteer group will want to check pages 37–41 in the cookbook for food hunted on the Kansas prairie.

4. Introduce Wilder's *On the Banks of Plum Creek* by explaining that the family left Kansas territory to live in a sod house in Minnesota. Share the two chapters "The Christmas Horses" and "Merry Christmas." Relate their family gift to today. What might a family join together to wish for? Anticipate the content of three chapters, "Grasshoppers Walking," "Rings of Fire" and "The Glittering Cloud." Ask volunteers reading this book to be sure to share the other two Christmases described in the book. They may want to dramatize part of the chapter "School" and "The Darkest Hour Is Just before Dawn." Be sure to add to the map the family's trip to Minnesota from Kansas territory.

5. In Wilder's *By the Shores of Silver Lake,* Ma and the girls take the train to the Dakota Territory, where Pa finds a homestead and builds a shanty on the claim. Share "The Night Before Christmas" and "Merry Christmas" chapters. Discuss why the family termed it the best Christmas ever. Mrs. Boast had brought popcorn as a surprise. Share the notes about popcorn making in Walker's *The Little House Cookbook,* pp. 214–15, and

if possible eat some as a class surprise after the chapter is read. Again, ask for volunteers to read this book and share excerpts with the class. Suggest they dramatize the scene when Grace was lost while the family was planting trees, pages 373–77, and after Laura found her, pages 281–83. Be sure to map their trip from Minnesota.

6. In Wilder's *The Long Winter,* the family moves to town to try to survive despite the extreme cold. Share "Merry Christmas" with the class. Compare the foods they shared for dinner with that of previous years. Suggest that the students who read *The Long Winter* dramatize scenes from "The Last Mile" when Cap and Almanzo go in the storm to buy wheat only to have the storekeeper try to double the cost when selling it to starving families.

7. Introduce Wilder's *Little Town on the Prairie.* Explain that Laura must now plan to be a schoolteacher so that Mary, who became blind as a result of scarlet fever, could go to a college for the blind in Iowa. As we find out in *These Happy Golden Years,* she becomes a teacher at 15 years of age. Read the chapter "The School Exhibition." After hearing it, let the class compare the exhibition with the type of program their school would have. Which would be more enjoyable for the students? Why? Let the children discuss why they think teaching methods and the content of the curriculum have changed so much since Laura's time. Tell the class that the last chapter title is "Unexpected in December." Let them explore what they think the chapter is about. Perhaps the students who read *Little Town on the Prairie* would like to dramatize scenes from that chapter.

8. The last book in the original Wilder Little House series illustrated by Sewell was *These Happy Golden Years,* in which Laura teaches her first school and later marries Almanzo Wilder. To introduce the book, "Managing" is a good chapter to show how she solved her teaching problems, and "The Night before Christmas" gives a feeling for "the nicest Christmas" of all. After reading the short chapter, let the class discuss problems a teacher at 15 would face teaching at a pioneer rural school. Compare this Christmas with the Wilders' earlier ones to see if the class agrees it is the nicest one of all. Suggest that those who read *These Happy Golden Years* may want to share Laura's experiences at "The Perry School," including how Laura was going to spend her salary. They may want to refer to "The Laura Ingalls Songbook" and include "Polly-Wolly-Doodle" in their sharing with the class.

9. Plan a Laura Ingalls Wilder party with another class in the school. The children will want to write invitations and plan a program, games, and refreshments. The chapter "Thirst Quenchers and Treats" in Walker's *The Little House Cookbook* provides refreshment ideas. The children may, for example, want to dra-

matize school scenes from various books, sing appropriate songs, and have a spelling bee as party entertainment. If anyone in the community has visited Mansfield, Missouri, he or she could be invited to come and describe the Wilder Museum. Perhaps that person brought back a Charlotte doll or a gingerbread recipe that could be shared.

FOLLOW-UP ACTIVITIES FOR INDIVIDUALS OR SMALL GROUPS:

1. Read Wilder's *These Happy Golden Years.* Write a paragraph comparing "A Cold Ride" with a 12-mile ride home from school today.
2. Read Wilder's *These Happy Golden Years.* List the strange, damaging effects of "Summer Storm." Check in the school library media center or public library for a book on tornadoes. Find other strange accounts of tornado damage. Share with the class. Talk also about the modern methods of warning that help to save lives in such storms.
3. Read Wilder's *Little Town on the Prairie.* Compare "The Birthday Party" with one that 13- or 14-year-olds would have today. How would the clothes worn, food, and games be different?
4. Read Wilder's *On the Banks of Plum Creek.* Make a list of Nellie Olson's character traits and give an example from the book to justify each trait listed. Now do the same for Laura. Which girl would you rather have as a school classmate? Why?
5. Read Wilder's *On the Way Home.* Trace their route on the class map. Pretend you are traveling that same route today. Check the distance and write a one-day diary account of a family traveling by automobile. Include where they stopped for lunch and where they stayed, what they ate, and any historical sights they saw or entertainment they enjoyed.
6. Read Wilder's *The Long Winter.* Write a paragraph describing some of the problems Laura and her family suffered in that long winter.
7. After hearing *Little House in the Big Woods,* make a model of the house or illustrate your favorite scene in the story.
8. Read Wilder's *The First Four Years.* The introduction says that this first draft was discovered after Laura's death. In what ways might the book have been different if she had revised it before publication?
9. Read Wilder's *West from Home.* Compare the sights and exhibits of the Panama-Pacific International Exposition with World's Fair exhibits today. What are major causes of the differences?
10. Read Wilder's *By the Shores of Silver Lake.* Share the events of "Pa's Bet" with the class. Be sure to include the cost of the

claim. Let the class estimate what 160 acres of farm land in DeSmet would cost today. Perhaps a call to a realtor would help answer the question. How would acquiring a farm be different today? What conditions made Pa say it was a bet?

11. Read Wilder's *Little House on the Prairie*. Select one frightening or exciting event and record it as Laura might have if she had been old enough to keep a diary.

12. Read Wilder's *Farmer Boy*. Suppose your parents or those of a family in the neighborhood decided to leave for a week and the children were left "Keeping House." Describe how the instructions of what to do and not do would differ from those in the story. Write a paragraph about an accident that could have happened as serious as blacking polish on the wall. Include how it was corrected so no one knew it had happened.

Problem Solving with Marilyn Burns

STUDENT OBJECTIVES:

- Recognize symmetry in everyday objects
- Take the steps necessary to solve a problem
- Discuss the importance of clocks in our daily lives
- Create a topological garden
- Practice magic with numbers
- Explore personal feelings about everyday situations
- Gain a better understanding of Hanukkah

RECOMMENDED READING:

Burns, Marilyn. *The Book of Think.* Illustrated by Martha Weston. Little, Brown, 1976.
    Children are guided to think in new ways in order to solve problems.

———. *The Hanukkah Book.* Illustrated by Martha Weston. Four Winds Press, 1981.
    By presenting the recipes and traditions of this holiday celebration, readers gain a new understanding of Hanukkah.

————. *I Am Not A Short Adult!* Little, Brown, 1977.
Children are stimulated to explore their feelings about home, school, work, and other everyday situations.

————. *The I Hate Mathematics! Book.* Illustrated by Martha Hairston. Little, Brown, 1975.
This collection of painless mathematical problems, puzzles, riddles, and teasers will entice even the most avid arithmetic haters.

————. *Math for Smarty Pants.* Illustrated by Martha Weston. Little, Brown, 1982.
This book is designed to help young people learn how to solve problems.

————. *This Book Is about Time.* Illustrated by Martha Weston. Little, Brown, 1978.
Time is explained through the introduction of clocks, time zones, calendars, nature's clocks, and ways the body adjusts to time.

GROUP INTRODUCTORY ACTIVITY:

In a letter from Marilyn Burns forwarded by Little, Brown, she provides an introduction to her writing that will have appeal to young people. She says that when she was in the eighth grade she kept a diary for the entire year, faithfully writing daily. After that year she was so exhausted by the experience that she did no writing for 15 years.

On the verso of the title page of *The I Hate Mathematics! Book,* Burns suggests that the ideas for this book came from a group of people who believe that learning happens only when it is wanted and that it can happen anywhere without fancy tools. Keeping this thought in mind, ask each student to bring a fruit or vegetable from home before Burns's books are shared. Introduce *The I Hate Mathematics! Book* and then turn to page 95 as the springboard for learning about symmetry in an enjoyable way.

Ahead of class, be sure to collect the following items: ripe bananas, rotten bananas, cutting board, paring knife, and wax paper. As the class meets, have them lay their fruit or vegetable aside for the moment. Begin the discussion by asking them to think about how many sides a banana has. What shape is a banana? Then show them a ripe banana in order to decide about the number of sides. Once this is established, ask them how many sides a rotten banana has. After gaining their attention by this activity, use the ideas on pages 95–100 for more fun.

One of the activities involves cutting up fruit to see the various patterns that are evident. When doing this activity, also use Tana Hoban's *Look Again* (Macmillan, 1971) so they can see how Hoban photographed various objects so the reader could see the patterns.

FOLLOW-UP ACTIVITIES FOR TEACHER AND STUDENTS TO SHARE:

1. Marilyn Burns suggests ways to open our minds to creative problem solutions in *The Book of Think.* To help students open their minds, begin with the warm-up exercises in Part 1. Ask questions such as "Without looking, what color of socks are you wearing?" "When you clasp your hands, which thumb is on top?" Now have each student take the quiz on page 15. Next, on an overhead projector or chalkboard, draw the nine dots as shown on page 23. Now ask the students to draw the nine dots and connect them with four straight lines (answer on page 24). This should whet their desire to use the book for more problem-solving fun.

2. Through the dialogue of five characters showing activities, stories, and games, Burns's *Math For Smarty Pants* helps young people learn how to take the steps necessary to solve a problem. The chapter entitled "Mathematical Stunt Flying" shows numerical loopings. The loop described on page 18 uses numbers and words. Have each member of the class start with number 39 and follow through the directions you give orally as indicated in the example. They will see that they could continue on with 4. Now have them each try a different number and follow your oral directions. Does each one conclude with 4? Have students try to figure out why the activity always ends up with 4.

3. Burns's *Math For Smarty Pants* has riddles that make you think. Try out the riddle on page 54 with the class. "On New Year's Day, January 1, some relatives came to visit the family of a mathematical smarty pants. 'How old are you?' the relatives asked. Smarty Pants answered, 'The day before yesterday I was 9 years old, and next year I will be 12 years old.' This was true." When was Smarty Pants's birthday? Explain your answer.

4. How many different kinds of clocks are there? Students can find the answer to this question in Burns's *This Book Is about Time.* Have students help prepare a bulletin board with pictures of all kinds of clocks or a time trip around the world (pp. 24–25). Discuss the reasons it is important to "keep time" in our society. Suppose that for one day, all the clocks in the world broke down. Have students discuss how this would change their lives or events in the world. After discussing these questions, have the students write a story about a world without clocks. More ideas can be found on page 46.

5. Children begin early to wonder who their real friends are, why they are liked or disliked, and if their parents like them as much as they like brothers and sisters. To help children begin to answer these questions, they need to know themselves. In Burns's *I Am Not A Short Adult!* many ideas for understanding

are given. To introduce the book, divide the class into pairs and share the Who-Am-I game on pages 13–14.

FOLLOW-UP ACTIVITIES FOR INDIVIDUALS OR SMALL GROUPS:

1. Follow the ideas on pages 22–24 in Burns's *The I Hate Mathematics! Book* and create a topological garden.
2. Read the poem "Eighteen Flavors" from Shel Silverstein's *Where the Sidewalk Ends* (Harper & Row, 1974). Using *The I Hate Mathematics! Book,* refer to pages 2–27 to figure out how many combinations and permutations you can make from the 18 flavors of ice cream.
3. "There Are at Least Two Ways to Look at Something" is a section in Burns's *The Book Of Think.* After reading these pages, answer the questions asked. Now attempt to draw your own optical illusion. For additional fun, examine Ed Emberley's *The Wizard Of Op* (Little, Brown, 1975).
4. Mother Goose had many problems to solve. Turn to page 70 of Burns's *The Book Of Think* and solve two of the problems given. Now, using books in the library media center, select three other rhymes. Write down each rhyme, the problem faced, and possible solutions.
5. Burns's *Math for Smarty Pants* has many activities designed for small groups and individuals. Try the calculator game for two.

   Select another group game from *Math for Smarty Pants* and play it with a friend. Then share it with your class.
6. Be a magician with numbers. Try the problem on page 111 in Burns's *Math for Smarty Pants.* Regardless of the numbers you use, you will always get 9. Try this mathemagic with your classmates.

   Read *Math for Smarty Pants* and find another math problem to share.
7. On page 46 of Burns's *This Book Is about Time* Marilyn Burns gives you a few clock riddles. After reading these, go to the library media center and locate three other jokes or riddles about time. Write them down and share them with your class.
8. Everyone is aware of time, particularly if the day seems to go on forever. For fun, make a list of 10 different reasons why you check a clock or watch during the day. Now make a chart like the one shown on page 10 of Burns's *This Book Is about Time* to keep track of when you checked the clock and what you were doing at the time.
9. On pages 18–19 in Burns's *I Am Not A Short Adult!,* there are five questions about situations in which there is no right or wrong answer. Working with a small group of classmates, answer

the questions and tell why you feel comfortable with your answers.

10. Using the questions on pages 18–19 of Burns's *I Am Not A Short Adult!* for ideas, write and illustrate your own book. For example, the question "What do you like most?" can be answered with "To play alone, to play with one good friend, to play with a few friends, to play with a big group of kids." Each of these answers should be illustrated so that the reader of the book you are writing can answer for himself/herself. Use the question "What do you like most?" again. This time, use foods, animals, or places to visit as answers from which the reader can choose. Make your book as long as you like, using your ideas for questions.

11. Dreidel is the most popular game played during Hanukkah. The game works for two or more players. On page 73 of Burns's *The Hanukkah Book,* a picture shows what a dreidel looks like. Directions for making three different types of dreidel are given on pages 76–82. Read the instructions; then make your own dreidel. After making the dreidel, turn to page 74 and learn how to play the game.

12. Read Burns's *The Hanukkah Book.* If you are not of the Jewish faith, list 10 facts you learned about Jewish traditions. If you are Jewish, ask your teacher if you can invite an adult friend to visit your class and explain some of the Jewish holidays.

The Book Friends of Robert Burch

STUDENT OBJECTIVES:

- Predict the outcome of a story
- Evaluate the techniques used to show characterization in a book
- Record a diary entry for a character
- Describe how illustrations affect the mood of a book
- Compare a school in rural Georgia 40 years ago with today's classroom
- Note the use of "cliffhangers" as a plot technique
- Explore feelings of older people about personal freedom

RECOMMENDED READING:

Burch, Robert. *Christmas with Ida Early.* Viking, 1983.
The Sutton children fail in their matchmaking attempts, but Ida Early, the housekeeper, helps them enjoy an amazing holiday season.

―――. *D.J.'s Worst Enemy.* Illustrated by Emil Weiss. Viking, 1965.
D.J. causes many problems for himself and his Georgia farm family before he sees a new role for his life.

―――. *Hut School and the Wartime Home-Front Heroes.* Illustrated by Ronald Himler. Viking, 1974.
Picking cotton, attending a cabin school, and serving a leadership role in her sixth-grade class is part of Kate's home front role during World War II.

―――. *Ida Early Comes over the Mountain.* Viking, 1980.
Rural Georgia during the Depression is made much more enjoyable for the Sutton children through the efforts of Ida Early, the housekeeper.

―――. *Queenie Peavy.* Illustrated by Jerry Lazare. Viking, 1966.
Queenie learns that facing the reality of a father in prison is better than senseless fighting back.

―――. *Skinny.* Illustrated by Don Sibley. Viking, 1964.
Before 12-year-old Skinny went to the orphan's home, he won the hearts of the hotel guests and staff.

―――. *Two that Were Tough.* Illustrated by Richard Cuffari. Viking, 1976.
An old man and a stray chicken establish the value of freedom for all.

―――. *Wilkin's Ghost.* Viking, 1978.
Alex betrays the friendship of Wilkin, who decides to postpone the dreams of riding the rails and escaping the rural Georgia of 1935.

BIOGRAPHICAL SOURCES:

For more information on Robert Burch, see *More Books by More People,* 60–67; *Something about the Author,* 1:38–39; *Third Book of Junior Authors,* 49–50; *Twentieth-Century Children's Writers,* 202–03; *Twentieth-Century Children's Writers,* 2d ed., 137–38.

GROUP INTRODUCTORY ACTIVITY:

Before introducing Robert Burch's books, be sure to tell the class that Burch lived in Georgia during the Depression, the setting of his books. Burch says that none of his characters are based on real people, although some of them may be a combination of people he knew. None of his characters are himself either, although he often uses the setting and economic circumstances that he knew first-hand. He usually begins a story by thinking about the central characters until they become real to him. Then he considers the plot, which evolves naturally out of character development and setting. He rushes into the first draft, putting the story on paper as quickly as he can. Then he spends months, even years, rewriting before submitting it for publication.[6]

Introduce *Ida Early Comes over the Mountain* by reading Chapters 1 and 2, "Taller Than Anybody" and "The Stew-Making Fool." With that brief introduction to Ida Early, let the children describe her appearance and identify as many character traits as they can. Let them discuss how Burch acquainted his readers with her so well in such a short time. Was it mainly through the description of her or her actions?

Characterize Aunt Earnestine. At this point, does the class think the Sutton children would rather have Aunt Earnestine or Ida as the housekeeper? Why? Recall the scene of Ida's arrival or the situation when Aunt Earnestine and Mr. Sutton are leaving for town. Let class members volunteer for parts and dramatize the scene. Discuss why they are able to recall the scene so vividly.

FOLLOW-UP ACTIVITIES FOR TEACHER AND STUDENTS TO SHARE:

1. Finish reading *Ida Early Comes over the Mountain* to the class. After reading the chapters "Schoolyard" and "After School," let the class discuss the situation. Was it realistic that Ellen and Randall react as they did when the classmates began to jeer Ida? Why did they not speak up for her? How did they feel when it was over? Can they ever completely make up for it with Ida? Would they react differently again in a similar scene? Before reading "Almost Thanksgiving," tell the class that it is a five-page last chapter. Let them suggest what they think is going to happen. After all who wish to do so have shared, read the last chapter. After the story is completed, recall Ida's character traits that have been suggested by the first two chapters. What additional character traits can they add to the list now that they know her better? As a follow-up ask the class members either to

illustrate a favorite scene or, pretending to be Ida, describe one situation as if Ida were telling it to a friend.

2. To introduce Burch's *Christmas with Ida Early,* read the first chapter, "The Christmas Turkey." Discuss the brief introduction to the first book given by Robert Burch in this sequel. Was it enough so that the reader could enjoy *Christmas with Ida Early* even if s/he had not read *Ida Early Comes over the Mountain?* Why didn't Burch describe the first story in more detail in this book? As a follow-up to this first chapter, ask the children to think of an earlier adventure Ida had, or one she made up but pretended to have experienced, and tell it as Ida might have told the family after the evening work was done. They may want to tape rather than write their stories. Suggest that after a few children have read *Christmas with Ida Early,* they may want to dramatize some scenes for the class.

3. To introduce Burch's *Wilkin's Ghost,* read Chapters 1 and 2, "The Hanging Tree" and "Storm." Look at the black-and-white illustrations. How do they contribute to the reader's appreciation of the mood and setting of the story? The last line of the chapter "Storm" is called a "cliffhanger." Let the children discuss the meaning of this word as it relates to literature. Why does the author end a chapter in this way? Have each explore what they think will happen next. What did Wilkin see? Discuss Wilkin's character. Was he showing determination or stubbornness to take the shortcut? Was he brave while under the tree? Discuss the meaning of colloquial expressions such as "outwhopper" and "a heap quicker," page 4, and "booger," page 5. Talk about expressions characteristic of the present time in your area.

4. After the class has read and heard Robert Burch's books, have them write a "My Favorite Burch Character Is..." paragraph. Ask them to give reasons for their choice. When all have written their paragraph, let a committee tally the results and make a composite list of reasons for liking each character.

5. Have a Friends-of-Robert-Burch party. Suggest that each student come dressed as a character from one of the books. Share scenes from some of the books; tell Ida Early stories; play checkers, tiddlywinks, and other appropriate games; and have popcorn or ice cream for refreshments.

FOLLOW-UP ACTIVITIES FOR INDIVIDUALS OR SMALL GROUPS:

1. Read Burch's *Christmas with Ida Early.* Make up a funny verse Ellen might have written about Preacher Preston. Now think up a more serious one she might have written about Ida Early.

2. Read Burch's *Christmas with Ida Early*. Recall how the class characterized Aunt Earnestine after hearing the first chapters of *Ida Early Comes over the Mountain*. Would you change or add to those traits now? If so, in what way? If she has changed, what caused the change?

3. Read Burch's *Skinny*. Write the letter Skinny will write to Miss Bessie just before he comes back to the hotel for the summer. Include things he has been doing, and a message for Roman and Peachy.

4. Read Burch's *Skinny*. Pretend that Calvin keeps a diary. Write his diary entry describing his visit to the hotel.

5. Read Burch's *Wilkin's Ghost*. What do you think will happen to Alex in the coming years? What do you think will cause Wilkin to go to Atlanta for the first time?

6. Read Burch's *Wilkin's Ghost*. Was the ending a surprise? Did you suspect Alex was the thief instead of Floyd? Would you have preferred a different ending? If so, what? If not, why not?

7. Read Burch's *D.J.'s Worst Enemy*. Why did Robert Burch give the book this title? What incidents helped D.J. to change and "join the family"?

8. Read Burch's *Hut School and the Wartime Home Front Heroes*. Make a list of all the events and activities that identified changes caused by living during the war.

9. Read Burch's *Hut School and the Wartime Home Front Heroes*. Compare school in rural Georgia in the early 1940s with your school today. Describe the likenesses and differences.

10. Read Burch's *Queenie Peavy*. Characterize her, giving an incident from the story to justify each conclusion you reach about character traits. A dynamic character changes before the end of the story. Did Queenie change? If so, in what ways? If not, why not?

11. Read Burch's *Two that Were Tough*. What did you find out about the feelings of old people by reading the book? Tell the plot of the story to an older person in your family or community. Does he or she have a similar feeling about freedom? Does the older person feel the story ended in the right way, or would he or she have changed the ending? If so, how? Share your interview with the class. In what ways can young people express their concerns about the aged in a positive manner?

Share a Shura Book

STUDENT OBJECTIVES:

- Assess characteristics of book characters
- Research the medicinal and food value of specific wild plants
- Identify and evaluate the theme in a story
- Research Civil War battle sites
- Write an imaginary letter to a newspaper editor
- Illustrate a favorite descriptive passage

RECOMMENDED READING:

Shura, Mary Francis. *The Barkley Street Six-Pack.* Dodd, Mead, 1979.
   Jane Todd's life is completely dominated by Natalie until Natalie moves away and Jane understands the problems created by the friendship.

———. *Chester.* Illustrated by Susan Swan. Dodd, Mead, 1980.
   In one week Chester and his unique family break all records on the block by being different from everyone else.

———. *Eleanor.* Illustrated by Susan Swan. Dodd, Mead, 1983.
   Chester's sister Eleanor devises an excellent plan for representing Millard C. Fillmore School in the field day.

———. *The Gray Ghosts of Taylor Ridge.* Illustrated by Michael Hampshire. Dodd, Mead, 1978.
   In an attempt to find a lost compass, Nan and Nathan come face to face with the gray ghosts haunting Taylor Ridge.

———. *Happles and Cinnamunger.* Illustrated by Bertram M. Tormey. Dodd, Mead, 1981.
   When Ilsa Von der Nagil becomes the Taggert family's new housekeeper, the mischievous fairies also arrive.

———. *Jefferson.* Illustrated by Susan Swan. Dodd, Mead, 1984.
   Jefferson's bad luck jinx changes after the neighborhood kids give him a surprise birthday party.

———. *Mister Wolf and Me.* Illustrated by Konrad Hack. Dodd, Mead, 1979.
   Thirteen-year-old Miles struggles to prove his dog's innocence when a wild dog kills a farmer's sheep.

———. *Pornada.* Illustrated by Erwin Schachner. Atheneum, 1968.
Francisco with his "good-for-nothing" pig puts his dreams and visions on paper and sells the artwork to keep his poor family alive during the harsh winter.

———. *The Search for Grissi.* Illustrated by Ted Lewis. Dodd, Mead, 1985.
The search for the cat Grissi unexpectedly brings together the whole neighborhood.

———. *The Season of Silence.* Atheneum, 1976.
Susie is given an opportunity to learn more about herself as she finds her routine and friends changed during her recovery from a serious illness.

BIOGRAPHICAL SOURCES:

For more information on Mary Francis Shura, see *Something about the Author,* 6:52–53; *Third Book of Junior Authors,* 264–65.

GROUP INTRODUCTORY ACTIVITY:

Set up a display of books by Mary Francis Shura. Introduce the class to *Chester* by reading humorous excerpts describing him and his remarkable family. If the children have shared *Chester* previously in the Friendship unit, have them recall events that indicate Chester's character. Discuss with the class why they might or might not like to have Chester's family in their neighborhood. One of Chester's unique characteristics is to wear a green sock on his left foot. As part of the Mary Francis Shura unit, plan with the class a "Sock-It-to-Me-Day" in which the class or entire student body each wears socks of any color, shape, or size in hair, on feet, or anywhere desired.

FOLLOW-UP ACTIVITIES FOR TEACHER AND STUDENTS TO SHARE:

Introduce Mary Francis Shura by telling the children that she writes about things she enjoys—families that allow children to be individuals, and animals, nature, and games. She likes "chuckles hidden so carefully that you have to listen twice."[7]

1. Read Shura's *Jefferson* aloud to the class. As you come to places in the story where the students find themselves in a possible money-making situation, stop reading and ask students for their

ideas on what activity will be carried out. After hearing all the troubles Jaime and his friends had raising money, have a class birthday party in honor of Jefferson. If possible, make the party special by finding ways to earn the money needed. Are there any ideas used by Jaime and his friends that would be appropriate? Students may want to invite another class to the party and share some of the plays or activities engaged in during the unit.

2. After a number of students have read Shura's *Chester,* let those students engage in a whopper contest. Who can tell a more interesting reason about why they were late to school than Chester did on page 58?

3. Read aloud *The Season of Silence* by Mary Francis Shura. In this novel, Susie begins to sketch the wildflowers she finds in Clary's meadow. After listening to Derek Born, she learns the names and uses of many of the flowers. Susie also discovers that Mrs. Clary has begun her own book, *Country Simples.* Have students research wildflowers in the library media center and make a class notebook, including illustrations and value of each, classified under Mrs. Clary's divisions of Healing, Food, and Magic.

4. Urge a group of students to read Shura's *Pornada,* in which Francisco's neighbor, Guido, makes a long journey in search of a special stone. Before a book discussion with them, share *The Treasure* by Uri Shulevitz (Farrar, Straus & Giroux, 1978). In the discussion, have students compare the journeys taken by the old man in each story. In what ways were they similar? Can they name any other stories in which a similar journey or quest is taken? Identify the theme in each book and evaluate which is more fully developed. Was descriptive language or illustrations and brief text a more effective way to develop the theme?

FOLLOW-UP ACTIVITIES FOR INDIVIDUALS OR SMALL GROUPS:

1. After reading Shura's *Chester,* list all of the traits that set Chester and his family apart from the other kids on the block.

2. In Shura's *Eleanor* Pogo Lambert, basketball star and Millard C. Fillmore Elementary School's only famous graduate, comes back to attend the field day events. After reading the story, find out which people who have attended your school are now famous in the community, state, or nation. Write up any information you can find out about one person and share with your class. If the person is still living, write to him/her asking what he/she re-members about attending your school. If the person responds, share the letter with your class.

3. The chapter headings in Shura's *Happles and Cinnamunger* are very descriptive of the events. After reading the book, write down why you think each chapter was given its title. For instance, why is one chapter named "And Doppelgangers"?

4. If you had been as lucky as Miss Floss in Shura's *Happles and Cinnamunger* to win a trip around the world, where would you choose to go and what would you want to see? After reading the story, use reference books to plot your travel route, identifying at least five cities you would visit and what you would plan to see in each place. Go one step further and figure out how much a trip like this would cost you if you had not won it.

5. The mysterious circumstances in Shura's *The Gray Ghosts of Taylor Ridge* center around a farm that had been caught in the strife of the Civil War over 100 years before. Nathan recounts how much he enjoyed going to the battle site at Lexington, Missouri. Go to the library and locate information on one of the following battles: Shiloh, Tennessee; Fredericksburg, Virginia; Chancellorsville, Virginia; Gettysburg, Pennsylvania; Vicksburg, Mississippi; or Richmond, Virginia. When did the battle take place? Who won? What was the significance or what was gained from this battle? Name the officers involved. Diagram the strategy used by either side or make a picture of the battle you researched.

6. The $10 gold coin found in Shura's *The Gray Ghosts of Taylor Ridge* was called the 1858 Gold Eagle. After reading the story, find out when this coin was issued and when it was discontinued. The Civil War brought many changes in our coinage. A new motto appeared in 1866 that we find on our coins today. What was it? Three commemorative half dollars, the Stone Mountain, Antietam, and Gettysburg, are reminders of the Civil War. Find out what you can about them and share with the class. An excellent source for your research is *Coins Have Tales to Tell* by Frances Williams Brown (Lippincott, 1966).

7. Read Shura's *The Search for Grissi.* Write an epilogue in which you tell how Grissi was found.

8. Read Shura's *Mister Wolf and Me,* which shows how emotionally attached Miles becomes to his dog in his struggle to save its life. Jordan Aggers, however, has evidence that makes him believe Mister Wolf is killing sheep and should be eliminated. Selecte either Miles's or Jordan's point of view and write an imaginary letter to the editor of Miles's hometown paper defending your position.

9. After reading Shura's *Mister Wolf and Me,* make a bibliography of dog stories, including author, title, publisher, and date of publication for each. Use the card catalog under the subject Dogs to find those owned by your library media center. You may want to include nonfiction books that identify breeds of dogs and give information about care. Remember, these books

have a Dewey number you may want to include instead of an F for fiction.

10. Jane Todd's father in Shura's *The Barkley Street Six-Pack* made up a whole alphabet of things to do on Barkley Street. Create an A-to-Z set of alphabet verses about games or ideas for using spare time enjoyed in your neighborhood. You may want others who have read the book to help you.

11. In Shura's *The Barkley Street Six-Pack,* Jane Todd learns about herself and gains self-confidence. After reading the book, list the reasons for this change in her character. Recall changes in Susie Spinner's character in *The Season of Silence.* Did the two girls experience any of the same changes? In order for a main character to be believable to the reader, that person must be fully developed. How does the author make both Jane and Susie believable?

12. In Shura's *Pornada,* Francisco and Pornada take time to appreciate the beauty in the world around them. After reading *Pornada,* locate passages with colorful, descriptive language used by the author to make you imagine Francisco's surroundings. Select one of these passages and illustrate it as you think Francisco might have done.

13. After reading Shura's *Jefferson,* select one day's activities described in the story and write a short play sharing those events. Get classmates to help you produce the play for the class. Videotape the play if possible so other classes can share it.

14. Select a scene from your favorite Shura story and make a reader's theater script. Share the scene with your teacher or library media specialist before writing to be sure it is appropriate for reader's theater. Duplicate copies of the script and ask classmates to share in producing it for the class.

15. Design a bookmark featuring your favorite Shura book so other students in the school will be curious and want to read her books. If several of your classmates make bookmarks, you may want to display them on a library media center bulletin board.

Myra Livingston, Poet and Editor

STUDENT OBJECTIVES:

- Recite a favorite poem to the class
- Write a limerick
- Discuss and analyze the mood created by a poem
- Compose and illustrate a concrete poem
- Examine the impact of figurative language in poems
- Recognize the difference between being a poet and the editor of an anthology

RECOMMENDED READING:

Livingston, Myra. *Celebrations.* Illustrated by Leonard Everett Fisher, Holiday House, 1985.
Sixteen different holidays are imaginatively presented in poetry and illustrations.

———. *A Circle of Seasons.* Illustrated by Leonard Everett Fisher. Holiday House, 1982.
Beautifully illustrated imaginative poetry makes the reader view the seasons in a new way.

———. *4-Way Stop and Other Poems.* Illustrated by James J. Spanfeller. Atheneum, 1976.
A variety of types of poems on subjects familiar to young people are included.

———. *How Pleasant to Know Mr. Lear.* Illustrated by Edward Lear. Holiday House, 1982.
Introduces Edward Lear and organizes his poetry around his likes and dislikes to enhance enjoyment and understanding.

———. *A Lollygag of Limericks.* Illustrated by Joseph Low. Atheneum, 1978.
A collection of 32 limericks inspired by English place names.

———. *The Malibu, and Other Poems.* Illustrated by James Spanfeller. Atheneum, 1972.
Forty brief poems reflecting observations and reactions to a variety of situations.

————. *Sky Songs.* Illustrated by Leonard Everett Fisher. Holiday House, 1984.
Fourteen sensitive poems, enhanced by striking double-spread illustrations, explore the moods of weather, sun, moon and stars.

————. *O Sliver of Liver.* Illustrated by Iris Van Rynbach. Atheneum, 1979.
Forty-two short poems to spark the reader's imagination.

BIOGRAPHICAL SOURCES:

For more information on Myra Cohn Livingston, see *Books Are by People,* 152–53; *Fourth Book of Junior Authors & Illustrators,* 231–32; *Something about the Author,* 5:116–17; *Twentieth-Century Children's Writers,* 794–96; *Twentieth-Century Children's Writers,* 2d ed., 490–91.

GROUP INTRODUCTORY ACTIVITY:

Myra Livingston says that she has loved books ever since she can remember and that she began writing poetry as soon as she could read. Her mother encouraged her to write about topics she knew well. Her first poems were published in *Story Parade,* a children's magazine. She wrote her first book of poems during her first year in college. Now she also edits poetry collections.[8]

Introduce poetry that Livingston has written or edited. Explain that the poetry in collections she edited was written by another poet or poets. Explore with the class what would be required to be a good editor of children's poetry collections. For example, they may suggest that an editor needs to be able to recognize *good* poetry; would need to read many, many poems; must know children's interests; and should select poems that stimulate imagination.

Introduce Livingston's book of poems *O Sliver of Liver* by reading "O Sliver of Liver." Talk about foods the children dislike. Let the class compose a poem using a student's suggestion of food for the first, fourth, and seventh lines.

Read "A Ghostly Conversation" as a choral. Explain to the class that each time you point to them they are to say no. The location of your hand from low to high will indicate the volume of each "No," with the lowest point as the softest response. When your hand sweeps across in front of you, they are to say "Boo," and to stop when your hand falls. Practice the "Nos" and "Boos" once before reading the poem.

Read the haiku "January." Let the class write a group haiku for April, July, and September, beginning with "Now here we are,

Spring," "Here we are, Summer," and "Now here we are, Fall." Remind the class that 5-, 7-, 5-syllable lines are needed.

Show and read the "concrete poetry" on pages 11, 24, and 41. Explain that concrete poetry is written in the shape of the subject of the poem. Give them a title such as "Snake" and let the class draw the shape and compose a poem recorded on the blackboard or a transparency. Suggest that each child write more concrete poems later and share with the class.

Read the haiku "Small Song" and share the illustration. Did the illustration help convey the meaning?

Tell the class that *O Sliver of Liver* will be on their reading table so they can enjoy other poems in the collection. They may want to copy other haiku that are not illustrated and draw appropriate pictures for a poetry bulletin board. Remind them to indicate Myra Livingston wrote them so that her haiku will not be confused with original poems written by class members.

FOLLOW-UP ACTIVITIES FOR TEACHER AND STUDENTS TO SHARE:

1. Introduce Livingston's *4-Way Stop and Other Poems* by reading "Spoiled Sister Song" as a choral. Divide the class in two groups. When you point, one group will say "I want what I want." The other group will say "I see what I want." Practice their saying the lines once before reading the poem. Read "Conversation with Washington" as a choral after assigning one student to say "What," another "How," etc. when you point to each one. Show the students "Old Glory" and read the poem. Does anyone remember the name for this type of poetry? "4-Way Stop," the title poem, is also concrete poetry. Share it with the class. Read "The Trouble Is ———." Let the class suggest other parental questions and orders that Myra Livingston might have used for the poem. Before reading "Paul Revere Speaks," ask the class to think of topics that Paul Revere might speak about. Read the poem. Think of a current person such as the President. What might the President's concerns be?

2. Read Livingston's *A Circle of Seasons* to the class, stopping to enjoy the beauty of the illustrations with each stanza. After sharing the entire poem, reread the verse beginning "Spring brings out her baseball bat." Have the children recall baseball terms used in describing spring. Reread to see if any were missed. Reread "Summer blasts off fireworks...." and discuss why that was appropriate for summer. After their comments, have them recall the exciting verbs that portray July 4. After "Autumn calls the winning toss...," the class will want to recall the verse. What did autumn tackle, block, and intercept? Think

about the meaning of "makes a last, long play." After "Winter blows a blizzard...," discuss why Fisher chose blue for the illustration. What mood is created? Recall the action words that contribute to that mood. In "Winter etches windowpanes...," we suddenly sense winter in what occupation? Let the class discuss phrases that contribute to the artist's impression.

3. Introduce *How Pleasant to Know Mr. Lear!* Explain to the class that the poetry was written by Lear and that only the introduction to the book and to each section were written by Myra Livingston. Share with the class the introduction to Lear, his appearance, likes, and dislikes. Then read "How Pleasant to Know Mr. Lear!". See how much of the real Lear is found in the poem. After sharing Livingston's commentary about "The Owl and the Pussy-Cat," pages xi and xii, and "By The Side Of The Ocean," page 80, read "The Owl and the Pussy-Cat." Discuss whether the Livingston introduction makes the poem more meaningful. Read "His Nose Is Remarkably Big," page 19, then share two or three nose limericks. Talk about the rhyme scheme of a limerick. Write a class "nose limerick." Read the introduction to "Pancakes and Chocolate Shrimps," page 90. Show the class the drawings of "The Dish Tree" on the following page. Ask each of the class members to write a limerick about one of Lear's pictures or make a food-related line drawing and write a limerick about it. Tell the class the book will be on the reading table so they can explore and enjoy more of Lear's poems.

4. Introduce the class to *A Lollygag of Limericks.* Explain that these were written by Livingston rather than by Lear as in *How Pleasant to Know Mr. Lear!*. Read the limerick on page 5 about the man on the Salisbury Plain, then read one of Lear's from *How Pleasant to Know Mr. Lear!,* in which the last line repeats the first. Let the class note the difference in the two limericks. Compare Low's illustrations with Lear's. In what ways are they similar/different? Read the limericks on pages 14 and 15 in *A Lollygag of Limericks.* Discuss other humorous things the Fellow of Wall might do in order to talk to people. What else might the widow of Chipping do because her memory is slipping? Suggest that class members write a limerick about one of their ideas for either of the two situations. After they write and illustrate with line drawings, they may be shared on a bulletin board in the classroom or library media center. Tell the class that these limericks are based on English place names. Suggest that they may want to read some limericks and see if they can locate the place by using an atlas map of England.

5. Introduce Livingston's *The Malibu and Other Poems.* Read "Get Lost." Discuss how the poetry form affects the mood of the content. Talk about their feelings when they want to be alone. Read "Theme with Variation." Ahead of time, put the lines that are the same on a transparency and, as a class, create a new

variation. Before reading "The Malibu," tell the students that Myra Livingston lives in Beverly Hills, California, and as the blurb to the book jacket indicates, she is, among other things, caught up in "beach bumming at Malibu." Discuss her feelings about "The Malibu" in winter, as evidenced in the poem. Tell them that the book will be on the reading table so they can read and enjoy others in the collection. Some student may want to illustrate one of his/her favorites for the bulletin board.

6. Introduce Livingston's *Sky Songs.* Read the explanation: "This art was prepared with acrylic paint, the same size as it appears in the book. The pictures were created on textured paper and then peeled from the back of the paper in preparation for laser light scanning." Show the class the illustration for "Noon." Ask the children what they think the poem is about after considering the illustration. Then read the poem. Discuss the mood created and what figurative language or unique concept inspired that mood. Share "Clouds" in the same way. Then show them the illustration for "Storm" and have them imagine the content before sharing the poem. Since the title is *Sky Songs,* see if they can anticipate the titles of the other 11 poems. Then read "Smog." Talk about the mood this creates. What message is Livingston giving by including this poem? Was poetry an effective way to deliver this message? Why/why not?

FOLLOW-UP ACTIVITIES FOR INDIVIDUALS OR SMALL GROUPS:

1. Read "Haiku for Halloween" in *4-Way Stop and Other Poems.* Think of another subject that could be used for a Halloween haiku. Write the poem and illustrate it.
2. Read *A Circle of Seasons* to yourself after hearing it read aloud. Which verse did you like best? Why? Include in your answer whether the season described is your favorite one. Did that influence your decision?
3. Read Livingston's introduction, "A Runcible Hat," page 57, in *How Pleasant to Know Mr. Lear!* and the poems in that section. Then write a limerick about a hat and make a line drawing about it.
4. Read the section "The Days of His Pilgrimage" pages 102–13 in *How Pleasant to Know Mr. Lear!.* Write a limerick about travel to a make-believe place or a mode of travel. Illustrate the poem with a Lear-like drawing.
5. Read the "Nonsense Cookery" recipes in *How Pleasant to Know Mr. Lear!,* pages 95–97. Write a humorous recipe and draw a picture of the treat that would result from following the recipe.

6. Read the limerick about the girl from Southend-on-Sea, page 27, in *A Lollygag of Limericks*. Find the story "The Princess and the Pea" in the library media center. Read it, then write another appropriate limerick inspired by that story. Share with your class.

7. Notice some of the funny place names in Livingston's *A Lollygag of Limericks*. Look at a map of your state. Find a humorous-sounding place name and write a limerick that seems appropriate for the name. Share with the class, pointing out the place name location on the map. You may want to research in the library media center or public library to find out the origin of the place name used.

8. Read the poems in Livingston's *Celebrations*. Write another appropriate verse for "New Year's Eve," "April Fool," and "Memorial Day" in the same pattern as that used by Livingston. Why is the "Memorial Day" poem more solemn than the other two?

9. Read "The New One" in Livingston's *The Malibu and Other Poems*. Think of a new joke to insert. Copy the appropriate lines and insert your new joke instead of the one used by Livingston. Illustrate and share with the class.

10. Read "Goldfish Whisper" in Livingston's *The Malibu and Other Poems*. Write a paragraph telling an incident recounted by a goldfish or create a "Conversation with a Goldfish" in poetry form.

11. Read Livingston's *Sky Songs*. Find a favorite poem and, using a poetry anthology from the library media center, find other poems on the same subject. Is your Livingston choice from *Sky Songs* still your favorite? Why? Why not? What different moods were created by different poets on the same subject? Why the difference?

American Folklore

STUDENT OBJECTIVES:

- Identify humor and exaggeration as a source of enjoyment of folktales
- Compare the qualities possessed by American tall tale heroes and heroines

- Learn and demonstrate techniques for effective story telling
- Write and produce a puppet play based on a tall tale hero
- Apply knowledge of the characteristics of a tall tale by writing an original story
- Listen to stories being told and assess the value of this form of communication

RECOMMENDED READING:

Chase, Richard. *Grandfather Tales.* Illustrated by Berkeley Williams, Jr. Houghton Mifflin, 1948.
    Mountain tales, with their unique blend of humor, come to life through such stories as "Sody Sallyrates," "Soap, Soap, Soap," and "Old One-Eye."

———. *The Jack Tales.* Illustrated by Berkeley Williams, Jr. Houghton Mifflin, 1943.
    Jack outwits everything from giants to wild hogs in 18 stories from the mountains of North Carolina.

Emrich, Duncan. *The Nonsense Book of Riddles, Rhymes, Tongue Twisters, Puzzles and Jokes from American Folklore.* Illustrated by Ib Ohlsson. Four Winds Press, 1970.
    These nonsense rhymes show the humor and spirit of the early settlers.

Keats, Ezra Jack. *John Henry: An American Legend.* Pantheon, 1965.
    Bold, vivid illustrations enhance the tale of this folk hero.

Kellogg, Steven. *Paul Bunyan.* Morrow, 1984.
    Humorous illustrations extend the brief text, which recounts the unbelievable adventures of the amazing lumberjack.

McCormick, Dell J. *Paul Bunyan Swings His Axe.* Caxton, 1936.
    Paul Bunyan comes to life through tales about the popcorn blizzard and the winter of the big snow, among others.

———. *Tall Timber Tales.* Illustrated by Lorna Livesley. Caxton, 1939.
    Twenty stories record the adventures of Paul Bunyan in the north woods.

Malcolmson, Anne. *Yankee Doodle's Cousins.* Illustrated by Robert McCloskey. Houghton Mifflin, 1951.
    Twenty-eight stories of heroes from the East, South, Mississippi Valley, and West are included in this collection.

Schwartz, Alvin. *Scary Stories to Tell in the Dark.* Illustrated by Stephen Gammell. Lippincott, 1981.
    Funny twists and scary endings characterize these stories of ghosts and skeleton-like creatures.

―――. *Whoppers, Tall Tales and Other Lies.* Illustrated by Glen Rounds. Lippincott, 1975.
This collection of folklore includes whoppers about farming, fighting, fiddling, and fishing.

Stoutenberg, Adrien. *American Tall Tales.* Illustrated by Richard M. Powers. Viking, 1966.
Eight accounts of the feats of famous folk tale heroes are presented.

GROUP INTRODUCTORY ACTIVITY:

Two well-known tall-tale heroes are Pecos Bill and Paul Bunyan. Read a story about either of them from Anne Malcolmson's *Yankee Doodle's Cousins.* Follow with a discussion of the following: What physical characteristics did the hero have? What was the setting of the story? What hardships or problems were encountered by the hero and how were they solved? Cite examples of humor and exaggeration. What symbols or objects come to mind when this tall tale hero is mentioned? What physical activity might the people have been doing when this tale was first told? Does this tale mean as much to us today as it did to the pioneers 100 to 200 years ago?

After the discussion, help the students locate folktales in the library through the subject entry in the card catalog. Ask each student to locate, check out, and read a tall tale. In a follow-up class session, they should be prepared to share the following information with the class: title of the book, name of the story if it was included in a collection, description of the main character, setting, at least two problems the hero encountered and how each was overcome, and an exaggeration in the story.

FOLLOW-UP ACTIVITIES FOR TEACHER AND STUDENTS TO SHARE:

1. If American folklore filmstrips and/or recordings are available, ask the library media specialist to set up an area in the media center where children can individually share the heroes in audiovisual format. A suggested sound filmstrip is *John Henry: An American Legend* (Guidance Associates, 1967, 45 fr., col., 14 min). Good sound recordings include *Johnny Appleseed and Paul Bunyan* (Caedmon, 1970, disc CDL 5-1321), *John Henry and Joe Magarac* (Caedmon, n.d., disc CDL 5-1318); and *Jackie Torrence: "The Story Lady"* (Weston Woods, 1982, disc WW 720 C).

2. Students should be urged to read at least five different stories of American folklore heroes and heroines in order to note similarities in the stories and the divergence of occupations in which they engaged. To help the class organize their data concerning each hero/heroine, make a large posterboard chart with columns in which children can list the character's name, occupation, characteristics, region in which he/she lived, and one exaggerated incident recounted in the story read. An alternative approach to the poster board format is to duplicate forms for each child to chart this information.

3. Have the students assist in developing a state story file. Make a 5″ X 8″ index card for each region of the United States. As stories are read by the teacher and students about regional characters, record the bibliographic information on the appropriate card. Also indicate where the book can be located—personal collection, school library media center, public library. This file will be valuable for future folktale units or for correlation with social studies units about the states.

4. Read aloud Ezra Jack Keats's *John Henry: An American Legend.* Then let students discuss the qualities that made John Henry a folk hero. What was his first outstanding feat? Show the illustrations again so children can study them. What techniques did Keats use to demonstrate his size and endurance? What symbolizes John Henry's strength? Since these stories were originally handed down by word of mouth, each illustrator used his/her own imagination in extending the story. Urge children to find another story about John Henry in available collections of folk tales and illustrate a favorite scene.

5. Ask the music teacher to work with the students and teach them songs about American folk heroes, such as "The Ballad of Davy Crockett" or "John Henry." One source for folk songs is Ruth Crawford Seeger's *American Folk Songs for Children in Home, School, and Nursery School* (Doubleday, 1948). If *Cobblestone* magazine is available, refer to pages 39–41 in the October 1982 issue.

6. Urge a group of students to dramatize a folk hero such as Johnny Appleseed. If available, refer to pages 537–48 in Sylvia Kamerman's *Dramatized Folktales of the World* (Plays, 1971) for scripts and suggestions. If time allows, the children may prefer to write their own play and dramatize it for the class.

7. Read to yourself pages 1–3 in Alvin Schwartz's *Scary Stories to Tell in the Dark.* Then turn the lights down low and read aloud "Me Tie Dough-Ty Walker." Keep the book in the classroom and challenge the students to read the stories on their own. Some may want to read or tell one of the stories to the class.

8. Using Duncan Emrich's *The Nonsense Book of Riddles, Rhymes, Tongue Twisters, Puzzles and Jokes from American Folklore,* set up a nonsense corner in the classroom. Put some riddles on note

cards with answers on the back so children can try to figure out the riddle before reading the solution. Set aside time for the students to read tongue twisters aloud. Go outside as a class or involve the physical education teacher in playing jump rope rhymes. Encourage the children to record favorite riddles or rhymes on the tape recorder. Before learning autograph rhymes, urge the students to ask their parents and grandparents if they recall autograph rhymes from their school days which the children can share with the class. Perhaps they have an old autograph album that can be brought to school and displayed.

9. *The Jack Tales* collected by Richard Chase includes episode after episode concerning the adventures of an unassuming hero named Jack. Read the preface to yourself to gain some background about these tales to share with the children. Read aloud to the class some of Jack's adventures. The colorful, descriptive language influences the storytelling quality, imaginative stimulation, and humor of these stories. To get students to listen for this colorful language, print out passages such as "Jack looked down the holler, saw a man about thirty-feet high comin' a-stompin up the mountain, steppin' right over the laurel bushes and the rock-clifts" (p. 7). After sharing *The Jack Tales,* suggest that today authentic folk tales are often collected from people who cannot read and have no radio or TV. Discuss why this could be important in the preservation of the original tales. If possible, have the class listen to Jackie Torrence's rendition of "Jack and the Varmints" on the recording *Jackie Torrence: "The Story Lady"* (Weston Woods, 1982, disc WW 720 C). Allow time afterward for them to discuss the storytelling techniques she used to hold their attention.

FOLLOW-UP ACTIVITIES FOR INDIVIDUALS OR SMALL GROUPS:

1. After having read several whoppers from Schwartz's *Whoppers: Tall Tales and Other Lies,* read other sources and see if you can find other versions of the same story. If B.A. Botkin's *A Treasury of American Folklore* (Crown, 1944) is in the reference section of your school or public library, it would be a good source to use. Ask your grandparents or elderly neighbors to tell you any whoppers they remember from childhood. Are any of their stories in the books you have read? Were there any differences in the stories?

2. Read or listen to at least three versions of the legend of John Henry. Write down the title, author, and call number of each source in which you located the story. List the characteristics of John Henry that seemed real to you and those that seemed

exaggerated. Identify the setting of each story. Where and why do you think the story of John Henry began? Share the information you have gathered about John Henry by doing a pantomime or monologue for the class that depicts his character traits.

3. Read at least two stories about Paul Bunyan in Dell McCormick's *Tall Timber Tales* or listen to a recording about Paul Bunyan if one is available. The stories are filled with exaggerations and comparisons, such as Paul Bunyan's footprints being so large that they filled with water and became lakes or that it took seven men to lift his axe. Write down the name of each story and list at least three exaggerations in each tale.

4. As you read or hear tales of Paul Bunyan, you meet some very colorful friends of Paul's. They have names such as Peter Puget, Chris Crosshaul, Cream Puff Fatty, and Hot Biscuit Slim. Using either names that begin with the same letter, such as Peter Puget, or names that describe the person's job, such as Hot Biscuit Slim, create five names that might represent a tall tale hero of today. Write a brief description of an activity each engaged in, such as the one McCormick records in *Paul Bunyan Swings His Axe,* page 32: "When Hot Biscuit Slim, the cook, made soup he rowed out into the center of the kettle with boatloads of cabbages, turnips and potatoes, and shoveled them into the boiling hot water."

5. Select one tall-tale character and think of as many of your own similes or comparisons to describe him/her as you can. For example, Annie Christmas was as tall as ———, Paul Bunyan's footprints were as large as ———, or Pecos Bill's whip sounded like ———.

6. Using the characters included in Malcolmson's *Yankee Doodle's Cousins* or a list prepared by your teacher, use the encyclopedia to find out which tall-tale characters actually lived. Make a list of those who actually lived, when and where they lived, and what they achieved. Select one and record how you think s/he became a tall tale hero or heroine.

7. Folktales are said to be a mirror of the people who tell them. The stories attempt to record both the wonders of nature and the human emotions of fear, joy, sorrow, and triumph evidenced by the people who told and listened to them. After reading "Johnny Appleseed: Rainbow Walker" in Stoutenberg's *American Tall Tales,* write a paragraph pointing out emotions identified in the story which mirrored the people who traveled the wilderness roads to the West, *or* make a diorama or picture depicting the beauty of nature shared in this tale.

8. Working in a small group, write your own puppet play based on the adventures of an American folk hero. Produce the puppet play for the class. Videotape the play if possible so it can be shared with parents or other students.

9. What if Mike Fink and Ol' Stormalong, John Henry and Joe Magarac, *or* Blackbeard and Pirate Jean Lafitte teamed up for an adventure together? After reading a story about each of the two you select, write your own tall tale of an adventure the two heroes might have had together.

10. Make a question-and-answer game or crossword puzzle using ideas from at least 10 of the tall-tale characters about whom you have read or heard stories. For example, "Who had a blue ox named Babe?" (Paul Bunyan) or "Who was the natural scientist from Nebraska?" (Febold Feboldson). Decide on the number of players and rules if you prepare a game. Share with the class.

11. In a small group, listen to the story "Sody Sallyraytus" on the recording *The Folktellers: Tales to Grow On* (Weston Woods, 1981, disc WW 711). Listen to the repetition and join in with the storytellers. After hearing this story, listen for the almost musical quality storytelling has in other stories on the recording. Each member of the group should read the "Sody Sallyraytus" story in Richard Chase's *Grandfather Tales* (pp. 75–79). Discuss the following with your teacher or library media specialist: What difference do you feel between hearing a story told and reading it silently? Which do you prefer? Why? What made you laugh in the story? What difference did you find between the Folkteller's version and Richard Chase's?

12. Read Steven Kellogg's *Paul Bunyan*. Study the illustration of Paul rocking in the cradle. List five specific problems caused by the waves.

    Make an illustration of another underground ogre Paul might have found. Name it, describe why people feared it, and tell how Paul got rid of it.

13. In the preface to *Grandfather Tales* Richard Chase says, "After you have learned the tales in silent print, shut the book and tell 'em." Select one of the stories from *Grandfather Tales* or *The Jack Tales* to tell to the class as a storyteller would. Discuss storytelling techniques with your teacher or library media specialist.

14. After hearing "Jack and the Varmints" told by Jackie Torrence on the recording *Jackie Torrence: "The Story Lady"* (Weston Woods, 1982, disc WW 720C) or reading it in Chase's *The Jack Tales,* decide what you would do if you were hired to get rid of a wild hog, a unicorn, or a lion. Using the tape recorder, explain what steps you would take to solve each problem.

Meet the Memorable Characters of Betsy Byars

STUDENT OBJECTIVES:

- Analyze plot, setting, theme, and character developed through book discussion
- Create appropriate titles for book chapters
- Discuss how problems encountered may help to develop character traits
- Analyze what makes characters credible
- Predict what will happen to a character
- Create a play or reader's theater script
- Conclude how conflict is important to plot development

RECOMMENDED READING:

Byars, Betsy. *The Animal, The Vegetable, and John D. Jones.* Illustrated by Ruth Sanderson. Delacorte, 1982.
Clara and Deanie find their vacation nearly ruined by intruders—their father's girl friend and her son John D. Jones.

———. *The Cartoonist.* Illustrated by Richard Cuffari. Viking, 1978.
Alfie's attic and his cartoons provide an escape from his family's problems until he is forced to face his own.

———. *The Cybil War.* Illustrated by Gail Owens. Viking, 1981.
Simon has long admired Cybil Ackerman, but thanks to his friend Tony Angotti, Simon's friendship with Cybil is nearly destroyed.

———. *The House of Wings.* Illustrated by Daniel Schwartz. Viking, 1972.
Sammie discovers a most unusual living situation while staying with his grandfather and a house filled with birds.

———. *The Night Swimmers.* Illustrated by Troy Howell. Delacorte, 1980.
Three lonely children, Retta, Johnny, and little Roy, find pleasure by escaping to a neighbor's pool at night until a near tragedy awakens their father to the needs of his family.

———. *The Pinballs.* Harper & Row, 1977.
Three children, Carlie, Harney, and Thomas J., who are in the same foster home, learn how to adjust and eventually trust each other.

———. *The Summer of the Swans.* Illustrated by Ted CoConis. Viking, 1970.
Sara, whose feelings change almost hourly, is totally wrapped up in herself until her retarded brother gets lost.

———. *Trouble River.* Illustrated by Rocco Negri. Viking, 1969.
Dewey finds trouble as he and his grandmother escape the Indians by going down Trouble River on his handmade raft.

———. *The TV Kid.* Illustrated by Richard Cuffari. Viking, 1976.
Lennie's world revolves around fantasies of television game shows until an accident nearly costs him his life.

BIOGRAPHICAL SOURCES:

For more information on Betsy Byars, see *More Books by More People,* 68–73; *Something about the Author,* 4:40–41; *Third Book of Junior Authors,* 55; *Twentieth-Century Children's Writers,* 215–17; *Twentieth-Century Children's Writers,* 2d ed., 148–49.

GROUP INTRODUCTORY ACTIVITY:

Introduce the unit on Betsy Byars by telling the children that although Betsy loved to read, she had no idea of writing as a career until she was alone much of the time while her husband was in graduate school. First she wrote for magazines, but as her children grew, she became a writer of books for young people. She finds her ideas in the things around her—in newspapers and in her children's school happenings. She writes mainly in the winter; in the summer she assists her husband in his hobby of hang gliding.[9] Present brief book talks on two or three of her books, and then read a few sentences from some of her other books to establish the conflicts and interest the children. Several suggestions for book talks follow. In *The Pinballs,* an introduction to the three children and their problems is appropriate, followed by dialogue showing the characters as they establish their relationships and become stronger (pp. 96–97), and ending with Carlie and Thomas J.'s decision on how to help Harvey (pp. 115–16).

In discussing *The TV Kid,* describe Lennie's home life and his addiction to the TV. When reading about Lennie's visit to the houses on the lake, include his thoughts on why it is OK to break in and watch television (pp. 34–35). Stop when Lennie is under the house and discovers the rattlesnakes (p. 55).

Describe how and why Sammy was left in the care of his eccentric grandfather in *The House of Wings*. The sighting of the injured crane, serving to create a bond between Sammy and his grandfather (portions of pp. 36–49) is important to the conflict solution. Stop reading and encourage the children to find out what happens when they discover that the crane is blind (p. 90).

In *The Animal, The Vegetable, and John D. Jones* Betsy Byars introduces two sisters whose vacation is nearly ruined by unwanted company. The origin of the title becomes evident (p. 32) as the girls call each other names while John D. Jones watches. Before leading up to Clara's being carried out to sea on the raft (p. 104), read a situation between the girls in which a relationship with John D. is established.

FOLLOW-UP ACTIVITIES FOR TEACHER AND STUDENTS TO SHARE:

1. Read aloud the adventures of 12-year-old Dewey and his grandmother in *Trouble River*. At the end of each chapter, stop and discuss the problems or conflicts that Dewey faces. By the end of the book, the students should recognize how conflict is important to the development of the plot. After completing the novel, have the students recall some of the conflicts Dewey had and how he solved them. What character traits did Dewey develop in facing these conflicts?

2. Have several copies of any of the following books by Betsy Byars available for at least four to six students to read before a scheduled book discussion: *The Pinballs, The Cartoonist, The Summer of the Swans, The Night Swimmers, The Cybal War,* and *The TV Kid.* At first, book discussions can be led by the librarian or teacher, but students may wish to lead later ones. In this type of book discussion, the following points should be considered:

   In literary analysis, character development means developing the main character with a multiplicity of human traits and emotions. For the character to be credible, there must be a unity of character and action. Terms that can be used effectively in referring to characters include "flat" (not well developed); "round" (well developed); "static" (do not change during the story), and "dynamic" (change as the story progresses). Have the children characterize the protagonist and/or other major characters, utilizing descriptions and events in the story to document their analysis.

   Plot is described as the series of events showing the character in action. Conflict is necessary in plot development. Conflict occurs when the protagonist (central character) struggles against an antagonist (opposing force or forces). These forces can be nature, society, another, or self. Have the students evaluate the plot, identify each conflict as self against ———. What were the solutions to each conflict?

Identify the setting (time and place) and determine whether it was necessary for the development of the story (integral) or of little consequence (backdrop). Urge students to justify their answer.

From what point of view did the author tell the story? Was it first person (told with "I" from the character's perspective) or omniscient (author telling story in third person so he/she can be "all-knowing" about a number of characters). Was the author's choice of point of view satisfactory for the readers? Why/why not?

Identify the primary theme that was the underlying message of the book. Students may determine there were also secondary themes. Were the themes implicit (not specifically stated) or explicit (stated in the text)?

What seems to be the author's purpose in writing the book? Was it for enjoyment only, for information, or was the author trying to present a specific message? What might have been a part of the author's background that caused this story to be written? Have students consult biographical information about Betsy Byars if it is available.

Teachers/librarians seeking additional information about approaches to analyzing books should consult Rebecca J. Lukens's *A Critical Handbook Of Children's Literature.*[10]

3. Betsy Byars's novels provide a means for readers to experience the lives of her fictional characters, to gain a better understanding of people, and to participate in the pleasure of reading. After students have been exposed to a number of books by Betsy Byars, bring the class together to discuss possibilities such as the following:

Which book characters by Betsy Byars seemed most believable? The student should answer by describing the person and giving at least two situations that contributed to his/her credibility.

Describe and discuss any similarities between characters in her books.

What conflicts and solutions can be found in her stories?

What similarities in conflict (self against self, society, nature, another person) can be found?

Discuss the various themes found in her books. Was the same theme evident in more than one?

FOLLOW-UP ACTIVITIES FOR INDIVIDUALS OR SMALL GROUPS:

1. If Betsy Byars were coming to visit your school, write down the questions you would ask her about herself and/or one of her books you have read.
2. Harvey in Byars's *The Pinballs* made a "Bad Things" list. After reading *The Pinballs,* make a list of problems encountered by Carlie or Thomas J. and the solutions they found to each.
3. Read Byars's *The TV Kid,* stopping on page 55 when Lennie hears the sound of a rattle. Now think about and predict what will happen to Lennie. Write your own account of what happens. Fold your paper and put it in an envelope to keep. Now finish reading *The TV Kid* and compare your account with Betsy Byars's ending.
4. Read Byars's *The Night Swimmers.* Pretend you are a newspaper reporter and you have been assigned to write an account of the incident involving three children who were sneaking into Colonel Roberts's pool at night to swim, as Reta, Johnny, and Roy did. Write the newspaper story recounting how little Roy nearly drowns.
5. In chapter 2 of Byars's *The Cartoonist,* one senses Alfie's enjoyment of his cartoons. Either think about an incident that has happened to you or create your own Super Hero's adventure and write a comic strip describing the situation. For information on how to write and draw cartoons, you may want to refer to a book in the library media center or public library such as *The Art of the Comic Strip* by Shirley Glubok (Macmillan, 1979) or *The Young Cartoonist: The ABC's of Cartooning* by Syd Hoff (Stravon Educational Press, 1983).
6. In Byars's *The House of Wings* Sammy learns how to feed and care for geese, a parrot, a crane, and an owl. Select three of the birds grandfather cared for and do the research needed to complete a chart showing how each bird gets food, moves, and communicates.
7. If you enjoyed Byars's *The House of Wings,* read *In Search of the Sandhill Crane* by Keith Robertson (Viking, 1973). Determine the primary theme in each of the two books.
8. After reading Byars's *The Summer of the Swans,* write your explanation of what Sara meant by the statement on page 119: "I have cried over myself a hundred times this summer," she thought. "I have wept over my big feet and my skinny legs and my nose. I have even cried over my stupid shoes, and now when I have a true sadness there are no tears left."
9. On pages 98-99 of Byars's *The Animal, The Vegetable, and John D. Jones,* Clara gives titles to unwritten books that describe her miserable vacation. Since Betsy Byars didn't give chapter titles

in this book, read *The Animal, The Vegetable, and John D. Jones* and write appropriate titles for each chapter.
10. Read Byars's *Trouble River* carefully, particularly noting dialogue. Select an event that has good character dialogue and a minimum of action, such as Dewey telling his grandmother about building the raft, and create a play or reader's theater script.

Hobbies

STUDENT OBJECTIVES:

- Construct a musical instrument
- Create a potato print
- Share a hobby with the class
- Develop a word puzzle
- Analyze the classification of various hobby books in the library media center
- Create an original cartoon character
- Apply sportsmath to sports events

RECOMMENDED READING:

Arthur, Lee; James, Elizabeth; and Taylor, Judith B. *Sportsmath: How It Works.* Lothrop, 1975.
Through a description of an actual football, baseball, basketball, hockey, and tennis game, the user is taught how to compute averages, percentages, and a variety of calculations.

Benjamin, Carol Lea. *Cartooning for Kids.* Crowell, 1982.
Demonstrates how to create simple cartoons using circles, dots, lines, and curves, as well as suggesting ideas to try.

Berndt, Fredrick. *The Domino Book.* Nelson, 1974.
Presents rules for domino games such as Seven-Toed Pete and Sniff, solitaire rules, and a variety of arithmetical puzzles using dominoes.

Cobb, Vicki, and Darling, Kathy. *Bet You Can't!* Illustrated by Martha Weston. Lothrop, 1980.
Presents more than 60 science impossibilities to fool the reader and a presentation of the scientific principles for each.

Cone, Fern Geller. *Crazy Crocheting.* Illustrated by J. Morton Cone, Ferne Geller Cone, and Rachel Osterlof. Atheneum, 1981.
Gives instructions for basic crocheting, ideas for correcting mistakes, and suggestions for special things to make.

Engler, Larry, and Fijan, Carol. *Making Puppets Come Alive.* Illustrated by David Attie. Taplinger, 1973.
Through photographs of hand puppets, basic finger, wrist, and arm movements are shared, followed by exercises and suggested improvisations.

Haddad, Helen R. *Potato Printing.* Crowell, 1981.
Demonstrates how a potato can be used to print pictures, designs, and messages on fabric and paper.

Hansen, Rosanna. *The Fairy Tale Book of Ballet.* Grosset, 1980.
Photographs and text depict three much-loved ballets—*Swan Lake, The Sleeping Beauty,* and *The Nutcracker.*

Judy, Susan, and Judy, Stephen. *Gifts of Writing.* Scribner's, 1980.
Suggests ways that creative writing and art can be combined to make stationery, books, cards, and a variety of holiday gifts.

Kohl, Herbert. *A Book of Puzzlement.* Schocken, 1981.
An exciting collection of over 300 games and puzzles involving words, sentences, nonsense, fables, songs, codes, and photographic writing.

Olcheski, Bill. *Beginning Stamp Collecting.* Walck, 1976.
A broad introduction to stamp collecting, as well as the role of dealers, auctions, clubs, and shows in assisting the young collector.

Wiseman, Ann. *Making Musical Things.* Scribner's, 1979.
Gives instructions for making a variety of musical instruments from easily acquired items, such as milk cartons, rubber bands, and plastic straws.

GROUP INTRODUCTORY ACTIVITY:

Introduce the topic of hobbies by suggesting that there are three types: collecting objects, making objects, and performing an activity. Let the class share what their hobbies are, categorizing each as it is shared.

Suggest to the class that you have pulled books representing all three types of hobbies—and there are many more in the school library media center. Then talk about why one might want to have a hobby. After the children share a number of ideas, talk about reasons why someone who has a hobby would want to read about it.

Introduce Hansen's *The Fairy Tale Book of Ballet* as a book about one type of hobby. Read the story of the ballet *The Sleeping Beauty,* facts about the dances, the music by Tchaikovsky, the makeup, and the costumes. Talk about the differences between the ballet version and the story as the class knows it. Why were changes made? Was the class surprised at any facts about the actors or makeup? Suggest that if anyone in the class has ballet or dancing as a hobby, they may want to read this and/or other books about ballet, then share their hobby with the class. Note that the book is classified in the 700s (the arts). Let the class justify this classification.

FOLLOW-UP ACTIVITIES FOR TEACHER AND STUDENTS TO SHARE:

1. To introduce Cone's book *Crazy Crocheting,* ask a person in the community to come to the class and demonstrate crocheting. After young people see how to get started, the book will be much more meaningful to them. Suggest that if one or more members of the class are interested, they could make some finger folk (puppets) and share a story with the class. An older member of the community who crochets might be willing to come back to the class and help in this endeavor. Note that this book is also classified in the 700s (the arts).

2. Introduce *Making Musical Things* by reading the poetry introduction. Show the class the variety of instruments Wiseman illustrates. Then suggest that the class make bottle cap, walnut, and button finger castanets. Let the class try out their instruments with appropriate music. Place the book in a music center and suggest that class members bring materials, make instruments, and share with the class.

3. Introduce *A Book of Puzzlement* by letting the class have fun with words. Using Kohl's introduction (p. 65), as a class, create a few new words with complete definitions. Suggest members of the class make other words with complete definitions for a class dictionary. Suggest they illustrate each and make it a picture dictionary. Introduce Lewis Carroll's word ladders. Read the directions (p. 45) and then, with one-letter substitutions, as a class try Carroll's challenge to Drive PIG to STY, etc. After the class understands the process, suggest that they make Carroll-type challenges. Tell the students that you will leave the book on the class library table. Urge them to use it to develop other word puzzles.

4. Introduce Judy's *Gifts of Writing* by suggesting that the class members make family trees, pages 18–21. Have each student

interview their parents, getting basic information about each ancestor, including (if possible) birth and death date, place of birth, where lived, occupation, if married, and names of children. Assist children in developing their basic tree and adding leaves. If someone in the community is interested in tracing histories, perhaps they will share their techniques with the class. Let the class have an idea of the variety of ideas that are in *Gifts of Writing.* Suggest that they may want to develop some of those ideas to share with the class.

5. At the close of the unit, have a Hobby Day. Urge those students who have hobbies to read a book about their hobby, bring the hobby, and share while introducing the book they read. Other students may become interested in that hobby as a result.

FOLLOW-UP ACTIVITIES FOR INDIVIDUALS OR SMALL GROUPS:

1. Read the section of Kohl's *A Book of Puzzlements* on "Crossword Puzzles and Thematic Word Squares," pages 73–83. Make a puzzle using hobbies or book characters as a theme. Share with the class.

2. Read "Lipograms" in Kohl's *A Book of Puzzlements,* pages 61–64. Select a poem and rewrite it, leaving out words containing a letter or letters you decide to omit. Retain the same meaning in the poem despite the substituted words. Share with the class.

3. Read about "Fortune Cookies" in Judy's *Gifts of Writing.* Make up the fortune, type or write on strips of paper, make the cookies using the suggested recipe, and share with the class.

4. If you collect stamps for a hobby, read Olcheski's *Beginning Stamp Collecting.* Share with the class new facts that you learned.

5. With two or three classmates, read Engler's *Making Puppets Come Alive* and practice techniques for moving puppets. Using hand puppets, teach these techniques to the class. Improvise a skit to share.

6. Using Haddad's *Potato Printing,* practice some of the suggested techniques. Then do some fabric or background printing to share with the class.

7. If science is a hobby of yours, read Cobb's *Bet You Can't!* Try some of the scientific impossibilities. Demonstrate your favorite to the class, explaining the scientific principle involved.

8. If you enjoy drawing, read Benjamin's *Cartooning for Kids.* Try cartooning a nursery rhyme, develop some note paper with a series of cartoon corners, or make a greeting card appropriate

for the month with your original cartoon character. Share with the class.

9. If you enjoy playing dominoes, use Berndt's *The Domino Book* to find rules for a new domino solitaire game. Explain the rules to the class and demonstrate the game.

10. Browse the library. Find a hobby book in each of the Dewey classifications from 300 to 900. Justify why each is classified as it is. Share the books and your reasoning for the classifications with the library media specialist, then with your class.

11. If you are a sports fan or enjoy playing football, baseball, basketball, hockey, or tennis, read Arthur's *Sportsmath*. Using a specific game currently being played, use the information about computing averages and other calculations to analyze the game. Share your findings with the class.

Culminating Activities after Fifth Grade and Up

Have young people as a group address the following:

Discuss book characters you have shared in this and previous years. What book and author does each represent? Why do you remember each?

What do you remember about specific authors? When did they begin to write? Where do they get their ideas?

What follow-up experiences did you enjoy the most? Did they help you remember the books?

What poems and poets do you recall? Can you say any short poems or portions of poems from memory? What is a parody? What is a concrete poem? How does figurative language affect your reaction to a poem? What is the difference between a poet and an anthologist?

What is the general arrangement of books in the library? In what hundred would natural science, history, and poetry be found? Describe a nonfiction book, give its title, and see if other class members can suggest in which hundred classification it will be found.

Read the students a short story. Critically analyze the story, letting students discuss the type of plot conflict, characterization, theme, setting, and point of view.

REFERENCES

1. Lee Bennett Hopkins, *More Books by More People,* (New York: Harcourt Brace Jovanovich, 1974), p. 179.

2. *Jean Craighead George,* (brochure)(New York: Harper & Row, August 1981), p. 1.

3. *Jean Craighead George,* p. 1.

4. Rebecca Lukens, *A Critical Handbook of Children's Literature,* 2d ed. (Glenview, IL: Scott, Foresman, 1982), p. 55.

5. D.L. Kirkpatrick, ed., *Twentieth-Century Children's Writers* (New York: St. Martin's Press, 1978), p. 1342.

6. Hopkins, p. 64.

7. Doris de Montreville and Donna Hill, eds., *Third Book of Junior Authors* (New York: H.W. Wilson, 1972), p. 264.

8. Doris de Montreville and Elizabeth D. Crawford, eds, *Fourth Book of Junior Authors & Illustrators* (New York: H.W. Wilson, 1978), pp. 231–32.

9. de Montreville and Hill, p. 55.

10. Lukens, pp. 28–174.

Appendices

Appendix I
Biographical Sources for
Authors and Illustrators

Books Are by People. By Lee Bennett Hopkins. New York: Citation Press, 1969. o.p.

Fifth Book of Junior Authors & Illustrators. Edited by Sally Holmes Holtze. New York: H.W. Wilson, 1983.

Fourth Book of Junior Authors & Illustrators. Edited by Doris de Montreville and Elizabeth D. Crawford. New York: H.W. Wilson, 1978.

The Junior Book of Authors, 2d ed. Edited by Stanley J. Kunitz and Howard Haycraft. New York: H.W. Wilson, 1951.

More Books by More People. By Lee Bennett Hopkins. Harcourt Brace Jovanovich 1974.

More Junior Authors. Edited by Muriel Fuller. New York: H.W. Wilson, 1963.

Something about the Author. Edited by Anne Commire. Detroit, MI: Gale Research. Vol. 1–39, 1978–1985.

Third Book of Junior Authors. Edited by Doris de Montreville and Donna Hill. New York: H.W. Wilson, 1972.

Twentieth-Century Children's Writers. Edited by D.L. Kirkpatrick. New York: St. Martin's, 1978, o.p.

Twentieth-Century Children's Writers. 2d ed. Edited by D.L. Kirkpatrick. New York: St. Martin's, 1983.

Yesterday's Authors of Books for Children. Vol. 1. Edited by Anne Commire. Detroit, MI: Gale Research, 1977.

Appendix II
Sources for Book Introduction Techniques

Baker, Augusta, and Green, Ellin. *Storytelling: Art and Technique.* New York: Bowker, 1977.
Basic ideas for the selection, preparation, and presentation of stories in a variety of settings.

Bauer, Caroline Feller. *Handbook for Storytellers.* Chicago: American Library Association, 1977.
Gives techniques for storytelling, multimedia storytelling, puppetry, and book talks.

———. *This Way to Books.* New York: H.W. Wilson, 1983.
Approaches to storytelling, book talks, poetry sharing, and language arts activities.

Champlin, Connie. *Puppetry and Creative Dramatics in Storytelling.* Austin, TX: Nancy Renfro Studios, 1980.
Using a variety of stories, the author identifies introduction, presentation, and follow-up activities.

Cianciolo, Patricia. *Illustrations in Children's Books,* 2d. ed. Dubuque, IA: William C. Brown, 1976. o.p.
Examines styles of art in children's books and ideas for sharing illustrations.

Cochrane, Louise. *Shadow Puppets in Color.* Boston: Plays, Inc., 1972.
Gives instructions for making shadow puppets, ideas for staging, and plays to produce.

Coger, Leslie Irene, and White, Melvin R. *Reader's Theatre Handbook,* 3d. ed. Dallas, TX: Scott, Foresman, 1982.
Gives instructions for selecting and preparing scripts, casting, and performing, as well as samples of scripts on both the elementary and secondary levels.

Coody, Betty. *Using Literature with Young Children,* 3d ed. Dubuque, IA: William C. Brown, 1983.
Ideas for storytelling, creative dramatics, poetry sharing, art experiences, and cooking fun.

De Wit, Dorothy. *Children's Faces Looking Up.* Chicago: American Library Association, 1979.
Includes techniques for story selection, sources, ideas for modifying tales, tips for tellers, and examples of story programs.

Engler, Larry, and Fijan, Carol. *Making Puppets Come Alive: A Method of Learning and Teaching Hand Puppetry.* New York: Taplinger, 1973.
Shows through photographs and description how the amateur can bring the puppet to life through movement as well as addressing basic elements of puppet presentation.

Huck, Charlotte S. *Children's Literature in the Elementary School,* 3d ed. New York: Holt, Rinehart & Winston, 1979.
Stresses understanding of children's growth patterns, awareness of children's literature, and the necessity for a children's literature program.

Lukens, Rebecca. *A Critical Handbook of Children's Literature,* 2d ed. Dallas, TX: Scott, Foresman, 1982.
Examines the importance of understanding character development, plot, setting, theme, point of view, style, and tone in developing experiences for children with quality literature.

Pereira, Nancy. *Creative Dramatics in the Library.* Rowayton, CT: New Plays, Inc., 1976, o.p.
Ideas for creative dramatics adaptable for both school and public libraries.

Renfro, Nancy. *Puppetry and the Art of Story Creation.* Austin, TX: Nancy Renfro Studios, 1979.
Practical suggestions both for the creation of simple puppets and their use in storytelling.

Sloan, Glenna. *The Child as Critic,* 2d ed. New York: Columbia Teachers College Press, 1984.
Justifies the provision of thought-provoking literature activities in the development of the child's ability to critically evaluate.

Spolin, Viola. *Improvisation for the Theater: A Handbook of Teaching and Directing Techniques,* rev. ed. Evanston, IL: Northwestern University Press, 1983.
Recognizes the importance of spontaneous creative responses and gives over 200 theater games to be used in stimulating creative expression.

———. *Stories to Dramatize.* Selected by Winifred Ward. New Orleans, LA: Children's Theatre Press, 1952.
Includes stories suitable for dramatization and techniques for presentation.

Appendix III
Directory of Publishers and Producers

Harry N. Abrams, Inc.
100 Fifth Ave.
New York, NY 10011

Addison-Wesley Publishing Co.
Reading, MA 01867

American Library Association
50 E. Huron St.
Chicago, IL 60611

Anchorage Press
P.O. Box 8067
New Orleans, LA 70182

Arista Corp.
P.O. Box 6146
Concord, CA 94524

Atheneum Publishers
597 Fifth Ave.
New York, NY 10017

Barr Films
P.O. Box 5667
Pasadena, CA 91107

Beginner Books. *See* Random
  House.

R.R. Bowker Company
205 E. 42nd St.
New York, NY 10017

Bowmar-Noble Publishers
Box 25308
1901 N. Walnut St.
Oklahoma City, OK 73125

Bradbury Press, Inc.
2 Overhill Rd.
Scarsdale, NY 10583

William C. Brown Publishers
2460 Kerper Blvd.
Dubuque, IA 52001

Caedmon
1995 Broadway
New York, NY 10023

Caxton Printers
Box 700
Caldwell, ID 83605

Children's Theatre Press. *See*
  Anchorage Press.

Citation Press. *See* Scholastic.

Clarion. *See* Houghton Mifflin.

William Collins Publishing Inc.
2080 W. 117 St.
Cleveland, OH 44111

Columbia Records
51 W. 52nd St.
New York, NY 10019

Columbia Teachers College
  Press
Columbia University
1234 Amsterdam Ave.
New York, NY 10027

Coward, McCann & Geoghegan
200 Madison Ave.
New York, NY 10016

Crowell. *See* Harper & Row.

Crown Publishers, Inc.
One Park Ave.
New York, NY 10016

Delacorte Press. *See* Dell.

Dell Publishing Company, Inc.
1 Dag Hammarskjold Plaza
245 E. 47th St.
New York, NY 10017

Dial. *See* Dutton.

Dodd, Mead & Company
79 Madison Ave.
New York, NY 10016

Doubleday & Company, Inc.
245 Park Ave.
New York, NY 10167

Droll Yankees
Mill Rd.
Foster, RI 02825

E.P. Dutton, Inc.
Two Park Ave.
New York, NY 10016

Farrar, Straus & Giroux, Inc.
19 Union Square W.
New York, NY 10003

Follett Publishing Company
1010 W. Washington Blvd.
Chicago, IL 60607

Four Winds Press
730 Broadway
New York, NY 10003

Gale Research Company
Book Tower
Detroit, MI 48226

Garrard Publishing Company
1607 N. Market St.
Champaign, IL 61820

Golden Press. *See* Western.

Greenwillow. *See* Morrow.

Grosset & Dunlap, Inc.
51 Madison Ave.
New York, NY 10010

Guidance Associates
The Center for Humanities
Communications Park
Box 1000
Mount Kisco, NY 10549-9989

Harcourt Brace Jovanovich, Inc.
757 Third Ave.
New York, NY 10017

Harper & Row, Publishers, Inc.
10 E. 53rd St.
New York, NY 10022

Holiday House, Inc.
18 E. 53rd St.
New York, NY 10022

Holt, Rinehart & Winston, Inc.
521 Fifth Ave.
6th Floor
New York, NY 10175

Houghton Mifflin Company
1 Beacon St.
Boston, MA 02108

Hubbard Press. *See* Rand
McNally.

Human Sciences Press, Inc.
72 Fifth Ave.
New York, NY 10011

Alfred A. Knopf, Inc.
201 E. 50th St.
New York, NY 10022

Lippincott. *See* Harper & Row.

Little, Brown & Company
34 Beacon St.
Boston, MA 02106

Live Oak Media
P.O. Box 34
Ancramdale, NY 12503

Lothrop. *See* Morrow.

McGraw-Hill, Inc.
1221 Avenue of the Americas
New York, NY 10020

David McKay Company, Inc.
Two Park Ave.
New York, NY 10016

Macmillan Publishing Company
866 Third Ave.
New York, NY 10022

William Morrow & Company,
  Inc.
105 Madison Ave.
New York, NY 10016

Thomas Nelson, Inc.
405 7th Ave. S.
Nashville, TN 37203

Helene Obolensky Enterprises,
  Inc.
Box 87
909 Third Ave.
New York, NY 10150

Oxford University Press, Inc.
200 Madison Ave.
New York, NY 10016

Pantheon Books, Inc.
201 E. 50th St.
New York, NY 10022

Parnassus Press. *See* Houghton
  Mifflin.

Parents Magazine Press *See*
  Dutton.

Penguin Books
40 West 23rd St.
New York, NY 10010

Philomel. *See* Putnam's.

Pied Piper
P.O. Box 320
Verdugo City, CA 91046

Plays, Inc.
8 Arlington St.
Boston, MA 02116

Prentice-Hall, Inc.
Route 9 West
Englewood Cliffs, NJ 07632

G.P. Putnam's Sons
200 Madison Ave.
New York, NY 10016

Rand McNally & Company
8255 Central Park Ave.
Skokie, IL 60076

Random House, Inc.
201 East 50th St.
New York, NY 10022

Rod & Staff Publishers, Inc.
Crockett, KY 41413

St. Martins Press, Inc.
175 Fifth Ave.
New York, NY 10010

Schocken Books, Inc.
200 Madison Ave.
New York, NY 10016

Scholastic, Inc.
730 Broadway
New York, NY 10003

Scott, Foresman & Company
1900 East Lake Ave.
Glenview, IL 60025

Charles Scribner's Sons
597 Fifth Ave.
New York, NY 10017

Scroll Press, Inc.
2858 Valeria Court
Merrick, NY 11566

The Seabury Press, Inc.
815 Second Ave.
New York, NY 10017

Simon & Schuster, Inc.
1230 Avenue of the Americas
New York, NY 10020

Stravon Educational Press
845 Third Ave.
New York, NY 10022

Taplinger Publishing Company,
   Inc.
132 West 22nd St.
New York, NY 10011

Troll Associates
320 Route 17
Mahwah, NJ 07430

Van Nostrand Reinhold
   Company, Inc.
135 West 50th St.
New York, NY 10020

The Viking Press
40 West 23rd St.
New York, NY 10010

Walck. *See* David McKay.

Walker & Company
720 Fifth Ave
New York, NY 10019

Frederick Warne & Company,
   Inc.
Two Park Ave.
New York, NY 10016

Franklin Watts, Inc.
387 Park Ave. S.
New York, NY 10016

Western Publishing Company,
   Inc.
850 Third Ave.
New York, NY 10022

The Westminster Press
925 Chestnut St.
Philadelphia, PA 19107

Weston Woods
Weston, CT 06680

The H.W. Wilson Company
950 University Ave.
Bronx, NY 10452

Windmill Books, Inc.
1230 Avenue of the Americas
New York, NY 10020

Index

Compiled by Linda Webster

This index contains authors, illustrators, and titles of books and nonprint media, as well as subjects.